Lifting up the Serpent in the Gospel of John

Lifting up the Serpent in the Gospel of John

The Cross as Restorative Justice

Allison R. deForest

Christian World Imprints

First Published in 2020 by

Christian World Imprints
Christian Publishing & Books from India
C-3, Wazirpur Industrial Area
Delhi-110052
cwidelhi2017@gmail.com
www.ChristianWorldImprints.com
Phone: +91 11 41526079

ISBN: 978-93-5148-482-0

Printed in India.

Dedication:

To Chris, my spouse, friend,
and faithful dialog partner,
who read every draft

To Donald and Dorothy, my parents,
who raised me to be curious and skeptical

To Mallory and Beau, my children,
who kindled the passion to work for justice

To all the scholars encountered in the course of this adventure –
particularly three mentors: Rev. Dr. Ann L. Fritschel,
Dr. Erik M. Heen, and Rev. Dr. J. Jayakiran Sebastian,
who allowed me to ask questions and
taught me how to seek answers.

Contents

Abstract

The strange resemblance that the author of the Gospel of John sees between Jesus and the serpent that Moses made, at God's command and in order to save Israel from the consequence of her rebellion, has long been a fascinating puzzle. Why does John call upon this particular scriptural story to describe Jesus' death on the cross? In what way is Jesus like the serpent?

This research work explores this puzzle in detail, beginning with how the figure of the snake functions in John's Gospel, followed by an examination of the story as told in Numbers twenty-one and a discussion of how the story of Moses and the serpent was read and retold by authors around the turn of the Era.

This exploration demonstrates that John's typology encompasses the whole of the Christ event: incarnation, crucifixion, resurrection and ascension. When one looks to the "lifted up" Christ, one sees both God and the consequence of humanity's refusal to trust God. Human failure and God's response are united. This a picture of "restorative" atonement. Looking to the cross opens a dialogue between offender and offended which leads to reconciliation and true forgiveness. By the Spirit, given by the resurrected Christ, reconciliation with God and others becomes possible.

This picture of what God accomplishes through the Christ event can add depth and nuance to the discussion of atonement theology that is occurring today, a discussion that calls into question the dominance of penal substitutionary atonement as the default explanation for how salvation is accomplished through Jesus' death and the retributive justice system that has been built in part upon this explanation.

Chapter 1

Introduction

Rationale

"The Bible says that Jesus died to save you from your sins." Often-heard phrases like this one raise two questions: *is* this indeed what the Bible says, and, if so, what does it *mean*? The Bible is an ancient and complicated set of texts and the myriad approaches to investigating it fall somewhere along a spectrum that ranges from treating it as a historical artifact to believing that one particular translation is literal truth.

One understanding of Christ's death that lies, latent and unexamined, in our current American consciousness can be illustrated by a door-hanger invitation to Easter worship.[1] The message on it can be summarized as follows. "You can know you will go to heaven" if you follow these four easy steps: 1) Recognize that, along with everyone else, you are not good enough to get into heaven on your own (Romans 3:23). 2) Realize that just as you earn wages for good work, you are punished for doing wrong and that punishment is "eternal death in a place called Hell" (Romans 6:23). 3) Believe the

1 The flyer was distributed by Lighthouse Baptist Church, 1349 Green St, Lehighton, PA, 18235, (610) 377-0641, www.lbclehighton.org. A copy of it is included in an appendix to this work.

announcement that Christ showed his great love for us when he paid the debt for our sin by dying on the cross (Romans 5:8). 4) Trust in Christ alone as your savior, because everlasting life is a gift that he purchased with his blood and that he freely offers to those who call on him by faith (Romans 6:23, Romans 10:13). A prayer is provided to help readers repent and ask Jesus to come into their heart and save them.

Many who feel anxious or insecure, who have been marginalized, abandoned, or abused in some way, tend to feel an acute need for comfort, security and affirmation. If at the same time, this source of consolation is simple and logical, easy to understand and hold onto – mentally satisfying – it becomes very compelling. The message that one is a horrible sinner in need of redemption resonates deeply with such people, but while it offers the hope of 'salvation', it also paralyzes them in feelings of unworthiness and worthlessness. The utterly logical and 'rational' presentation meshes well with the way post-enlightenment people have been taught to organize knowledge and yet, while this belief system can instill great devotion to scripture and sometimes even the discipline of reading it; as knowledge increases, so do the questions. The 'gospel' offered above is simple and logical; it seems to offer hope for love and acceptance, but ultimately it reinforces low self-esteem and provides a counterfeit rationale for marginalization. This 'gospel' also requires an act of will, a *decision* to be loved and forgiven and, in response, to feel trust. But love, trust, and forgiven-ness are feelings that grow from a foundation that has often been denied to oppressed outsiders, one that this rational 'gospel' itself denies. Such feelings cannot be understood and manufactured by those already struggling to find acceptance and peace within themselves and in their world.

One context, among others, that displays this personal dilemma in many ways is a small town, just south of the eastern Pennsylvania coal region. This place mourns its past as a prosperous mill town, protected (or isolated) by the Blue Mountain from the economically prosperous Lehigh Valley. The people here suffer from a certain amount of low self esteem—they are the ones left behind after the mills and mines have closed and the companies with their wealthy owners, seeking to cut costs and maximize profits, have moved on.

People here cling tightly to the safety of their traditional values and ways of being church. They mourn the passing of a life that they perceive as having been better (whether in reality it was or not) than what they experience now. They often don't seem to think well enough of themselves to demand better from their medical care, their educational system, or their government. Their understanding of God comes from the penal substitutionary atonement theory that is in the air they breathe and from a church become social institution that sustains itself by collecting dues and keeping track of membership through rigidly enforced requirements. They tend to believe in an unexamined way that the Bible is a set of propositional truths that support this thinking. People in this context have internalized that, though God loves them, God and the church demand something of them. The demands are, in their minds, for their own good, but they are demanded because people are unworthy, despicable creatures, deserving only of God's just punishment. This stern, harsh God mirrors their social and economic environment. It is an image of God that reenforces a devotion to the institution of church in the 16.3% of the population that still cares about church,[2] while it leads to despair, dependence, and drug abuse in the large part of the population that has been disenfranchised by their inability to live up to the churches' standards for giving and behavior. Neither group has any desire to open the Bible and rethink what is written there. For them the Bible has been distilled down to a simple, logical message, to be accepted as it was passed down, and a set of rules to be followed or discarded, based on the circumstances or leanings of the autonomous individual making the decision. This same dynamic applies to to any of a number of groups who want to take their faith seriously but have been marginalized and denied opportunity to become fully integrated into the life of the church for any number of reasons.

Popular christian music concerts seem to manipulate people in a similar way. Participants are called to whip up feelings of unworthiness so that the 'gospel' of Jesus taking God's punishment

2 "Baseline Assessment for Visioning Process," Prepared for St. John's Lutheran Church, Mahoning Valley, PA by Spiritual Levity, August 2014, Appendix I, 15.

on one's behalf can once again be good news. The audience is given the opportunity to repent and renew their commitment alongside of those who are invited to repent and commit themselves to Christ for the first time. The rest of the concert can then be a time of praise and adoration to the God who has rescued properly repentant humanity. This experience too raises questions. Christians always have a need to acknowledge sin as well as repentance and renewal, but does God desire God's people to regularly crawl back into the darkness of despair and self-loathing that a life in Christ lifts them from? If penal substitutionary atonement is a love story between God and God's creation, it is a very strange love story indeed.

Thus the American 'gospel' of penal substitutionary atonement offers a simple, understandable solution to the problem of broken relationship, but one that is ultimately at cross-purposes with what it claims to achieve. It asks a person to produce, from their own mind and heart, an indestructible trust in a fundamentally untrustworthy object – a cold, calculating, infinite bean counter; a God who cannot forgive until all the boxes are checked and the recompense is complete (by Christ on the repentant sinners behalf). In addition it asks one to accept, as acceptable to God, a particularly violent blood sacrifice for one's sins and those of others. Blood sacrifice is, in our current context repugnant, perhaps because it is not well understood. But the violence of the cross has been used as the rationale for an incalculable number of violent deeds done in Christ's name, including the crusades, the Holocaust, and abuse of women.[3]

This depiction of the relationship between God and creation does not correspond well with the Gospel of Jesus Christ as set forth in the roughly 8,000 verses of the New Testament. Instead, it is a strange brew that bubbled up from a mixture of ancient atonement theories, read out of their original context, and Common Sense realism, a philosophy coming out of Scotland and important to the development of political theory at the time America gained her independence from Britain. Common Sense philosophy grounded everything in "human intuitions of the external world and of the

---

3 David J. Lose *provides a very readable critique of penal substitutionary atonement in his dialogical Making Sense of the Cross* (Minneapolis: Augsburg Fortress, 2011), 110-126.

mind"[4] and made human reason the foundation for understanding God and scripture. The quintessentially American exposition of salvation through Jesus Christ, rehearsed on the afore mentioned door hanger, in no way adequately expresses the complex and nuanced dialogue that is contained within the Bible about what God does for humankind in the person and work of Jesus. It is the hope that this study in the theology of Jesus' saving life, death, resurrection, and ascension expressed through the typology of the bronze serpent in the Gospel of John will contribute to a wider dialogue both about atonement theology and about how one develops theology as scripture is read.

This author's close and intertextual reading of John's Gospel, with particular regard to the typology between Jesus and Moses' bronze serpent, suggests that Restorative justice is a useful lens with which to engage the question of what God accomplishes on behalf of humanity through the Christ event.

Restorative justice is "a theory of justice that emphasizes repairing the harm caused or revealed by criminal behavior [that] is best accomplished through cooperative processes that include all stakeholders."[5] Restorative justice seeks to heal all parties involved in an offense: victims, offenders and communities.[6] It does this by considering three basic conceptions. The first, encounter: bringing all "stakeholders" – offender, victim, and other affected members of a community – together in various configurations of mediated conversation to discuss not only what happened, but what contributed to it and what resulted from it. In John's Gospel one is confronted with one's offense through Jesus as the serpent (John 3:14). Seeing God in the incarnate Jesus, crucified because of humanity's rejection, yet risen and ascended, leads human offenders to confront their offense and their victim in order to find healing. When Jesus greets his disciples on the first Easter evening and

4 Mark A. Noll, "Common Sense Traditions and American Evangelical Thought." *American Quarterly* 37:2 (1985), 218.

5 Daniel W. Van Ness and Karen Heetderks Strong, *Restoring Justice: An Introduction to Restorative Justice* (New York: Routledge, 2015), 44. See also the body of work by Christopher Marshall.

6 Van Ness and Strong, *Restoring Justice*, 45.

breathes the Spirit into them, he gives them the following charge, "If you forgive the sins of any, they are forgiven them; if you retain the sins of any, they are retained" (John 20:23). Here, Jesus commissions his followers to continue the commission that he had from God, freeing those captive to the sin of the world and retaining the sin of unbelief in those who reject the one sent from God to protect their own power and privilege until they can be moved, perhaps like Nicodemus and Joseph of Aramathea, to a new place. The second is reparation, the group of stakeholders decides on what can be done to repair the harm. As with Jesus and Peter, following Peter's denial of his discipleship (John 21:15-19), a dialogue takes place to determine what actions will move offender and victim beyond their fractured relationship. Finally, transformation, the stakeholders work together to find processes that allow life to be lived in a way that makes the offense less likely to occur again.[7] In John, the disciples are given the power of the Holy Spirit in order to deal with sin and to love one another.

Retributive justice operates on the principle that pain will vindicate. In practice, however, this is often counterproductive for both victims and offenders.[8] Even if an offender experiences pain, without dialogue, this liberates neither the victim nor the offender. Often the offender begins to feel that they are a victim of the system, while the original victim receives little or no response or recourse at all. In the current criminal justice system of the United States, the offender relies heavily on a defense lawyer, who as often as not tries to obtain an out-of-court settlement. This means that innocence or guilt is never determined. In addition, the victim of a crime is often sidelined from the process because all crime is deemed to be against the state. Victims may never have the opportunity to confront their victimizers at all.[9] Current studies also show that pain does not work particularly well as a deterrent. Statistics from many western

7 Van Ness and Strong, *Restoring Justice*, 43-44.

8 Van Ness and Strong, *Restoring Justice*, 52.

9 Van Ness and Strong, *Restoring Justice*, 10-11.

countries show that recidivism (reoffending) rates are alarming.[10] Retributive justice has not proven to restore offenders nor satisfy their victims. Communities too continue to suffer from both the disenfranchisement of victims and the effects of crime.

In a theological system that similarly says that pain vindicates and that the pain can fall on an innocent to remove the consequences from the guilty, there is much that goes unaddressed. The assumption that sin is an offense against God allows for the working out of justice between God and the offender. This ignores, however, any others affected by the offense. The "sinner" can go free without ever reconciling with those they have sinned against. No societal factors that may have impacted the offender and made the offense possible (or likely) need be addressed either.

In Anselm's feudal context, in which a temporal Lord held absolute sway over his serfs, Anselm's picture of the honor due to the Lord may have made some sense. In Luther's late Medieval/ early Renaissance context, where the church held nearly absolute power, demanded penance and offered indulgence, Luther's 'happy exchange'[11] was indeed a word of freedom. But in the current North American context, where only the criminal justice system deals with serious infractions, penal substitutionary atonement, which tells people that Christ has removed the consequences of their sin, leaves a huge vacuum. There is no other public forum, other than perhaps the educational system, where how one treats ones fellows is addressed. Since the dimension of reconciliation within a community is ignored, the forgiveness that one receives from God feels hollow and insincere.

---

10 Timothy Gorringe reports that 70% of adult males in Britain reoffend within four years. (Timothy Gorringe, *God's Just Vengeance* (Cambridge: Cambridge University Press, 1996), 249. Van Ness and Strong report that two centuries of attempts to reduce recidivism by rehabilitation have been disappointing (Van Ness and Strong, *Restoring Justice*, 5).

11 Luther describes this 'happy (or joyous) exchange' in *The Freedom of a Christian.* Luther says that while the human soul is full of sins, death, and damnation, Christ is full of grace, life, and salvation. When faith steps in the soul's sins, death and damnation become Christ's and Christ's grace, life and salvation become the soul's. (Timothy J. Wengert, *The Freedom of the Christian, 1520* (Minneapolis: Fortress, 2016) 500.

Restorative justice takes consequences as seriously as retributive justice does. The effects of an offense are addressed in this model by bringing all the parties together. The victim, offender, and community meet face-to-face to talk about how the offense has affected everyone. Safe space is created for dialogue, understanding, repentance, forgiveness, and the creation of strategies to change the community situation for the better. Violence is sidelined because no unrelated pain is needed. Cycles of violence are broken because violent acts are not met with violence in return. The difficult and costly work of reconciliation, done between all those affected by the offense, moves all toward understanding and healing. Community is restored through the process.

In John's Gospel, Jesus descends into humanity's situation, in order to become the victim of humanity's rejection, a rejection that had been going on since the beginnings of humanity according to the Old Testament witness. In Christ, God becomes a part of human society. Jesus, though he has all the power of God within him, becomes the passive, non-retributive recipient of humanity's rejection of God. God becomes one who, from within humanity, is in a position ask for restoration and to offer real forgiveness. In turning to Jesus on the cross, humanity comes face-to-face with its rejection of God; its failure to believe that God dwells in its midst as promised. In Jesus, humans must face their propensity to go their own way and take divine matters into their own hands with disastrous results. But God's response to human rejection does not come from far off and high above. Jesus has descended into a dialogue that includes all parties – the victim, the offenders, and the community whose structure both allowed for and provoked the offense. The risen Christ, by the Spirit, provides the ability for all the parties to work toward reconciliation and transformation. The ascended Christ draws all creation up into God restoring and reconciling all. In John, all this is accomplished through the 'lifting up' of the Incarnate One.

To see this in John's Gospel, sin, judgment, justice, and salvation need to be understood on John's terms. In John, sin is the failure to see God in Christ. This is first expressed implicitly in the prologue where John tells his readers/hearers that the Word "came to what was his own, and his own people did not accept him" (John 1:11). It is stated again more explicitly in John 15:24, "If I had not done among them the works that no one else did, they would not have sin. But now they have seen and hated both me and my Father." Again in John 16:8-9, John tells us that Jesus will ἐλέγξει (bring to recognition of wrongdoing) the world about sin "because they do not believe (πιστεύουσιν) in me." Thus sin in John is not as much any moral failing as it is a rejection of God that fractures the relationship between God and God's people. This fractured relationship is what Jesus overcomes in his life, death, resurrection and ascension. The arc of the Christ event reveals God in a way that human eyes and hearts can 'see' and thus restores the relationship between God and the world (κόσμος) that God 'so loves.' Judging or judgment in John, as will be demonstrated later in this research, is more descriptive of a state of being than it is an action. The Greek word, usually translated as both judging; judgment; and, occasionally, as condemned, is κρίσις – crisis. For John being judged or under judgment is the opposite of having eternal life, also expressed as salvation. This is perhaps best expressed in John 3:14 - 21:

> And just as Moses lifted up the serpent in wilderness, so it is necessary that the Son of Man be lifted up, that everyone who has faith in him may have eternal life. For God loved the cosmos in this way, that God gave the only unique Son, so that everyone having faith in him, might not be destroyed, but might have life eternal. For God did not send the Son into the cosmos in order to judge the cosmos, but so that the cosmos might be saved through him. The one who has faith in him is not judged (or perhaps does not judge one's self), but the one who does not have faith in him has already been judged (or has already judged one's self) because that one has not trusted in the name of the only unique Son of God. And this is the judgment, that the light has come into the cosmos and humanity loved the darkness rather than the light because their works were evil. For anyone who does poorly hates the light and does not come towards the light, so that their works will not be exposed (ἐλεγχθῇ), But

> the one doing what is true comes toward the light, so that it can be seen that those works are done in God (Author's translation).

So eternal life is a life of doing works "in God," in the light. Being under judgment is living (doing works) that one desires to keep hidden in darkness, away from God and the light. In Jesus' final prayer, John has Jesus pray, "And this is eternal life, that they may know you, the only true God, and Jesus Christ whom you have sent" (John 17:2). Salvation in John is living this eternal life, no longer under judgment.

When we understand these terms as John defines them, we see that in his Gospel salvation comes about when one sees God in Christ. This often begins, as will be seen in John's narrative, when the characters come face to face with Jesus and either receive or reject the God who sent him.

Thus John's narrative suggests that in the Christ event (his life, death, resurrection, and ascension) offenders are called to face the one (and the ones) whom they have offended. They are given space to hear and understand the pain that they have inflicted. They are given the power and the opportunity to redress those harms and plan for a new future. God enters into the human struggle as a member of the human family, a victim of its propensity toward violence, to become part of the circle of dialogue that provides accountability to both the offender and the offended and restores the relationship between them and their community.

Scripture does not present any one definitive explanation of what God accomplishes through the cross of Christ. The book of Hebrews uses the image of Jesus as both priest and sacrifice in a Day of Atonement ritual. Paul seems to give a fairly succinct statement in Romans 3:25, "whom God put forward as a sacrifice of atonement by his blood, effective through faith," but one's understanding of this statement hinges on the interpretation of the Greek word ἱλαστήριον (translated as "sacrifice of atonement" in the NRSV) which continues to be the subject of much scholarly debate.

The image of God's justice uncovered in essentially all of the Old Testament narratives, including that explored in the close reading of the story of Moses and the bronze serpent in Numbers, is largely one of restorative justice.[12] God's intent in God's actions in the Wilderness wandering, in God's speaking through the prophets, and even in the catastrophic events of the Assyrian and Babylonian conquests, was to instruct Israel and bring her back into right relationship with her God. The trouble inflicted was intended to confront Israel with her wrongdoing and turning away – her lack of trust – in a way that promoted a return. This return would allow the community to move forward in the direction of God's promise.

John's Gospel shows much of this same concern. We see this perhaps most strikingly in the epilogue, when Jesus confronts Peter with his denial and questions him three times in order to restore his sense of call as a disciple (John 21:15-19). But it is also in evidence throughout the Gospel. Jesus' encounter with the woman of Samaria is another example. In their dialogue, the woman is brought to an acknowledgment of her past – whether sinful, as a loose woman, or painful, as one who has been passed from man to man, can be debated – but it is this recognition of the truth of her personhood in the presence of God that empowers her to return to her community as a witness to Christ. Nicodemus is similarly confronted with his failure to understand, especially as a teacher of Israel. The arc of his story implies that he too becomes a follower of Christ. The healing of the man by the pool of Bethzatha involves an invitation by Jesus to the man to examine his past. The man does not do so and he ends up setting off the hostility of "the Jews" towards Jesus. In John 6, Jesus returns God's people to the Old Testament context. He gives them bread from heaven and confronts them in their seeking only to fill their stomachs. He challenges them to trust him to the extent that they will eat his flesh and drink his blood. At this point in the story only the twelve remain, all the other would be disciples go away. The long section at the Festival of Booths shows Jesus calling to the people to see God working in him, but in this dialogue "the Jews" fail over and over to face their rebellion and return to God.

12 Van Ness and Strong also point out that the Hebrew Scriptures are focused on restoration of the individual and the community. (Van Ness and Strong, *Restoring Justice: An Introduction to Restorative Justice*, 6-7).

The woman caught in adultery, though not original to John's Gospel, finds a fitting home here because her encounter with Jesus shows the restorative pattern; a face-to-face acknowledgment of her failure before God leads to forgiveness, reconciliation, and new life. The delayed face-to-face meeting between the man born blind, where he finally "sees" Jesus (John 9:35-38) is the capstone of that story's contrast between trust and the blindness of unbelief. "The Jews" are confronted with their blindness but do not turned to be healed. After the death of Lazarus, both Mary and Martha are asked to consider their faith in the presence of Christ. This is an interesting reversal because they see themselves as the offended and Jesus is the offender. They both confront Jesus with their knowledge that he could have healed their brother if he had arrived before Lazarus' death. They are subsequently shown that Jesus has power over death and a new level of trust is offered to them. But following the death of Lazarus the rejection of Jesus by "the Jews" is solidified and the plan to put Jesus to death is set in motion. The final great irony, that the rejection of God by the people of God leads to the saving of the world, comes to pass. When the Incarnate One is "lifted up," human rebellion meets God's unfailing love in the person of Jesus. The irony that 'lifting up' in John means both the crucifixion of Jesus and his return to the glory he shared with his father through his resurrection and ascension, invites John's readers/hearers to see that what is salvific is the entire arc of the Christ event. The cross, important and essential as it is, cannot be separated from the incarnation, resurrection and ascension.[13]

Judgment, in John, is a gift from God, intended to turn God's people around. It promotes dialogue so that the pain is not everlasting. When, after the resurrection, Jesus breathes his spirit into his disciples, his words address their new ability to deal with sin (John 20:22-23). The Spirit gives the disciples the power to forgive or to retain sins, to move beyond their fractured relationship with God and thus with one another. The Spirit gives the disciples the power to

13 Gail O'Day highlights this point in her commentary on John 3:14. (Gail R. O'Day), "John" in *The New Interpreters Bible: A Commentary in Twelve Volumes, Volume IX* (Nashville: Abingdon Press, 1995), 552.

build the new community of God. Penal substitutionary atonement tends to put off retribution into the eschatological future, but in John's Gospel, judgment and reconciliation are real-time events.

The liturgy of the church also promotes restorative justice. The rite of confession and forgiveness, both individual and corporate, is focused on restoring the relationship between believers and God. In its corporate expression, the liturgy expresses that sin is not only against God; community restoration is one of the goals of the rite.

The author of John's Gospel says that any one who believes in the "lifted up" Son of Man will be able to have eternal life (John 3:14). If, as discussed above, in looking to Jesus, lifted up just as the serpent was lifted, humanity comes face to face with both its failure to trust that God has its best interest at heart; and God's response to that failure, what does this say about what God accomplishes through the Christ event? To this author, it speaks of restorative justice.

The hypothesis that restorative justice can help make sense of the scriptural witness is supported by the work of Timothy Gorringe. Gorringe traces in detail the long history that connects the crucifixion of Jesus with retributive justice.[14] He critiques the role that Anselm's satisfaction theory (which was later developed into penal substitution by Calvin) has had in both the establishment and enforcement of laws in the western world. This conflation, says Gorringe has made it seem reasonable to people of faith to shore up the power of the rich and oppress the poor.[15] He believes that satisfaction theory retains its power because there are ways in which it is true to human experience – the need to exact or make some sort of payment for wrongdoing does help to deal, at least temporarily, with the guilt and violence that are felt on both an individual and collective level.[16] Beginning with the writings of the Old Testament and other ancient law codes, Gorringe demonstrates that law was seen as divinely given to make communal living possible. The complex relationship between sin and crime, morality and legality, which arise when humans live together,

14 Timothy Gorringe, *God's Just Vengeance* (Cambridge: Cambridge University Press, 1996), 6-7.

15 Gorringe, *God's Just Vengeance,* 1-5.

16 Gorringe, *God's Just Vengeance,* 11.

also underlies the relationship between atonement theology and legal practice.[17] Critiques by such as Tolstoy, Nietzsche, and Girard demonstrate how the image of Christ on the cross, originally "an icon of the wickedness of judicial punishment, became the focus of its legality" and taught western society that offenders must suffer for their offenses.[18] Gorringe points out that there are and always have been alternatives to satisfaction theory, such as those offered by Abelard and those who followed him. Next Gorringe explores the idea of retribution in the Old Testament. He finds three episodes in which retribution seems to be God's response to breaches of taboo (Achan's keeping of the spoils of Jericho (Joshua 7), Saul's killing of the Gibeonites in 2 Samuel 21 and David's taking of the census in 2 Samuel 24.)[19] In all other cases Gorringe sees that the image of suffering, though not necessarily separated from guilt or penalty is educative, not punitive.[20] He emphasizes the ambiguity involved in ancient sacrificial rites which are difficult to understand in our current context, but blood imagery, taken up in the book of Hebrews and perhaps by Paul, provides the power that fuels satisfaction theory. For Gorringe, the Pentateuch, which weaves cultic, moral, and criminal law tightly together, is foundational for the development of penal theory in the West.[21] The activity of God in judging sin became equated with human judges punishing offenders.[22] But Gorringe believes that the writings of the New Testament, based on their Old Testament foundation, deconstruct retributive justice.[23] He seeks to demonstrate the the New Testament can be read in ways that do not support the theory of satisfaction. Following Rene Girard, Gorringe believes that later interpreters of the New Testament turned the story of protest against judicial cruelty into one that validated it.[24] Gorringe

17 Gorringe, *God's Just Vengeance,* 22.

18 Gorringe, *God's Just Vengeance,* 23.

19 Gorringe, *God's Just Vengeance,* 34.

20 Gorringe, *God's Just Vengeance,* 44.

21 Gorringe, *God's Just Vengeance,* 40.

22 Gorringe, *God's Just Vengeance,* 44.

23 Gorringe, *God's Just Vengeance,* 58.

24 Gorringe, *God's Just Vengeance,* 81.

continues to trace the relationship between the development of Anselm's satisfaction theory and it's critique by Abelard that have led to the current system of punishment and prison in many western countries. This system is firmly rooted in the idea that retributive punishment pays a debt owed to society for crimes against the community and takes the acts of offenders seriously.[25] Retribution theories appeal to the need for order, a sense of justice, and a need to make sense of suffering and feelings of guilt.[26] But for Gorringe, retributive theory cannot deal with the realities of a society made up of unequals.[27] The cross of Christ reveals the true nature of human political power and the way that religion underwrites that power. It also reveals God's mercy because God does not judge humans, humans judge themselves. Gorringe understands that ultimately God even allows humanity to pass judgment on God, though God is beyond human condemnation, thus the trial and punishment of Jesus in some sense condemns all other trials and punishments.[28] Following Moltmann, Gorringe understands that God becomes a victim in order to stand in solidarity with victims so that they always have rights with God.[29] What Jesus does on the cross, according to Gorringe is "the absorption of violence, the redefinition of power, and the establishment of the possibility for forgiveness."[30] Gorringe sees that God accepts offenders without condoning their offenses, requiring that the offender own up to what has been done. God invites the offender into a community of reconciliation and thus encourages the offender to live a new life. Through the sacraments of the church, "a community founded upon betrayal and the survival of betrayal," God declares the offender to be free from past offenses and invites the offender into the life of a disciple.[31] The author of the Gospel of John might expand say this to include not just the cross,

25 Gorringe, *God's Just Vengeance,* 229.
26 Gorringe, *God's Just Vengeance,* 231.
27 Gorringe, *God's Just Vengeance,* 333.
28 Gorringe, *God's Just Vengeance,* 237.
29 Gorringe, *God's Just Vengeance,* 239.
30 Gorringe, *God's Just Vengeance,* 247.
31 Gorringe, *God's Just Vengeance,* 268.

but also the incarnation, resurrection, and ascension, and then say Amen.

It is the thesis of this research work that when one reads John's Gospel through the lens of restorative justice one can recover some of its unique emphases. One sees in the Christ event (the incarnation, crucifixion, resurrection and ascension), humans who offend by their rejection of God, meeting the offended one. Called to face their offense and their victim, humanity is offered the opportunity to dialogue about their wrong doing and what contributed to it, to receive forgiveness from the one they have offended, and to bring together the community of God to find ways to offer restitution and reconciliation. Ultimately it is the resurrection and ascension which allow retribution to be set aside. When God brings new life out of death and the things that have been lost are restored, the only thing left to be accomplished is reconciliation.

The Christ event saves us because in the incarnation, life, death, resurrection, and ascension God enters into God's creation in a new way. God is no longer outside of creation but has become part of it. Jesus dies violently (again sent by God the Creator and willingly) because we die violently; not in our place but with us. Thus Jesus enters the circle of restorative justice as a victim. He works through the whole mess of why we sin and hurt one other. Because Jesus was raised, we can receive the Spirit and be given the power to live as God calls us to live now and into eternity.

The research will proceed as follows. The remainder of this chapter will provide an introduction to the methodology to be used, including brief discussions of scriptural theology, narrative criticism, irony, rhetoric and intertextuality. It will also introduce some public theology questions and set the limits of the research. Chapter 2 will present a close reading of the sections of John's Gospel that refer to the figure of Jesus as the serpent, drawing on the techniques of irony, rhetoric, and intertextuality as discussed in Chapter 1. Chapter 3 will step back to look at Numbers 21 and other relevant passages in the Old Testament seeking to demonstrate that the reading of John presented in Chapter 2 is a responsible reading when set in the larger context of scripture. Chapter 4 will examine the writings of other ancient authors who use the image of the serpent on the pole, again to check if the reading provided here is coherent in the wider context of the First Century of the Common Era. Finally, Chapter 5 will return to the question at the heart of this research: does John, using the figure of Jesus as the serpent, provide another way to understand how God accomplishes salvation through the Christ event; an understanding that can deepen the dialogue about atonement that is currently taking place in our society? The question will be answered affirmatively. John's Jesus offers "restorative" justice to the world.

Methodology

It needs to be said at the outset that this work is intended to be a confessional reading of the Gospel of John, that is a reading from inside the church for the benefit of the church in the world. It takes the literature of the Bible seriously as sacred literature that speaks to realities beyond history and science, as it has spoken in the past. It is possible that only a confessional reading can be expected to adequately understand the literary device of typology as used in John 3:14, as will be discussed below. Following Ellen Davis, the work attempted here intends to help the people of God interpret their experience, be moved by Scripture, and trust the Bible as one reliable guide for their life.[32] At the same time this work seeks to benefit from the best that biblical scholarship can offer by taking seriously the context in which the Gospel of John was written. This work stands on the shoulders of others and seeks to honor their intelligence, diligence and faithfulness.

The following sections discuss the umbrella of Scriptural Theology under which this work will take place and the specific critical methods that will be used to explore the typology expressed in John 3:14.

Scriptural Theology

'Scriptural Theology,' which might be considered synonymous with 'Theological Interpretation of Scripture' or 'Biblical Theology,' depending on how these terms are understood, is, in the current

32 Ellen F. Davis, "Teaching the Bible Confessionally in the Church," in *The Art of Reading Scripture*, ed. Ellen F. Davis and Richard B. Hays (Grand Rapids: Eerdmans, 2003), 9-10.

climate of biblical studies, difficult to define. The intent in this research is to explore one scriptural depiction of Jesus' death, resurrection, and ascension: that given in John 3:14 by the phrase, "And just as Moses lifted up the serpent in the wilderness so must the Son of Man be lifted up…"[33] in an attempt to understand better what God accomplished through the Christ event, the purview of "atonement" theology. As an exercise in Scriptural Theology, this research seeks to bring together the disciplines of biblical studies and constructive theology, long divided by the currents of history, in a way that explores the meaning of a biblical text for the church in service to the world. It attempts to use the best tools of both disciplines while neither bracketing out the question of faith nor using exegesis to support any particular piece of doctrine. The presupposition behind the work is that there is a God who has been truly witnessed to by the sacred writings of the Old and New Testaments and who has done something decisive for humanity through the incarnation, cross, resurrection, and ascension of Christ. This author locates herself within a credal faith tradition, so it is unavoidable that there is a latent bias behind this work. However it is not the goal of the work to bolster any existing theology – the intent is to let the text speak about God with its own voice into the current context as much as is possible. All readers of scripture have lenses, shaped and polished by their experience, education, and temperament. This work is the result of a close reading of John's Gospel followed by an examination of its Old Testament roots and literature produced in roughly the same time period. The work has suggested that "restorative justice" is a powerful lens through which to view the Gospel; a lens that allows new light to shine from the Gospel and lift up Jesus again before the world. While historical-critical and literary-critical tools will be used, the answers that are sought are neither historical or literary. No philosophical defense of the existence of God or justification of faith claims will be attempted, though in keeping with John Collins' exhortation, the moral and ethical impacts of atonement theology

33 Scriptural quotations are taken from the NRSV unless otherwise noted.

on the current American context, where this author is located, will be examined.[34]

New books and articles are continually becoming available and two sections of the Society of Biblical Literature have been devoted to Theological Interpretation of Scripture.[35] A brief summary of some of this discussion, including this author's viewpoint, follows.

A ground breaking narration of how biblical scholarship arrived at the current state, which Scriptural Theology tries to address, was provided by Hans Frei.[36] Frei described how the rise of rationalism and the scientific method made it impossible for interpreters to encounter scripture in the way that they had prior to the Reformation. A wedge was driven between the reality depicted in the texts and the reality of the world around the interpreter. The nature of miraculous and numinous elements as well as internal contradictions within scripture had always raised questions for interpreters, but in the enlightenment climate of humanism and rationalism, those questions eroded the truth claims of scripture. How could the Bible be true if it did not accurately reflect what history and archeology were discovering about the ancient world? Such questions about what Scripture is and how best to read it are pressing now for any interpreter of biblical texts and the range of answers to these questions is almost as broad and various as the number of interpreters. Is the Bible the verbally inspired word of God, essentially dictated by the Holy Spirit and intended to be interpreted literally as a rulebook for how to live the Christian life? Or is the Bible an entirely human document that provides a window into the history of an ancient culture and religion that has, through

---

34 John J. Collins, *Encounters with Biblical Theology* (Minneapolis: Augsburg Fortress, 2005), 6.

35 Stephen E. Fowl, *Theological Interpretation of Scripture* (Eugene, Oregon: Cascade Books, 2009), Kindle Electronic Edition: Introduction, Location 34.

36 Hans W. Frei, *The Eclipse of the Biblical Narrative: A Study in Eighteenth and Nineteenth Century Hermeneutics*. (New Haven: Yale University Press, 1974). Other helpful and readable summaries of this history are offered by James L. Kugel in the first and final chapters of his *How to Read the Bible: A Guide to Scripture Then and Now* (New York: Free Press, 2007), 1-46 and 662-689 and John Sandys-Wunsch, *What Have They Done to the Bible? A History of Modern Biblical Interpretation* (Collegeville: Liturgical Press, 2005).

the vagaries of history, had a huge impact on the culture and thought of the West? Or is it something in between? If the Bible is to be taken seriously as an important object of study in the twenty-first century, what are appropriate methods and goals for its study? How can a present day interpreter use the best of the discoveries of the past and avoid some of the pitfalls that are so apparent in twenty-twenty hindsight?

James Kugel illustrates this historical shift by noting the change in assumptions about Scripture that has occurred from those of the ancient interpreters, including the New Testament writers, to those of post-enlightenment interpreters. Kugel first summarizes the unwritten assumptions lying behind the work of all ancient interpreters. They assumed that the text was fundamentally: first, cryptic (it might say one thing and mean another) second, lessons directed at the *current* reader; third, perfectly harmonious (containing no errors or contradictions) and finally divinely given (containing God's direct speech through God's prophets).[37] But, Kugel points out, after the tectonic shifts in western thinking brought about by the Reformation, the Renaissance and the Enlightenment, Spinoza outlines a procedure for reading the Bible that almost entirely dismantles the ancient four assumptions. For Spinoza, according to Kugel, understandings of scripture: first, come from the words of Scripture alone, traditional interpretations are suspect; second, come from understanding the language and world of ideas out of which the scriptures were written without the influence of current prejudices or preferences; third, should be literal until this becomes impossible, in which case a metaphorical interpretation is allowed; fourth, depend on the process of how a particular biblical book came to be written and the life situation and personality of its human author; and finally, have to recognize that there are contradictions and multiple viewpoints, so that the important task is to find areas of common agreement and discard the contradictory material.[38]

This change in assumptions led to dramatic changes, not only in how Scripture was read, but also in how it was viewed. Scripture

37 Kugel, *How to Read the Bible*, 14-16.

38 Kugel, *How to Read the Bible*, 31-32.

changed from a *subject* that addressed its readers to an *object* of study.[39] Biblical theologians like J. P. Gabler, followed by William Wrede developed a program that sought to end the "the inappropriate combination of the simplicity and ease of biblical theology with the subtlety and difficulty of dogmatic theology"[40] Gabler defined biblical theology as "conveying what the holy writers felt about divine matters,"[41] separate from dogmatic theology, which was what theologians philosophized about divine things. Biblical theology was fixed and divinely inspired. It could be discovered through a historical exercise conducted on Scripture; biblical theology was then available for theologians to produce their work, which was inevitably conditioned by the location of the theologian. For Gabler, the task of the biblical theologian was to discover the theology of the writers of Scripture by careful interpretation and comparison of the ideas of the various authors of scripture[42] in order to determine those "which have to do with the unchanging testament of Christian doctrine, and therefore pertain directly to" contemporary humanity.[43]

William Wrede further developed and critiqued Gabler's ideas and the method they produced, continuing to make distinctions between biblical authors as well as the Old and New Testaments,[44] and emphasizing that biblical theology is a purely historical endeavor.[45]

39 Kugel, *How to Read the Bible*, 666.

40 J. P. Gabler, "On the Proper Distinction Between Biblical and Dogmatic Theology and the Specific Objectives of Each" tr. John Sandys-Wunsch and Laurence Eldredge in *Johann P. Gabler on Biblical Theology*, http://jimhamilton.info/wp-content/uploads/2012/05/Gabler-ProperDistinction-BiblicalTheology.pdf, 495 (Accessed on July 2015).

41 Gabler, "On the Proper Distinction Between Biblical and Dogmatic Theology and the Specific Objectives of Each," 496.

42 Gabler, "On the Proper Distinction Between Biblical and Dogmatic Theology and the Specific Objectives of Each," 498.

43 Gabler, "On the Proper Distinction Between Biblical and Dogmatic Theology and the Specific Objectives of Each," 500.

44 William Wrede, "The Task and Methods of "New Testament Theology," in T*he Nature of New Testament Theology: The Contribution of William Wrede and Adolf Schatter*, pp. 68-116, ed. trans. Robert Morgan (London: SCM Press, 1973), 68.

45 Wrede, "The Task and Methods of "New Testament Theology," 69.

Wrede believed that a careful scholar can discover "only what was" leaving all his own thought behind.[46] Wrede wanted to eliminate consideration of the canon as a later construct conditioned by the historical situation of the church fathers.[47] Wrede did not feel that it was possible to determine the individual views of the individual New Testament writers – there was not enough writing from most of them[48] – instead he believed that a more general picture could be obtained. Wrede was also critical of literary methods that found connections between documents,[49] feeling that they overemphasized the details in individual documents.[50] For Wrede, "the type is more important than the variant and what is wanted is the general widespread view that influences the individual cases."[51] There is a poignancy to the absolute confidence that both Gabler and Wrede express in their work. Phrases like "self -evident" and "of course" abound. They were absolutely certain that with hard work, their end could be achieved: that the single coherent theology, expressed in disparate pieces by the authors of the New Testament, could be discovered.

David Steinmetz, among others, provides a useful critique of the method proposed by Gabler and Wrede. Steinmetz, like Kugel, recalls the wisdom of the ancient interpreters, a wisdom that noted the multivalent meanings of any given text. For Steinmetz, "meaning involves a listener as well as a speaker" and "the meaning of historical texts cannot be separated from the complex problem of their reception and the notion that a text means only what its author intends it to mean is historically naive [...] To attempt to understand those original meanings is the first step in the exegetical process, not the last and final step."[52]

---

46 Wrede, "The Task and Methods of "New Testament Theology," 70.

47 Wrede, "The Task and Methods of "New Testament Theology," 71.

48 Wrede, "The Task and Methods of "New Testament Theology," 74.

49 Wrede, "The Task and Methods of "New Testament Theology," 79.

50 Wrede, "The Task and Methods of "New Testament Theology," 81.

51 Wrede, "The Task and Methods of "New Testament Theology," 90.

52 David C. Steinmetz, "The Superiority of Pre-Critical Exegesis," in *The Theological Interpretation of Scripture: Classic and Contemporary Readings*, ed. Stephen E. Fowl (Cambridge: Blackwell, 1997), 36.

It may be useful at this point to contrast the procedures to be followed in this research with those recommended by William Wrede. This project attempts to reconnect biblical exegesis and theology – particularly atonement theology – not by using the scriptural text to support an already existing doctrinal formula, but to let the text speak to its readers/hearers with its own voice about what God accomplishes for humanity in Christ. The project pays attention to the specific details of a specific author of scripture, believing that the author uses those details to convey something important about the Christ event.[53] The project also seeks intentionally to find connections between various scriptural writings; it seeks to bring together what historical-critical methods have separated, particularly the writings of the Old and New Testaments, recognizing that only when we seek to understand how and why the writers of scripture made these connections, can we begin to understand what they were saying about Christ.

In the post-modern context, where one is confronted with many different perspectives and many other faiths, Gabler and Wrede's projects do appear historically naive. Thus, while current biblical exegesis owes a great debt to the work of these scholars and all those who followed them in their discoveries of the historical context behind the scriptural texts, what this research seeks to do is something different. For this work, the view of scripture that is most fitting was articulated by Martin Luther in his Prefaces to the Old Testament: "here you will find the swaddling clothes and the manger in which Christ lies."[54] The Bible is a whole that came to be through a complex process of human agency, led by God. Historical as well as literary methods are useful in letting it speak. Non-canonical sources can also be helpful in this investigation, though they are distinct from the Bible itself. The product of the investigation that is this work, is as historically conditioned and human as is scripture itself – though also, hopefully, led by God. It is intended to contribute to

53 Not that Wrede would disagree with this idea, but Wrede would want to downplay the detail in favor of a broad general picture. See Wrede, "The Task and Methods of "New Testament Theology," 84.

54 Martin Luther, "Prefaces to the Old Testament" in *Luther's Works*,Volume 35 (Philadelphia: Muhlenberg Press, 1960), 236.

an ongoing dialogue. It is hoped that it will produce suppositions and further questions that can move the Christian community a step closer in its relationship to God.

The specific critical methods and features of the Johannine narrative to be used and explored in this study: narrative criticism, irony, rhetoric, intertextuality, and typology will now be discussed in some detail.

Narrative Criticism

Literary-critical methods of biblical interpretation begin with the assumption that "the form and specific articulation of any given text must be taken with the utmost seriousness and not regarded as incidental or extraneous." Thus literary critical methodologies provide "access to questions of the mode and arena of God's presence that are not within the range of traditional historical-critical method.[55] Narrative critical methods attempt to read the text in its final form and in terms of its own story-world.[56] The narrative, in this case the Gospel of John, is examined in terms of the techniques used to align the reader's perception of the world with the worldview of the narrative.[57] Thus the story's plot, characters, setting, point of view, and time frame can be analyzed in order to understand how they convey meaning and affect the reader's understanding of the subject matter. Narrative criticism will be the most important exegetical methodology of this research, chosen for two reasons. First the object of the investigation is the theology of the text – not the history of the text's production, the world behind the text, or the original author's intent. While these are interesting points of investigation, their resolution involves a great deal of uncertainty and leads one away from the primary goal of this work. Secondly, narrative criticism allows one to understand the meaning of a part

55 Gail R. O'Day, *Revelation in the Fourth Gospel: Narrative Mode and Theological Claim* (Philadelphia: Fortress Press, 1986), 2.

56 David M. Gunn, "Narrative Criticism," in *To Each Its Own Meaning: Biblical Criticisms and their Applications*, ed. Steven L. McKenzie and Stephen R. Haynes (Louisville: Westminster John Knox, 1999), 201.

57 R. Alan Culpepper, *Anatomy of the Fourth Gospel: A Study in Literary Design* (Philadelphia: Fortress Press, 1983), 4.

of a narrative within the context of the whole. Thus it avoids the practice of proof-texting; a practice that starts with a pre-determined theological conclusion and mines various texts for support for that conclusion. For the purposes of this study, the final form of John's Gospel as received through tradition will be studied and its narrative unity will be assumed. This narrative unity has been asserted by many scholars and need not be demonstrated here.[58] Also, for the sake of convenience, the implied author of the Fourth Gospel will be referred to as "John." This is not meant as a commitment to any particular theory of who the author of the Gospel was. This author's preference is that "John" was an otherwise unknown disciple of Jesus, not one of the twelve, who resided in or near Jerusalem and thus had experience of the parts of Jesus' life and ministry that took place near there. Whether or not his original material was revised or redacted by later followers is beyond the scope of this inquiry.

The aspects of John's narrative that are of particular interest to this study are the literary structure and major themes of John's Gospel (to be discussed in Chapter 2); John's use of irony and how it holds in tension two very different images of the crucifixion of Jesus; John's rhetoric and how it functions to affect the reader/hearer; and John's use of scripture, in this case the Old Testament, in service of his portrait of Jesus as the definitive revelation of God.

Irony

Gail R. O'Day has done a considerable amount of work on how irony functions in the Gospel of John. She describes two ways to consider irony and locates herself somewhere between the two. The first focuses more on literary questions and is exemplified by R. Allan Culpepper and Paul Duke. Culpepper identifies six themes that are treated ironically in John: the rejection of Jesus, the origin of Jesus, Jesus' identity, Jesus' ministry, Jesus' death, and discipleship. For Duke, irony functions both as part of the Johannine polemic against "the Jews" and, more importantly, as supporting the Johannine

58 Significant studies that accept the narrative unity of John's Gospel include the work of R. Allan Culpepper, Gail R. O'Day, Andrew T. Lincoln, George Parsenios and Jo-Ann A. Brant.

witness with a strong, though indirect appeal.[59] The second focuses more on theological questions and is best exemplified by George MacRae. For MacRae, the Johannine perception of an incongruity between appearance and reality is a dramatic irony that creates distance between the readers/hearers and the events in the narrative. This distance, created by the post-Easter knowledge injected into the narrative, expresses John's own insight into the meaning of Christ in the world and involves the reader in the challenge of faith.[60] O'Day is interested in both how John uses irony to express his theology and how its use impacts the reader.

Successful irony depends on some level of shared knowledge between the reader/hearer and the author.[61] It is the Post-Easter perspective, intertwined throughout John's Gospel that provides this. John stresses two levels of comprehension of who Jesus is and these two levels recur over and over in John's dualism as will be shown in the narrative reading presented in Chapter 2.[62] But John's dualities do not function as a simple either-or; they operate simultaneously. The real meaning is present in the expressed meaning in an unexpected way.[63] Over and over the reader is asked to size up both levels of meaning and make the correct mental move. Jesus uses this same dynamic in his speech, continually challenging the perception of his hearers in a way that leads to misunderstanding. The readers/hearers of the narrative are given interpretive keys that the characters in the narrative do not have. This creates the irony and draws the reader/hearers in as they work to interpret the story and Jesus' words. For O'Day, this is why Jesus comes both to judge and not to judge.[64] The dynamics of revelation are created and recreated by this narratival orchestration. The communication process is as important as the content of the communication. Revelation is not static and fixed, but

59 O'Day, *Revelation in the Fourth Gospel*, 3.

60 O'Day, *Revelation in the Fourth Gospel*, 6.

61 O'Day, *Revelation in the Fourth Gospel*, 7.

62 O'Day, *Revelation in the Fourth Gospel*, 7-8.

63 O'Day, *Revelation in the Fourth Gospel*, 8.

64 O'Day, *Revelation in the Fourth Gospel*, 9.

dynamic and generative, and John's Gospel itself allows the reader to experience that revelation.[65]

Irony can be distinguished from other forms of figurative speech because it always includes "some kind of opposition between the two levels of meaning, either contradiction, incongruity, or incompatibility."[66] In allegory or metaphor, even if one misses the second level of meaning, the story still advances. This is not true of irony. With irony, the levels of meaning are in conflict and the correct reading always involves awareness of the incongruity between the literal and intended meaning.[67] For irony to succeed, the author has to establish a relationship with the audience. They must share the same knowledge and perceptions. This relationship is built and strengthened through sharing ironies, so another function of irony is to build an alliance between the author and the reader/hearer; an alliance that in turn builds community among those who share the reading/hearing experience.[68]

O'Day believes that despite its apparent attempts to conceal, the irony in John draws the readers/hearers into participation in John's vision of Jesus, allowing them to "see," thus irony is revelatory language. It reveals by asking the reader/hearer to make judgments about the relative value of the stated and intended meanings.[69] "John's mode of presentation renders the object of that presentation: the literary form in which Jesus is presented as revelation in John is inseparable from the Johannine theology of revelation."[70]

Rhetoric

Both Jo-Ann Brant and George Parsenios have noted the dramatic quality of John's Gospel. Brant sees in the so-called Johannine anti-language, i.e., "word plays, ambiguity, and misunderstanding, dualism, and irony," the characteristics of the language of Greek

65 O'Day, *Revelation in the Fourth Gospel*, 10.

66 O'Day, *Revelation in the Fourth Gospel*, 23.

67 O'Day, *Revelation in the Fourth Gospel*, 24.

68 O'Day, *Revelation in the Fourth Gospel*, 30.

69 O'Day, *Revelation in the Fourth Gospel*, 31.

70 O'Day, *Revelation in the Fourth Gospel*, 32.

tragedy.[71] John's Gospel is also dramatic in that it gives the narrator a small role and frequently carries the plot through the speech of the characters; that is, the language shows rather than tells. Though the Fourth Gospel is not a play, readers/hearers *experience* it; they become its audience.[72] Brant notes that the attractiveness of this hypothesis in the past has been that it preserves the literary unity of the Gospel and that it provides a softening of the anti-Jewish polemic, the portrayal of "the Jews" is less problematic if they are seen as characters in a drama. These advantages may be true, but more importantly for Brant, to respect the literary context is to allow ambiguity and paradox to usurp certitude and clarity. The Gospel presents a struggle to understand who Jesus is and what God is doing. It is not a collection of creedal statements that can be ripped from their context.[73] Brant points out that in the first century of the Common Era the performance of Greek and Roman tragedies took the form of private readings in homes. This social context suggests to Brant that a public presentation of the Gospel through a reader may explain the presence of the theatrical conventions observed in the Gospel.[74] The prologue to the Gospel makes sense in this context and, like a prologue in Greek tragedy, it prepares its audience to follow the plot. John's prologue "initiates the audience into the privileged realm of knowing that makes irony possible, orients the audience to the broader narrative in which the action is situated and prepares it to enter the action in medias res, and calls the audience into being and gives it a role."[75]

George Parsenios also notes the similarities between John's Gospel and Greek tragedy, particularly in the legal language that combines features of ancient rhetoric and ancient drama.[76] Parsenios

---

71 Jo-Ann Brant, *Dialogue and Drama:Elements of Greek Tragedy in the Fourth Gospel* (Peabody: Hendrickson, 2004), 3.

72 Jo-Ann Brant, *Dialogue and Drama:Elements of Greek Tragedy in the Fourth Gospel* (Peabody: Hendrickson, 2004), 3.

73 Brant, *Dialogue and Drama*, 7.

74 Brant, *Dialogue and Drama*, 15.

75 Brant, *Dialogue and Drama*, 17.

76 George Parsenios, *Rhetoric and Drama in the Johannine Lawsuit Motif* (Tübingen, Mohr Siebeck, 2010), 1.

notes that John displaces Jesus' trial before the Sanhedrin in such a way that Jesus' entire life is a legal contest played out before the leaders of Israel, the testimony of which frames the Gospel from start to finish.[77] Parsenios demonstrates that "legal rhetoric and tragic drama represent twin modes of discourse" born together in ancient Athens that continued "to resemble and relate" as they matured and meet again in a unique way in the Gospel of John.[78] John uses "this forensic character of tragedy" because it illustrates that "the line that separates guilt from innocence is the difference between appearance and reality." John demonstrates the innocence of Jesus by showing that his "guilt was only apparent, not real."[79] But the disparity between appearance and reality goes even deeper than Jesus' innocence or guilt in John, for the appearance in the drama is that Jesus is on trial throughout the book, while the reality is that Jesus' presence puts the world on trial and the judgment against Jesus is his vindication and triumph.[80] Parsenios also notes John's use of a double meaning for the word ζητέω; the ones who have been seeking Jesus earnestly, like seekers of wisdom in ancient Israel, "find" Jesus, but those who are already convinced that he cannot be the Messiah seek him in a legal, prosecutorial way. "Sapiental and legal traditions [...] represent opposing responses to Jesus," though Parsenios qualifies this assertion in an appropriate way, pointing to John's creative appropriation of the traditions available to him.[81] The opposition is between appearance and reality, sight and blindness, and knowledge and ignorance, all readily recognizable elements in John's narrative.[82] For Parsenios, the signs in John are evidence that should lead to acceptance of Jesus – a blending of legal rhetoric and tragic recognition.[83] This blending of legal and dramatic rhetoric

77 Parsenios, *Rhetoric and Drama*, 1-2.

78 Parsenios, *Rhetoric and Drama*, 2.

79 Parsenios, *Rhetoric and Drama*, 28.

80 Parsenios, *Rhetoric and Drama*, 29.

81 Parsenios, *Rhetoric and Drama*, 82.

82 Parsenios, *Rhetoric and Drama*, 61.

83 Parsenios, Rhetoric and Drama, 88.

function to draw the reader/hearer into the narrative to judge and to be judged along with the characters in it.

Intertextuality

Intertextuality – a reference to an earlier text within a later one[84] – will also be an important exegetical focus of this study. The Gospel of John employs a large number of quotations from and allusions to the scriptures of ancient Israel, most probably the Septuagint.[85] How John uses these allusions to shape his story of Jesus' life from within his first-century Jewish worldview will be an essential component of this research.

Here it becomes necessary to discuss appropriate terminology. It is important to acknowledge that the collection of writings that Christians tend to call the Old Testament is also the scripture of Judaism. Many scholars refer to it as the Hebrew Bible to express respect for the history of that tradition apart from the rise of Christianity and its later assumption of political power that has had such dire consequences in human history. There is great value in the scholarly movement that wants to understand the Hebrew Bible in its own right before reinterpreting it in the light of the Christ event. These two readings need to be held in tension and in dialogue. One important interest of this research is how the early followers of Christ, many of them Jewish, interpreted his life, death, resurrection and ascension in light of their own scripture, which they probably read in Greek. It was these interpretations that became incorporated into the scripture of Christianity. Therefore for the purposes of this work, the terms Old and New Testament seem most appropriate.

In this regard, it is also important to acknowledge the difficulty in using the terms "Jew" and "Christian" during the time frame of many of the writings considered here. It is probably fair to call the writer of the *Epistle of Barnabas* and Justin Martyr 'Christians' because they seek in their writings to distance themselves, often in

84 Richard B. Hays, *Echoes of Scripture in the Letters of Paul* (New Haven: Yale University Press, 1989), 14.

85 Andreas J. Köstenberger, "John" in *Commentary on the New Testament Use of the Old Testament*, ed. G. K. Beale and D. A. Carson (Grand Rapids: Baker Academic, 2007), 417-418.

hostile ways, from the Jewish tradition. Philo and the author of the Wisdom of Solomon and the later rabbis may be described as Jewish, although, given the complexity of Second Temple Judaism even that title is a bit ambiguous in the time around the turn of the Era. The authors of Ezra, Nehemiah, Esther, and 1and 2 Maccabees do refer to the Jews (either with the substantive adjective 'Ιουδαῖος or as some subset of the nation of Ιουδα) and so that title will be used descriptively when appropriate. The term 'Ιουδαῖος was also used in the wider Roman culture to describe residents of Judea and those associated with them by ancestry, but for the writers of the New Testament itself both terms are problematic. The distinction between Judaism and Christianity that we experience today did not exist then. The very first followers of Jesus would have considered themselves as Jewish as any who considered Abraham, Isaac and Jacob to be their ancestors. While the Gospel of John explores a sharp and painful conflict between the followers of Jesus and those labeled "Ιουδαῖος,' this conflict reflects two different factions within a single tradition, which goes a long way towards explaining the bitterness of the fight. It is difficult to find appropriate language to express the distinctions within this period of time. Throughout this work the attempt will be made to use nuanced language that is not too cumbersome.

Quotations, Allusions, and Echoes

It is convenient to classify references to the Old Testament in the New Testament in terms of quotations, allusions and echoes. Quotations are often, though not always, introduced with a citation formula such as "it is written" or this "was to fulfill." Another criteria to identify a quotation is as a combination of words that could not have occurred in the form they do without knowledge of a prior occurrence.[86] Care should be taken in interpreting quotations to examine if they are direct or subtly modified to fit the quoting author's purposes. Allusions pick up on a few key words and are woven more completely into the fabric of the newer composition. It is occasionally difficult to know if an allusion is really intended

86 Steve Moyise, *The Old Testament in the New: An Introduction* (New York: Continuum, 2001), 5.

by the author and always difficult to know exactly how an allusion is to be interpreted. Should the entire context of the earlier passage be considered in the later passage or not? An echo is fainter still, a hint that the author is (perhaps intentionally) using the idioms or expressions of an earlier scriptural author.[87] Again interpretation of how much these echoes shape the author's meaning is difficult, but they can hint at the background of the author's thought.

Richard Hays provides some useful guidelines for understanding scriptural echoes including: availability, volume, recurrence, thematic coherence, historical plausibility, history of interpretation, and satisfaction.[88] These criteria can help examine the scriptural echoes associated with the sections of John's Gospel important for illuminating John's understanding of the meaning of Jesus being "lifted up."

Allegory and Typology

Hans Frei described typology as a natural extension of literal biblical interpretation. Because the writers of the New Testament read their Scripture as referring to actual historical events that tell a single story depicting the temporal sequence of which they were a part, they understood that earlier biblical stories or figures were types of later stories and events or patterns of meaning. The customary use of typology was to show that the persons, events, and prophesies of the Old Testament were fulfilled in the New Testament. "Figuration was at once a literary and a historical procedure, an interpretation of stories and their meanings by weaving them together into a common narrative referring to a single history and its patterns of meaning."[89] Typology is interested in two (or more) formally similar narratives. It adjusts them into the one real temporal sequence of which they are both a part. The emphasis is on the whole of the narrative sequence into which each individual story is shaped. The stories are figures of one another, but they retain their independent and self-contained

87 Moyise, *The Old Testament in the New*, 5-6.

88 Richard B. Hays, *The Conversion of the Imagination: Paul as Interpreter of Israel's Scripture* (Grand Rapids: Eerdmans, 2005), 34-45.

89 Frei, *The Eclipse of the Biblical Narrative*, 2.

status, each being literally descriptive and all forming a literal narrative.[90] Typological interpretation did not require a statement of the nature of the causal or temporal connection between the two types. It established the connection by sheer juxtaposition, noting the similarities and the order of ascending climax. The link between type and antitype "can be established only by narration and under the conviction of the primacy of the literal, grammatical sense."[91] For exegetes like John Calvin and Martin Luther, typological interpretation set forth the unity of the canon of Old and New Testaments as a single cumulative and complex pattern of meaning.[92] Typology only works if the narration is assumed to describe real events, objects or persons and if those figures are contained in the same stream of history. The interpreters themselves are part of this stream and can understand the typology only by garnering a sense of the narrative from the inside.[93]

Typology, as practiced by the Church fathers, may also give insights into the interpretive methods of the writers of the New Testament. As described by O'Keefe and Reno, typology moves beyond the analysis of particular words and images towards larger, unifying patterns within the Bible. Because they understood scripture to be part of the divine economy, the fathers understood that the whole Bible contained an ordered sequence that was structured by the figure of Christ. Typological exegesis explored the larger coherence of scripture and described its architecture. It allowed the fathers to develop a unified reading of the Old and New Testaments and provided a means to bring Christian practice and experience into God's economy as revealed in scripture. It was, according to O'Keefe and Reno, the most important interpretive strategy for early Christianity.[94] Types transcend distances of space and time and create a sense of participation in a unified reality, thus typological interpretation of the Bible is present in every century of

---

90 Frei, *The Eclipse of the Biblical Narrative*, 28.

91 Frei, *The Eclipse of the Biblical Narrative*, 31.

92 Frei, *The Eclipse of the Biblical Narrative*, 33.

93 Frei, *The Eclipse of the Biblical Narrative*, 36-37.

94 John J. O'Keefe and R. R. Reno, *Sanctified Vision: An Introduction to Early Christian Interpretation of the Bible* (Baltimore: Johns Hopkins, 2005), 69.

Christian history.[95] The success of a typology doesn't depend on any direct correspondence between history and the present; typology is an appeal to a common type. If one knows the narrative from which the type comes, the typology will need no explanation.[96] A good typology allows the reader/hearer to enter into the experience of the type directly without an extended explanation. The association of the type and antitype, discloses the common element, which becomes visible to the reader/hearer. "The dense particularity of the two sides of the typological interpretation does all the work of illumination"[97] and this illumination works both ways, shedding light on both the type and the antitype.

Leonhard Goppelt claims that "typology is the method of biblical interpretation that is characteristic of the [New Testament]."[98] He points out that Paul is the first to use type (τύπος) as a term for the prefiguring of the future in prior history (Romans 5:14). For Goppelt, typological interpretation is only appropriate if it uses historical facts – persons, actions, events, and institutions that are considered to be divinely ordained as types (representations) of future realities that will be greater and more complete.[99] This sense of heightening and completion makes typological interpretation particularly appropriate for eschatological writings.[100] The task for a contemporary reader of typology is to determine the viewpoint of the New Testament writer rather than any objective method of interpretation.[101] Goppelt notes that typology relies on history and a sense of consummation that arose in the early church because the scholarship of Palestine took seriously the literal meaning of the Old Testament and shut itself off from the non-Jewish world to some extent.[102]

---

95 O'Keefe and Reno, *Sanctified Vision*, 70.

96 O'Keefe and Reno, *Sanctified Vision*, 71.

97 O'Keefe and Reno, *Sanctified Vision*, 72.

98 Leonhard Goppelt, *Typos: The Typological Interpretation of the Old Testament in the New* (Grand Rapids: Eerdmans, 1982). 4.

99 Goppelt, *Typos*, 17-18.

100 Goppelt, *Typos*, 57.

101 Goppelt, *Typos*, 18.

102 Goppelt, *Typos*, 41.

Goppelt believes that John's Gospel reveals an attitude toward the Old Testament that presupposes a typological approach. John's Jesus emphasizes that scripture testifies about him and he uses scripture to interpret the salvation that he brings.[103] Goppelt believes that Jesus' work moves on the level of creation typology; the redemptive gifts of the Old Testament that give life and announce new creation are related to Jesus typologically. The Gospel gives continuous indications of a comprehensive typological approach.[104]

Allegory, according to O'Keefe and Reno means literally in Greek "other speak." Allegories claim that the plain or obvious sense of a text is not its full meaning. The words, events, and characters of the allegory stand for another realm of meaning that needs to be decoded. Allegorical interpretation reads the text like a map; it is a reading laid over the text rather than found in it.[105] Frei understands allegory to be the attachment of a free-floating meaning pattern to a narrative or event without any intrinsic connection between the time-bound picture and its allegorical meaning.[106] For Goppelt, allegory seeks to find in the ideas and phrases of a text "in addition to the literal sense of the text, and, at times, to the exclusion of it," another different and presumably deeper meaning. The historicity and the literal meaning of what is reported is of no consequence for allegorical interpretation (while for typology they are foundational).[107] The allegorist, however, would not see the double meaning as something forced upon the text, rather the allegorical interpretation would be intended and given in the text and understood through a divinely inspired process.

The difference between typology and allegory can be clearly demonstrated by comparing what Philo of Alexandria and the author of John's Gospel do when they reinterpret the story of Moses and the bronze serpent for their respective audiences.

---

103 Goppelt, *Typos*, 179.

104 Goppelt, *Typos*, 180-181.

105 O'Keefe and Reno, *Sanctified Vision*, 90.

106 Frei, *The Eclipse of the Biblical Narrative*, 29.

107 Goppelt, *Typos*, 18.

Philo was a Jewish exegete of Jewish texts, but he was very much a Hellenistic thinker. In his interpretations he greatly expands the biblical text, adding dialogue and giving the characters Greco-Roman qualities. His characters thus become personifications of moral virtues and vices. His allegorical readings of the Pentateuch draw on Greek philosophy, particularly Platonic philosophy.[108] Philo is thought to have been extremely influential, perhaps in the writing of the New Testament itself, but most certainly on Christian thought. "Philo's allegorical method and interpretations helped 'scripturize' Hellenistic philosophical concepts that would eventually become key to Christian theology."[109]

Philo deals with the story of Moses and the Bronze serpent in two places in his extant corpus: in his *Allegorical Interpretations II* and in *Husbandry*. Both of these works are in the style of a commentary, the Pentateuchal text is cited and an exposition follows. *Allegorical Interpretation II* is a commentary on Genesis 3:8b-19 and *Husbandry* is a commentary on Genesis 9:20-21.[110]

In both commentaries the serpent on the pole that Moses made is described allegorically as temperance, which is the antidote to the serpent of pleasure, the serpent that tempted Eve. The passages in Philo are too long to practically present a translation here, but his argument beginning with *Allegorical Interpretation* 2.71,[111] commenting on Genesis 3:1, runs something along these lines: God created mind (Adam) and outward sense (Eve). Pleasure – which brings these two things together was a third creation spoken of symbolically under the emblem of the serpent. The form of the

108 George W. E. Nickelsburg, "Philo among Greeks, Jews and Christians," in *Philo und das Neue Testament: Wechselseitige Wahrnehmungen*. ed. Roland Deines and Karl-Wilhelm Niebuhr (Tübingen: Mohr Siebeck, 2004), 58-59.

109 William Yarchin, *History of Biblical Interpretation: A Reader* (Peabody: Hendrickson, 2004), 19.

110 Peder Borgen, *Philo, John and Paul: New Perspectives on Judaism and Early Christianity* (Atlanta: Scholars Press,1987), 33.

111 Philo, Allegorical Interpretation II, English Text, *The Works of Philo,* Completed and Unabridged. New Updated Edition. Translated by C. D. Yonge. Copyright © 1993 by Hendrickson Publishers, Inc. Electronic text prepared by Oaktree Software, Inc. Version 1.1.

serpent is appropriate for pleasure because of its many windings – five in fact: sight, hearing, touch, taste, and smell – and pleasure is most intense when it arises from the connection between a man and a woman (mind and outward sense). The multitude of serpents that bite the Israelites on their way from their corporal habitations (that is Egypt) are the entanglements of immoderate pleasure that lead to death (2.77). Here Philo refers to the story in Numbers 21 quoting verse 7 from some version of the Septuagint: "ὅτι ἡμαρτήκαμεν, ὅτι κατελαλήσαμεν κατά κυρίου καί κατά σοῦ. εὖξαι οὖν πρός κύριον, καί ἀφελέτω ἀφ᾽ ἡμῶν τούς ὄφεις"[112] (2.78) As a remedy for the serpent of pleasure – the serpent that came to Eve – God commands Moses to make the serpent that is the word of temperance, saying "ποίησον σεαυτῷ ὄφιν καί θές αὐτόν ἐπί σημείου" (2.79). Philo goes on to explain details in the Numbers text such as the presence of the reflexive pronoun σεαυτῷ in God's command and why the serpent is made of bronze, even though that material is not specified in the command. Here Philo writes in much the same way that later Rabbis will. He pays meticulous attention to the text and feels called to dwell on its every feature, though his allegorical interpretations sound much more Hellenistic than Jewish. After this discussion he again quotes God's command in Numbers 21:8 "ὃν ἂν οὖν δάκῃ ὄφις, πᾶς ὁ ἰδών αυςτόν ζήσεται." Philo then draws widely on the Pentateuch to further explicate this issue. He uses the description of the wilderness in Deuteronomy 8, including the scorpions and serpents and water from the rock. He brings in Moses' rod and the serpent that it became in Exodus 4:3 and he discusses Jacob's blessing of Dan as a serpent in Genesis 49:16.

For Philo, "it can only be he who has clearly seen temperance and God, who is safe from death" (2:82). He makes the point that temperance can operate apart from God, but that it will not be enough. Not only temperance, but also the spiritual seeing of God saves from death:

112 Philo, Greek Text, *Works of Philo*, The Norwegian Philo Concordance Project, Copyright © 2005 Peder Borgen, Kåre Fuglseth, Roald Skarsten, Updated portions copyright © 2009 OakTree Software, Inc. Version 2.9.

> for if the mind that has been bitten by pleasure, that is by the serpent which was sent to Eve, shall have strength to behold the beauty of temperance, that is to say, the serpent made by Moses in a manner affecting the soul, and to behold God [himself] through the medium of the serpent, it shall live (2:81).

Philo's argument in *Husbandry* falls along much these same lines, though it is more practical and less spiritual. Philo is commenting on Genesis 9:20-21 by describing the different roles in agricultural work. Here temperance is equated with patient endurance:

> He, then, who with sound judgment contemplates the appearance of patient endurance, even if he has been previously bitten by the allurements of pleasures, must inevitably live; for the one holds over his soul a death to be averted by no prayers, but self-restraint proffers him health and preservation of life; and temperance, which repels evils, is a remedy and perfect antidote for intemperance (Husbandry 98).

The need to see God is not emphasized here, perhaps because of the more practical nature of the subject.

Philo, working with a version of the Septuagint, is very interested in the features of the narratives of Numbers 21 along with a wide range of other serpent related texts from the Pentateuch. It is interesting that despite his intense interest in the details of his text, he feels no need to warn against the worship of false gods; rather his concern is with overindulgence in pleasure. The serpent on the pole, allegorized to be a solution to the problem created by humanity's reaction to the serpent that persuaded Eve, is not a threat to the proper worship of the one true God; instead it makes it possible. Seeing the serpent on the pole saves one's life because one can then practice temperance and thus see God.

John's typological use of the story told in Numbers 21:4-9 stands in stark contrast to Philo's complex and detailed description of the other realm of meaning arising from the Septuagint text. John's allusion is a one-liner: "And just as Moses lifted up the serpent in the wilderness, so must the Son of Man be lifted up." In classic typological fashion the two events are juxtaposed, held up side by side before the readers/hearers. John implies that the second event, Jesus' 'lifting up', is the same *type* of thing as Moses lifting the bronze serpent that he had made at God's command. But Jesus' 'lifting up' is a heightening, an intensifying of that event.

Both Philo and John assume that their readers/hearers know the story told in scripture.[113] Philo relates the results of his interpretive work in great detail, but John uses typology. To understand his meaning we will need to import the story of Numbers 21 into the text of the Gospel and listen to its resonance there, in the context of the Gospel as a whole, in the hopes of identifying what is typical in the two accounts that would have inspired John's use of the story.

Hellenistic or Jewish?

As the literary elements of John's Gospel are examined, one other issue needs to be considered, particularly in conjunction with the typology in John 3:14: is the Gospel of John primarily Jewish in character or Hellenistic? Gail O'Day says that "John [...] belongs to and derives from the complex and multi-faceted cultural and intellectual milieu of first-century Judaism."[114] The preceding discussion certainly bears out this opinion. While scholars like Brant and Parsenios highlight the Greek influences in John's use of rhetoric and drama, John's continual references to Jewish scripture, and particularly his frequent use of the device of typology, which points to a literal and historical reading of scripture, show that John's perspective is also very Jewish. As Parsenios points out, "the two streams of Judaism and Hellenism [...] merge into a single style of discourse in their creative appropriation by John into the Fourth Gospel."[115] John has

113 While it is evident from his direct quotation, that Philo is referring to a Septuagint manuscript, John's source is much less certain. Andreas Köstenberger includes a fairly detailed summary of John's apparent sources (Köstenberger, "John," 417). It will be assumed, for lack of a better option, that John also knows the story from Numbers 21:4-9 as told in the Septuagint.

114 Gail R. O'Day, "John" in *The New Interpreters Bible: A Commentary in Twelve Volumes, Volume IX* (Nashville: Abingdon Press, 1995), 505.

115 Parsenios, *Rhetoric and Drama*, 47.

his own unique 'Hellenistic way of saying Jewish things'[116] and the best way to understand his meaning is to take seriously what he says and how he says it. This is the task that this work seeks to undertake.

What follows is a survey of the literature on John's Gospel with a particular focus on the typology between Jesus and Moses' bronze serpent: "And just as Moses lifted up the serpent in the wilderness, so must the Son of Man be lifted up, that whoever believes in him may have eternal life. (Καί καθῶς Μωϋσῆς ὓψωσεν τόν ὄφιν ἐν τῆ ἐρήμῳ ὂυτως ὑψωθῆναι δεῖ τόν υἱόν τοῦ ἀνθρώπου, ἳνα πᾶς ὁ πιστεύων ἐν αὐςτῷ ἒχῃ ζωήν αἰώνιον.) (John 3:14-15) Of particular interest to this discussion is how closely Jesus is correlated with the snake and the nature of the snake itself.

Literature Review

It is striking that Rudolf Bultmann, the scholarly giant who sparked much of the conversation that continues today on John's Gospel, can fully realize and discuss the paradox of the exaltation and yet humiliation of the Incarnate One (see further discussion below) and how it confronts humanity in a way that causes judgment, without ever mentioning Moses or the serpent that he "lifted up." Bultmann's worldview apparently does not allow for miraculous healing, nor does his view of Scripture, even as the source of salvation history[117] necessitate any nod to the Old Testament roots of the story of Jesus.

There is some scholarly debate over just how much John has the crucifixion in view when he describes Jesus as 'lifted up.' John Romanowsky explores the Christological aspects of the three 'lifted up' sayings in John. He concludes that the double meaning of ὑψόω in these sayings indicates that John goes beyond a merely theological statement that the exaltation of Jesus is revelatory. John also wants

116 This phrase is not original. It arose from discussions in a course entitled "Historiography and Self-Definition in Early Judaism and Christianity" taught by Annette Yoshiko Reed at the University of Pennsylvania in the Spring of 2013. If it was a quotation from a particular source, I have not been able to retrace it.

117 Rudolf Bultmann, *The Gospel of John: A Commentary* (Philadelphia: Westminster, 1971), 424.

to emphasize the crucifixion as a historical fact.[118] For Romanowsky the lifting up statements are used to indicate that Jesus reveals God with a unique authority and a person's free response to this revelation is their salvation or judgment, life or death.[119] He argues, following Moloney, that while the typology between the 'lifting up' of Jesus and the Moses' lifting up the serpent participates in an anti-Jewish polemic in John, the most obvious connection is with the crucifixion as Jesus' 'lifting up.' It is the opinion of this author and of the scholars discussed below, in agreement with Romanowsky, that John ironically has both crucifixion and exaltation in view.

C. H. Dodd concludes that, similar to the interpretations of the Numbers 21 incident in both the Wisdom of Solomon and Philo, the transaction of Moses lifting the bronze serpent in John "symbolizes the attainment of life through the vision (or knowledge) of God," an interpretation that, according to Dodd, is not dissimilar to the rabbinic interpretation, but also fits in with non-Jewish Hellenistic ways of thinking as evidenced by the Hermetic literature.[120] But though Dodd draws a rather direct comparison between seeing God and seeing the snake, and notes Philo's correlation of Moses' serpent and the serpent "that tempted Eve," he does not reflect further upon the nature of these serpents or elucidate how they might typologically reflect upon the nature of God in Christ.

Most scholars note the importance of the spatial correspondence between the lifting up of the bronze serpent and the 'lifting up' of the Son of Man, but do not attribute much importance to the fact that it was a serpent that was lifted up. Malina and Rohrbaugh emphasize that "what is important in the anti-language imagery is the spatial dimension."[121] Wayne Meeks describes the comparison of the 'lifting up' of the serpent by Moses and the 'lifting up' of the Son

118 John W. Romanowsky, "When the Son of Man is Lifted Up: The Redemptive Power of the Crucifixion in the Gospel of John" *Horizons* 32/1 (2005), 100-101.

119 Romanowsky, "When the Son of Man is Lifted Up, 102.

120 C. H. Dodd. *The Interpretation of the Fourth Gospel*, Cambridge: University Press, 1953), 306-307.

121 Bruce J. Malina and Richard L. Rohrbaugh. *Social-Science Commentary on the Gospel of John* (Minneapolis: Fortress, 1998), 85.

of Man as a clear case of typology, but it is the act of 'lifting up' that is typological; an action of Moses is parallel to an action associated with Jesus. For Meeks, John's main thrust is that what takes place through Jesus is correlated with but superior to what was enacted by Moses. The result of both events is the giving of life; the bronze serpent saved the Israelites from snake bite, but the Son of Man gives eternal life to those who believe in him.[122]

Many commentators note the double meaning of the Greek word ὑψόω in John 3:14. The verb can mean both "lift up" and "exalt." Raymond Brown, among others, draws out the Old Testament allusions in John's use of ὑψόω as coupled with his description of Jesus' crucifixion as his hour to be glorified. Of particular importance in this regard is the echo of the Suffering Servant oracles in Isaiah, most notably Isaiah 52:13 "See, my servant shall prosper; he shall be exalted (ὑψωθήσεται. and lifted up (δοξασθήσεται...." Brown believes that John conflates the story told in Numbers with the Suffering Servant theme to prove that Jesus' 'lifting up,' as both execution and vindication, was predicted in scripture.[123] Brown also notes the use of the serpent story in the Wisdom of Solomon and the Epistle of Barnabas and its interpretation in the Targums.[124] Gail O'Day believes that ὑψόω describes Jesus' crucifixion as his exaltation. This point is crucial to her understanding of John's soteriology. O'Day understands that John uses the ironic twist of recalling the story of Moses and the bronze serpent to fuse Jesus' crucifixion, resurrection and ascension into one continuous event. The allusion to Moses and the serpent illustrates the Son of Man's ascent to heaven following his descent from heaven as described in the Prologue (John 1:1-18). The crucifixion, resurrection and ascension are Jesus' return to the Father. The descending/ascending motif is related to birth from above in John 3 and it will be heard again when John revisits the 'lifting up' of Jesus in John 8:28 and 12:32-34.

122 Wayne A. Meeks, *The Prophet-King: Moses Traditions and the Johannine Christology* (Leiden: Brill, 1967), 291-292.

123 Raymond E. Brown, *The Gospel According to John I-XII: A New Translation with Introduction and Commentary* (Garden City NY: Doubleday, 1966), 146.

124 Brown, *The Gospel According to John i-xii*, 133.

O'Day suggests that the irony of the crucifixion as exaltation is also key to understanding John's attraction to irony, a literary device prominent throughout the Gospel.[125] O'Day also notes that the lifting up of the serpent in Numbers 21 is salvific, but like Brown, declines to explore further any possible correspondence between Jesus and the serpent. Malina and Rohrbaugh also note the irony of John's seeing Jesus' humiliating death as exaltation, but disregard any possibility of a comparison between Jesus and the serpent.[126] D. Moody Smith refers to John's allusion to Numbers 21 as "a classic typology" but declares that the analogy only applies to Jesus' 'lifting up', saying: "Of course, comparisons of Jesus with the snake are misplaced; the analogy applies only to being lifted up." For Moody Smith, Moses is the type of Christ because of his saving work and the element that is Christian in this typology is the emphasis on belief.[127] But even though John has a broad interest in comparing Moses and Jesus, Moody Smith's reading here is neither careful nor consistent enough. This typology does not compare Jesus to Moses, it compares Jesus with the serpent. Because John's Gospel is so rich and careful in its detail, it is important to explore this aspect of the comparison as well as all the others.

Andrew Lincoln and Andreas Köstenberger both note the double meaning of ὑψόω, but for both of them the typological comparison refers to the action of looking up. For Köstenberger, "Jesus likens the restoration of the people's physical lives as a result of looking at the bronze serpent to the people's reception of eternal life as a result of "looking" in faith at the Son of Man."[128] He adds the caveat that, as is said in the Wisdom of Solomon 16:6-7, it is not the person's faith, but God, in whom the person has faith, who saves. Lincoln believes that the statement in John 3:14 contributes to a lawsuit motif that runs very strongly throughout John's Gospel. Here, just as everyone who was bitten by a serpent, but looked at the bronze serpent lived,

125 O'Day, "The Gospel of John," 552.

126 Malina and Rohrbaugh. *Social-Science Commentary on the Gospel of John*, 85.

127 D. Moody Smith, *John* (Nashville: Abingdon Press, 1999), 97-98.

128 Köstenberger. "John," 435.

so everyone who receives the witness about the Son of Man receives a positive verdict of life.[129]

D. A. Carson, though he says that Jesus is in quite a different category from the snake, includes the aspect of punishment in his interpretation of the typology. For Carson, the snakes in the story told in Numbers 21 were sent as punishment for the persistent murmuring of Israel against God and the snake on the pole was God's gracious provision of life for those who had been bitten. This aspect of punishment will need to be investigated in the progress of this work. Carson does not draw out its implications in his commentary. He sees that there are two connections that John is making by comparing Jesus' 'lifting up' to that of the serpent. The first is the gracious granting of life, presumably to those who are being punished by means of death. The second, and deeper point of connection for Carson, is the act of 'lifting up' itself. In this regard, Carson also notes the double meaning of ὑψόω and his argument runs along the same lines as Brown and O'Day. Carson also wants to emphasize the distinction between Jesus and the bronze snake in that the snake was simply an object, in fact an object that had to be destroyed, when the Israelites came to see it as magical (2 Kings 18:4), while Jesus *is* himself the resurrection and the life and those who believe have life *in him* (author's italics).[130]

William Countryman also states that the snakes in the wilderness were sent as punishment for the people's rebellion and he notes the ambiguity of the snake in the Numbers story – both destroying and healing. Jesus' mission, in Countryman's view, carries a similar ambiguity in that it is intended for salvation of the rebellious cosmos, but can lead to judgment for those who reject Jesus. For Countryman, Jesus' 'lifting up' is his return to the Father and the purpose of his ascent and descent is to call humanity back into right relationship to its Creator. Jesus mission makes this right relationship, which is true and everlasting life, available to those who are or become doers of the truth. For Countryman then, the typological relationship is between

129 Andrew T. Lincoln, *Truth on Trial: The Lawsuit Motif in the Fourth Gospel* (Peabody: Hendrickson, 2000), 69.

130 D. A. Carson, *The Gospel According to John* (Grand Rapids: Eerdmans, 1991), 201-202.

the whole event in Numbers and Jesus' mission. While Countryman notes the ambiguity of the comparison, he does not provide further detail.[131]

While other scholars note the predicament of the Israelites as they interpret the typology in John, most do not include explicitly the aspect of punishment. Moody Smith describes the snakes in the Numbers account as being sent against the Israelites because they were rebellious.[132] Molony refers to the Israelites in Numbers 21 "suffering in their sinfulness."[133] Köstenberger states that God sent the snakes to judge rebellious Israel.[134] While this description strengthens the sense of typology between the Numbers event and the event of Jesus, it leaves one with the question, what does judgment mean for John?

Charles Gieschen uses the typology between the bronze serpent and Jesus to support his argument that John's Gospel teaches that the death of Jesus was an atonement for sin. He notes that the 'lifting up' of Jesus indicates the crucifixion and he notes the "intentional and profound double meaning to the verb ὑψόω [... that] Jesus will be literally "lifted up" in the crucifixion [and] he will also – in this very action of humiliating sacrifice – "be exalted" by the Father in order to show forth his divine identity for all to see and be drawn to him."[135] While much of Geischen's analysis is insightful and in line with other interpretations, this author finds the description of the crucifixion as a humiliating *sacrifice of atonement* to be a startling case of eisegesis. The crucifixion was indeed humiliating, but that John saw it as a atoning sacrifice is precisely what needs to be demonstrated to make Gieschen's argument complete. He backs up this supposition by referring to the gracious action of God in instructing Moses to place the bronze serpent on the pole to bring healing to Israel, yet a sacrificial element is entirely absent from the

---

131 L. William Countryman, *The Mystical Way in the Fourth Gospel: Crossing Over into God* (Harrisburg: Trinity Press, 1994), 34.

132 Moody Smith, *John*, 98.

133 Francis J. Moloney, *The Gospel of John* (Collegeville: The Liturgical Press, 1998), 95.

134 Köstenberger, "John," 435.

135 Charles A. Gieschen, "The Death of Jesus in the Gospel of John: Atonement for Sin?" *Concordia Theological Quarterly* 72 (2008), 250.

Numbers 21 account – the bronze serpent was not a sacrifice, indeed it was never a living serpent. Gieschen also believes that the element of sacrifice is drawn into John's account through the echo of Isaiah 53 with its pairing of exaltation and glorification and the reference to Jesus as the Lamb of God who takes away the sin of the world (John 1:29). These Old Testament echoes certainly need to be considered, perhaps particularly with reference to the question of sacrifice, and they will be revisited in Chapters 2 and 3 of this work.

James Charlesworth strongly affirms the typology between Jesus and the serpent, but claims that the analogy "is unthinkable if the serpent symbolizes evil."[136] He believes that the problem modern scholarship has with a comparison between Jesus and the serpent is due both to a natural revulsion to snakes and to a reception history of serpents as negative symbols because of a conflict during the fourth century between Christianity and the Cult of Ascelepius.[137] Charlesworth uses a number of arguments to support his interpretation of the typology. He examines the grammar of John 3:14-15 and concludes that καθώς and οὕτως are comparison words and the syntax and poetic structure of the passage demonstrate that the comparison is between the serpent and Jesus.[138] Charlesworth supports this argument by surveying the writings of an extensive number of early church commentaries.[139] But, though he holds up Augustine, Basil "the Great," Ephrem Syrus, and John Chrysostom as writers who affirm the typology between Jesus and the serpent, Charlesworth has to explain away the fact that all these interpreters viewed the snake as a negative figure. While Charlesworth notes the use of irony in John's Gospel, he puts forth the claim that the serpent would have been a positive symbol to John, the Judaism of his time, and in the wider Greco-Roman world as a symbol of life and eternal life. He argues, primarily from an examination of serpents in ancient literature and iconography, that the serpent would have been considered to be divine and immortal. He adds evidence that

136 James H. Charlesworth, *The Good and Evil Serpent: How a Universal Symbol became Christianized* (New Haven: Yale University Press, 2010), 362.

137 Charlesworth, *The Good and Evil Serpent*, 367.

138 Charlesworth, *The Good and Evil Serpent*, 376-377, 382-384.

139 Charlesworth, *The Good and Evil Serpent*, 376.

the serpent was viewed positively in Greek, Egyptian, Syrian and Phoenician thought in order to interpret the typology to be a claim that it is Jesus who brings eternal life.[140] Charlesworth certainly demonstrates that it was possible to view serpents in a positive light in the First Century CE, but it takes more than this to determine if John saw serpents in this way. The First Century was a time of great religious diversity, even within Judaism itself, and while John was certainly influenced by his cultural setting and Hellenized in his literary artistry, as has been discussed above, it is not a foregone conclusion that he would have adopted wholesale the religious views of cults, particularly those of Rome, with whom the Judaism of the First Century, as evidenced in the New Testament, was sometimes in an uneasy synchronicity, but more often diametrically opposed. Charlesworth also seeks to demonstrate that the view of serpents was positive in the Old Testament. His arguments in this regard will be discussed in Chapter 3. Charlesworth grounds his belief that John views serpents as symbols of life and eternal life based on connections that are speculative at best: 1) that there was Pool of Serpents mentioned by Josephus, 2) there was a cult of Asclepius at Bethzatha (where Jesus healed the man who had been ill for thirty six years (John 5)) when Jerusalem became a Roman city, and 3) the extant myth that Caesar Augustus was portrayed as a son of god because a serpent impregnated his mother. But Charlesworth also points out that the Gospel of John is particularly aligned with Palestinian Judaism, so much so that it is a particularly good source for study of the historical Jesus.[141] This fact would indicate that the best way to understand Johannine symbolism would be through Palestinian Judaism, not Greco-Roman culture. Charlesworth has done an exhaustive amount of research on the topic of snakes in the ancient world and he makes a strong case that the typology in John compares Jesus directly with Moses' serpent, but this author remains unconvinced that John would have seen the serpent purely, or even primarily, in a positive light.

---

140 Charlesworth, *The Good and Evil Serpent*, 373-375.

141 James H. Charlesworth, "The Historical Jesus in the Fourth Gospel: A Paradigm Shift?" in *Journal for the Study of the Historical Jesus* 8 (2010), 40.

Ronald Marshall sees quite clearly that the typology of John 3:14 compares Jesus and the serpent in way that is intended to "offend." For Marshall, following Robert Kysar, 'the lifting up' of the Son of Man is "the Johannine theology of the cross in a nutshell!"[142] Marshall backs his argument by examining the interpretations of past theologians, notably Augustine, and Martin Luther. These interpretations are interesting and instructive, but are later interpretations that move beyond the period that this research seeks to examine. Marshall's discussion does push back against those scholars who deny the parallel between Jesus and the serpent. He also successfully demonstrates, mainly through quoting Luther, that Jesus as the serpent fits the tenor of both John and Numbers 21. For Marshall, the image of the serpent was meant to be troubling to the Israelites and that in John, Jesus on the cross is meant to be ironic. But then Marshall uses these interpretations to say that John intends the serpent typology to say that Jesus 'lifting up' was a sacrifice that satisfied God's wrath. He qualifies this by saying God is satisfied not because of Jesus' suffering, but because of his obedience, and that "the magnitude of Jesus' unique suffering is deemed sufficient by God [Godself] to surmount the defamation of [God's] holiness and the provocation of [God's] wrath."[143] While the direct correlation of Jesus and the serpent seems to this author to be the best way to interpret John's typology, Marshall's subsequent argument again appears to depend on later theologies being read into this text. One needs to decide if the dualism in John portrays a God whose wrath needs to be satisfied. This discussion will be revisited in Chapter 5.

Craig Koester gets much nearer the mark when he discusses how Jesus' saying that the Son of Man must be lifted up just as Moses lifted up the serpent in the wilderness "reveals how something resulting from opposition to God can be transformed into a means of giving life with God." For Koester "both the serpent on the pole and the Messiah on the cross display the results of human sin and alienation

---

142 Ronald F. Marshall, "Our Serpent of Salvation: The Offense of Jesus in John's Gospel" in *Word and World*, XXL, 4 (Fall 2001), 386.

143 Marshall, "Our Serpent of Salvation," 393.

from God:"[144] the serpent because it was a visible reminder of the sin of the people when they spoke in mistrust against God and Moses and the Messiah because the people sinned by acting in unbelief and having him put to death. In both cases God transformed these results of sin into a means of giving life. When the snakebitten people in the wilderness were confronted by what was killing them in the serpent on the pole, they were restored to health. In John's Gospel, when people turn to Jesus they are confronted by the sin that is killing them and they receive eternal life.[145] Yet, while the 'lifting up' saying does certainly say something about God's power to transform evil into good, there is something a bit vague and unsatisfying about Koester's explanation of the typology. He has the snakes coming as a consequence of the sin of the people and Moses' lifting up of the bronze serpent as an act of obedience, but while the coming of Jesus may be seen as a consequence of humanity's sin (though it is a strange way of seeing it) the lifting up of Jesus was hardly an act of obedience on the part of those who actually did the lifting up. There is more to be said.

What if Jesus as the antitype of the *evil* serpent is precisely the point? It would fit very well with the irony John has already employed in linking Jesus' crucifixion with his exaltation and glorification. Also, if Jesus is the antitype of the serpent, then Nicodemus, a representative of both the Jewish authorities and an example of blindness (John 3:1-17), is the antitype of the unfaithful Israelites who grumble in their hardship and fail to appreciate God's providence.

Ultimately the best way to come up with a coherent understanding of what the typology between Jesus and the serpent means is to examine what it contributes to the narrative of John's Gospel. The next chapter of this work will build on the insights given by such commentators as Brown, Moloney, and O'Day and explore the typology that Charlesworth demonstrates in order to give a thick description of the work of Jesus as expressed in the Gospel

144 Craig R. Koester, *The Word of Life: A Theology of John's Gospel* (Grand Rapids: Eerdmans, 2008), 44.

145 Koester, *The Word of Life*, 45.

of John. The many possible layers of meaning that are revealed will, hopefully, broaden the current understanding of Jesus' death both as it was depicted in the First Century and as it is interpreted in the present day.

Implications for Public Theology

The ubiquity of penal substitutionary atonement was observed in the rationale for this work. It is also pointed out by David Lose in his study, *Making Sense of the Cross.*[146] Martha Schull Gilliss notes the "controversial "celebration" of sacrificial and substitutionary models of the atonement – specifically their focus on wrath and punishment" and raises the feminist and womanist "critique that neither ethical existence nor salvation can be possibly be founded on these models."[147] For Gilliss, atonement, "at-one-ment," embraces both Jesus' death and resurrection, "the full spectrum of gracious divine actions that make the creation "at one" again with God.[148] She also emphasizes that, "Christ has done something for us that we cannot totally account for using the images available to us," and stresses that multiple images are necessary to describe the spiritual and pastoral dimensions of atonement.[149] Gilliss describes the short comings of penal substitutionary atonement theory: that 1) the death of Christ overshadows the redemptive significance of the whole of the Christ Event, incarnation, death, resurrection, and ascension. 2) the Trinitarian nature of atonement is muted, and 3) the central message of freely given grace is overshadowed by the emphasis on propitiation for sin and assuagement of wrath.[150] Gilliss follows Kathryn Tanner in saying that Christ did not come to "engrave [his] lowliness into the world as its final good."[151] In this author's experience, penal substitutionary atonement offers initial comfort to

---

146 David J. Lose, *Making Sense of the Cross,* 126.

147 Martha Schull Gilliss, "Resurrecting the Atonement" in *Feminist and Womanist Essays in Reformed Dogmatics* (Louisville: Westminster John Knox, 2006), 126.

148 Gilliss, "Resurrecting the Atonement", 125.

149 Gilliss, "Resurrecting the Atonement", 125.

150 Gilliss, "Resurrecting the Atonement", 127.

151 Gilliss, "Resurrecting the Atonement", 128.

"disturbed consciences" (to use a phrase from Martin Luther),[152] but it also, in practice, requires that a person retain a sense of guilt and unworthiness in order to continue to experience the 'grace' that this theory proposes. As noted earlier one can see this dynamic in Christian concerts and in evangelical styles of worship. There is an emotional 'law/gospel' dynamic in which first, the participant focuses on his/her sinful unworthiness, second the 'good news' of God's sacrifice of [his] Son is re-presented, and then the worship or concert switches to praise and celebration. It can be a very cathartic experience, but it is also an experience that seems to require constant repetition. Does a person really need to dwell there? Or does this constant demand to return to a place of abasement have consequences that reach into every aspect of public life? This is not to advocate a form of sanctification here. Christians still commit acts (or fail to commit acts) that fracture their relationship with God, with each other, and with the creation. But Martin Luther's *simul iustis et peccator* (simultaneously justified and sinful) seems a healthier formulation than the dynamic of repeated degradation that penal substitutionary atonement requires. A punitive view of justice seems to allow, or even encourage, seeing the sinner as less than human. For Timothy Gorringe, criminal and social justice are correlative as are poverty and crime.[153] Social deprivation is one of the strongest motivators of crime. While no society will be, in this present reality, crime free; a just society will also be one that experiences a reduction in criminal behavior. A society that has denied social justice cannot have a legitimate criminal justice system, since its system will be upholding an unjust status quo. Issues of criminal and social justice are also bound up with how a society understands relationship, authority, and education. Societies that emphasize personal freedom and individual responsibility tend to favor retributive justice as a way to maintain control. More communal societies tend to focus on public duty, social responsibility and participation in the economy and do

152 Martin Luther, *Luther's Works, Volume 34: Career of the Reformer IV*, ed Lewis William Spitz (Minneapolis: Augsburg, 1960), 336-337.

153 Gorringe, *God's Just Vengeance*, 251.

not expect criminal justice to solve their problems.[154] For Gorringe, the most constructive attempts at improving justice are ones that attempt conflict resolution – bringing aggrieved parties together in the presence of a mediator – built on the assumption that all crime represents a breach of relationship.[155] Encounters between offenders and victims reduce the offenders' strategy of denying responsibility and respect the victim's experience of the crime. Offenders can receive forgiveness and perhaps experience new levels of trust. These strategies retain both offender and victim as part of the community and do not isolate them. Responsible reparation may be part of these encounters. Mediation and apology replace antagonism. This in turn can reduce the tendency of the offender to feel like a victim of an unfair system, which displaces the need to take responsibility for one's actions.[156] These processes place the community, not the offender, at the center of the process. Healthy local communities are essential to the success of these mechanisms of justice. The breakdown of such communities, due to advances in transportation and technology, are added difficulties; as is the market driven nature of existence in western society.[157] The challenge that Gorringe sees is the need to structure a genuine community where material goods and values are held in common; where those who are different are not marginalized or oppressed and are not controlled by false norming. For Gorringe, the church can contribute to the struggle to create such community as it has throughout its history. The church as an imagined community, alongside existing communities, can engage with them in a dialogue about what it might mean to respect the stranger, allow for difference, and make sure that all are provided for. Of course the church throughout history can also be critiqued for not living up to its inscripturated values. Key to these values, for Gorringe, is the kind of forgiveness that does not let people off the hook, but instead restores people to community by recognizing that

154 Gorringe, *God's Just Vengeance,* 253.

155 Gorringe, *God's Just Vengeance,* 253.

156 Gorringe, *God's Just Vengeance,* 255.

157 Gorringe, *God's Just Vengeance,* 261.

guilt is mutual.[158] Recognition of guilt and responsibility is implicit in acts of forgiveness and this kind of forgiveness can change both the past and the future.[159] "Forgiveness is prevenient," for Gorringe, "it enables reparation, expiation, 'atonement.'" Forgiveness is an act of love and as such is unconditional. Forgiveness is also a struggle that has to be prayed for and won. It is not sentimental, it is part of the way of the cross.[160] It is the only thing that breaks the cycle of disrespect which breeds disrespect and alienation which causes alienation.[161]

Dwelling or abiding in John's Gospel is in line with the picture that Gorringe presents. For John, one is to abide in God and the community of believers, a place where judgment is in the past. Again, in the present reality, abiding in God is not a permanent, continuous state, but it expresses a very different hope than does penal substitutionary atonement.

In addition to Gilliss' critique that substitutionary atonement theories overemphasize violence as a solution to humanity's problems, it is also disturbing that they promote a monolithic image of justice as retributive. The only solution to an infraction is punishment; without punishment forward movement is impossible. While this author has no wish to deny that there are serious consequences to all levels of what one might call sins – both of omission and commission –consequences and punishment are two different things. Consequences can teach and shape. What can punishment really accomplish? Punishment is thought to deter, but this idea is debated. The ELCA social statement on the death penalty states that capital punishment makes no provable impact on the breeding grounds of violent crime, pointing out that research on the deterrent effect of punishment gives at best mixed results and many proponents of the death penalty have abandoned deterrence as an argument.[162] Can punishment promote healthy relationships? It seems that

158 Gorringe, *God's Just Vengeance,* 262-265.

159 Gorringe, *God's Just Vengeance,* 266.

160 Gorringe, *God's Just Vengeance,* 267.

161 Gorringe, *God's Just Vengeance,* 268.

162 Evangelical Lutheran Church in America, *A Social Statement on: The Death Penalty,* (1991), 3, see also, n10.

it can only create distance. If the only solution to the problem of human disobedience is punishment, and even if that punishment is laid on Christ rather than guilty humanity, the gulf between God and God's creation becomes greater, not less. And if God, as God has demonstrated in Christ, can raise the dead, then the physical effects of sin and division can be repaired without punishment being exacted, what remains to be accomplished is the reestablishment of fractured relationships.

A further difficulty with penal substitutionary atonement is the literal way that it draws on scripture for its support. While the language of sacrifice and sin is certainly a part of Scripture and cannot be ignored, these are only two themes among many, one voice among a multitude. The complex dialogue between wondering voices within scripture is not honored adequately in most presentations of this atonement theory.

The results of the deficiencies in both this theory of atonement and how it is presented are writ large in the current social context. In a small town that struggles with the many challenges of the social and economic changes inherent in the move from an industrial/mining past to an uncertain future in our increasingly global and technological world, people who are on assistance or are afflicted with the collateral damage inflicted by poverty and addiction are believed to deserve their suffering, regardless of its social origins, because of the perception that their nature is entirely sinful. Attempts at solutions to these ills tend to be mainly on the law enforcement side (punishment of offenders), with little attention to root causes, cures, or prevention. Violence is often acceptable as it becomes part of the cycle of retributive punishment. Dialogue is often noticeably absent.

The current examination of John's Gospel aims at stretching many of these constraints. John speaks to us of Jesus entering into the world in a way that draws all people into God. John uses tension and misunderstanding to call each reader/hearer to question themselves and their standing with God and in their community, and John presents his theology through narrative, in a way that resists summarization and monolithic thinking. (An approach that this author will need to take to heart!) One of the goals of this research is to contribute to as public a dialogue as possible, a dialogue that encourages gathering together around story telling and accompaniment, where each can see themselves and the other at the foot of the cross that brings God's love and life into the pain of all people, and then find themselves drawn up into the communion that is eternal life in God.

Limitations of the Research

As was discussed above, the focus of this work will be to use the narrative elements of the Gospel of John to explicate the work of Jesus. Historical-critical elements will be included where they contribute to an understanding of the narrative. Text-critical issues will be beyond the scope of this investigation and the unity of John's Gospel as a coherent narrative will be assumed.

The 'Son of Man' is an important theological title for Jesus in the portions of John's Gospel that are the focus of this investigation, but a thorough exploration of this title is an apt subject for a work on its own. Only a brief statement of this author's interpretative choices will be given. The title Son of Man is also problematic in a work such as this, which seeks to bring scripture into dialogue with a variety of contextual readings including feminist and womanist. The exclusively male language for both humanity and God employed in that title can be seen as reinforcing traditions that have marginalized and oppressed women for centuries. However, it is difficult to retain the importance of this phrase as a title if one expands the language within it and to some interpreters it is seen as theologically problematic or even ridiculous or to do so. Within this work the title 'Incarnate One' will be used as a counterpoint to those citations that use the title 'Son of Man.' The title 'Son of Man' itself seems to be an Old Testament allusion, drawn most directly from Daniel 7:13-14, where the "one like a human being" (υἱός ἀνθρώπου) comes to the Ancient One and is given dominion, glory and kingship. It may also have some resonance with God's address to Ezekiel (υἱέ ἀνθρώπου) throughout that book. In the Gospel of John, Jesus stands in a unique relationship to God; he is the μονογενοῦς and the Word made flesh, the unique and complete revealer of God. John's portrayal of Jesus was an important part of the impetus to develop the doctrine of the Trinity and the two natures of Christ. "Incarnate One" expresses some of the nuances in John's depiction of Jesus without the exclusive, male-gendered language.

A comprehensive discussion of the relationship between John and the synoptic gospels is important and interesting, but beyond the scope of this research. However, salient differences and resonances between the Fourth Gospel and the other three will be discussed when they help to highlight a particular emphasis in John.

The work will not attempt a complete history of interpretation of John 3:14-15. It will focus on exploring the theological atmosphere in and around the time when the Fourth Gospel was written, testing whether the interpretation put forth might have been possible at the time of John's writing. Therefore, interpretations of the story of Moses and the bronze serpent written in and around the first century CE will be discussed along with a brief summary of it's use the writings of the early rabbinic tradition and early church.

Conclusion

O'Keefe and Reno give, as an example of typology, the Martin Luther King Jr. quote, "I have been to the mountain top and I have seen the promised land."[163] With these few words, King elegantly, powerfully, poignantly (and even prophetically – he speaks these words the day before he was assassinated) connects the civil rights movement in America with the Exodus of Israel from Egypt. Despite incredible distances of space, time, and circumstance, this typology works. It provides a meaningful context in which to understand the struggle. Regardless of whether or not one is an expert in the history of the ancient Middle East or even considers Moses to have been a real person, King's sentence transforms the black struggle for equality into a journey of faith led by a flawed but divinely inspired leader.

Interpreters of John 3:14 face an interesting challenge. Scholars understand how typology works. They can readily identify John's comparison of Jesus and the serpent as a typology, and yet they are still somewhat at a loss to identify the layers of meaning that are evoked by the comparison. This challenge is evidenced by the

---

163 O'Keefe and Reno, Sanctified Vision, 70.

number of differing ways, discussed above, in which the typology is considered. Which of all the layers of meaning are the most important? Can any features of the Numbers story be excluded from John's account? What is the shape or pattern of the story of Moses and the bronze serpent that was resonant for the hearers/readers of John's Gospel? Was the typology John's own creation, woven from motifs he inherited from his traditions and reworked on the basis of his conviction that Jesus was indeed the 'unique one' (μονογενοῦς) of God? Was he utilizing a tradition that he inherited as part of his Jewish heritage? Was it an idea prevalent in the Greco-Roman world surrounding him?

As with the Dr. King example mentioned above, there is no way to determine which layers of meaning are intended, no court that can determine which interpretation of the typology is absolutely correct. One can no more ask King which features of the Exodus story he had in mind than one can ask John. But one can read the rest of their work and seek to hear their words, first in light of their context and then in one's own, in a way that honors what they wrote and their place in a common story. That is what this research seeks to do. To hear John speak in his context and ours and to honor, though not uncritically, the place of his words in the story of our place. The goal of the next chapter, then will be to examine John's typology in the context of John's own work.

Chapter 2

The 'lifting up' of the Incarnate One in John's Gospel

Because of the allusive (and thus elusive) nature of the meaning of a typology, especially when it is read apart from its original context, it will be important to examine how Jesus as the antitype of the bronze serpent functions within John's Gospel. It will be demonstrated that this typology is important to the Gospel structurally, rhetorically, and thematically. The typology of the 'lifting up' of the Incarnate One (ὁ υἱός τοῦ ἀνθρώπου) 'just as' the serpent was lifted up is woven throughout the Gospel of John, occurring explicitly three times: in John 3:14, John 8:28 and John 12:31-32.

This chapter will first explore where this theme occurs within the structure of John's narrative and how it contributes to an interpretive lens for each section of the narrative in which it occurs. Next, each reference to the 'lifting up' of Jesus will be explored in detail. Possible layers of meaning from the events recounted in Numbers 21 will be brought into the context of John's narrative. How these layers of meaning add to John's marked rhetorical strategy, particularly irony, employed throughout John's Gospel and perhaps centering most strongly in John 3, will be explored.[164]

164 Gail O'Day suggests that John 3:14 "Contains a Key to the Theological Grounding of the Evangelist's Attraction to Irony," O'Day. "John", 552.

Finally, the Fourth Gospel is constructed like a thick tapestry with the threads of many different themes or motifs woven throughout. The 'lifting up' of the serpent incorporates facets of many of these themes and so becomes one of the most important threads that holds the Gospel together. It will be demonstrated that the typology of the serpent does in miniature what the Fourth Gospel intends to do as a whole – it lifts Jesus up to the community and the world, so that God can be seen and known (John 14:7) and it signals a decisive turning point in God's relationship to humankind. From this point on those who see and know God in Jesus can have eternal life.

The 'lifting up' of the Incarnate One in the Structure of John

The narrative structure of the extant form of John's Gospel can be divided into four major sections: the Prologue, the Book of Signs, the Book of Glory, and an Epilogue.[165] What follows is a relatively brief overview of the shape of the gospel. An outline is included in the Appendix. The Prologue (John 1:1-18) introduces the reader to the Word of God and the testimony of John the Baptizer and announces many of the recurring themes of the Gospel: 1) the victory of light over darkness, 2) belief through testimony, 3) the coming of the light and its rejection by many who might have been expected to receive it, 4) becoming children of God by birth from God, 5) the glory of God seen in the human flesh of the Word, 6) the relationship between the Father and the Son, and 7) the transcendence of the grace and truth of Jesus over the Law given through Moses. The Book of Signs runs from John 1:19 through John 12. It contains stories of some of the signs that Jesus performed during a three-year ministry, punctuated by discourses that reflect on those signs; conversations between Jesus and various characters that he encounters; and confrontations between Jesus and his opponents. The Book of Glory consists of John 13-20 and contains the depiction of Jesus' final night with his disciples, including his farewell discourse and final prayer, followed by the passion narrative and the witness to the resurrection. John 21, the Epilogue, is comprised of a final scene with Jesus and the

165 See Brown, *The Gospel According to John i-xii*, 146. I have yet to find a scholar who disagrees significantly with this outline.

disciples. It provides a foretaste of eschatological abundance and reconciliation and portrays two different types of commissioning – Peter's, to feed Jesus' sheep, and John's, to bear witness. All three references to the 'lifting up' of the Incarnate One occur in the Book of Signs. Many commentators suggest that the three 'lifting up' statements in John's Gospel are analogous to Jesus' three passion predictions in the synoptic Gospels.[166]

The Book of Signs

The Book of Signs can be further divided into smaller subsections. First, following the Prologue, the remainder of the first chapter of John, beginning in John 1:19, contains the witness of John the baptizer and the gathering of the disciples.

Cana to Cana (John 2-4)

Next, John 2-4 presents the Cana to Cana *inclusio,*[167] which opens with the sign at the wedding in Cana and closes with healing of the official's son, described as the second sign that Jesus performs after he returns from Judea to Cana (John 4:46,54). This section also includes Jesus' sign in the Temple, his nighttime encounter with Nicodemus and his conversation with the Samaritan woman at the well. All these vignettes highlight different responses to Jesus in a non-hostile setting.

During the wedding at Cana, Jesus' mother has absolute trust in Jesus' ability and willingness to resolve the difficulty of the lack of wine, a trust that she uses to motivate the servants to act on Jesus' word. The disciples see his 'glory' and believe in him, on some level, when he changes water into wine. When Jesus disrupts the marketplace aspects of the Temple, "the Jews" question his authority, asking for a sign. But they refuse to even consider the possibility of the sign when it is given. This vignette links Jesus' death and resurrection to the Temple in some as yet not elucidated way. A brief interlude in John 2:23-25 indicates that many people believed in

166 For example: O'Day, "John," 552; Moody Smith, *John,* 99, 174, 241; Brown, *The Gospel According to John i-xii,* 146.

167 Explored in depth by Francis J. Moloney in *Belief in the Word: Reading the Fourth Gospel: John 1-4* (Minneapolis: Fortress, 1993). 194-196.

Jesus because they saw his signs, but Jesus would not entrust himself to them because he knew what was in all people. Nicodemus is thus introduced as a person who professes to know something about Jesus, but one to whom Jesus does not entrust himself. Nicodemus and Jesus are at cross-purposes throughout their conversation. The conversation is about the birth from above (ἄνωθεν) that allows one to see the kingdom of God. However, Nicodemus gets confused by the second meaning of ἄνωθεν – "again" – and asks how a grown man can re-enter his mother's womb. Nicodemus, a teacher of Israel, is bewildered by his encounter with Jesus. The leader and teacher of "the Jews" fades from this portion of the narrative without demonstrating either belief in or rejection of Jesus, only plaintive confusion.

Following the encounter with Nicodemus the reader is privy to a conversation between John the Baptizer and his disciples, sparked by a question regarding baptism. The John of the narrative represents a person of authentic faith as he testifies to Jesus as the bridegroom, rejoices in Jesus' coming, accepts his own subordinate role as a witness, and articulates the proper response to Jesus: a belief that certifies that God is true and gives eternal life. Next, in contrast to Nicodemus, who remains in darkness at least for now, Jesus' encounter with the Samaritan woman, by far a less likely disciple, results in an awakening faith and a willingness to bring others to see Jesus. The outsider of outsiders, a woman of Samaria, becomes a witness to Jesus as the Messiah and leads her whole village to faith in him.

The final episode within the Cana-to-Cana frame is the story of the official who journeys from Capernaum to ask Jesus to come and heal his son, but turns toward home at Jesus' word that his son will live. His trust is confirmed when his slaves meet him with the news of his son's healing. He and his entire household "believe." The official (βασιλικός), possibly a Gentile, demonstrates a deep faith in Jesus.

It is in the same *inclusio*, in John 2:4, that the idea of Jesus' hour, both of glorification and death, is introduced. John's connection of Jesus' death to his glorification weaves the great Old Testament theme of the כְּבוֹד-יְהוָה (kavod YHWH) – the glory of God as God's visible presence throughout the wilderness journey; at Sinai, in the

Tabernacle, and later in the Temple – into John's narrative. The crucified one is God's visible presence with and Word (λόγος) to humanity.

The 'lifted up' theme is introduced in John 3:14-15: "And just as Moses lifted up the serpent in the wilderness, so must the Son of Man be lifted up, that whoever believes (ό πιστεύων) in him may have eternal life." These words are spoken by Jesus to Nicodemus as part of the conversation that occurs at night during the first Passover mentioned in John. Set in the Cana to Cana *inclusio* then, the 'lifting up' typology illustrates having life by believing/trusting/having faith in Jesus. John uses it here to tell his readers/hearers that those who turn with authentic faith to the crucified, resurrected, and ascended Christ are those who receive the birth from above.

Jesus as the Temple (John 5-10)

John 5-10 depicts Jesus as the antitype of the Temple. In this section of the Book of Signs, Jesus describes himself by using something central to the meaning of four important festivals. The first is a Sabbath, a reminder of God's work and rest in creating (John 5). Jesus' healing of the man by the Pool of Bethzatha demonstrates that he is Lord of the Sabbath, working because his Father is still working. It is this sign that sets off open hostility between Jesus and "the Jews." Next comes a Passover, the second in John. Here Jesus is out in the countryside, not in Jerusalem. He is shown typologically to be the bread from heaven as he feeds five thousand with five loaves and two fish. At the Festival of Booths (John 7:10-52, 8:12-59) Jesus declares himself to be living water and the light of the world, the two foci of this annual celebration of God's provision for Israel on their wilderness journey. The final festival is Dedication; probably what is now called Hanukkah. With its overtones of the renewal of Israel, Dedication becomes the context for the restoration of sight to the man born blind as well as the Good Shepherd discourse (an echo of Ezekiel's prophesy that the Lord will become the shepherd of Israel (Ezekiel 34:15) and replace the peoples' hearts of stone with hearts of flesh (Ezekiel 11:19).

By setting Jesus' words and actions in the context of Israel's history as represented in Temple rituals, John shows that Jesus is the presence of the God who is at the heart of Israel's worship. Jesus' presence provides the blessings that the presence of God in the Tabernacle/Temple provided to Israel. This section also shows his opponents reacting with increasing hostility. Up to Chapter 5, responses to Jesus were either positive or confused. Beyond it there is growing opposition. By the end of Chapter 11 "the Jews" have sought to stone and arrest Jesus many times and the plot to put him to death for the sake of the people has been developed.

The context for John 8:28, the second 'lifted up' prediction, is at the Festival of Booths/Tabernacles. Following Jesus' declaration that he is the light of the world (one of Jesus' numerous ἐγώ εἰμι statements, echoes of the name that God reveals to Moses at the burning bush (Exodus 3:14)), and a trial scene with the Pharisees, who question the validity of his testimony because he testifies to himself, Jesus refers again to his being lifted up: "When you have lifted up the Son of Man, then you will realize that I am he." By employing another ἐγώ εἰμι statement in a section that highlights Jesus as the incarnate presence of God, John stresses that it is in Jesus' return to the Father (the cross, resurrection, and ascension) that one knows the Father and sees what the Father is doing. Here, the second occurrence of the 'lifting up' theme reinforces the idea, introduced in John 2:4, that the glory (the presence and majesty) of God will be seen in Jesus when his hour has come.

What follows this declaration is an extensive dispute with "the Jews" in which they begin, in their opposition to Jesus, to renounce their own heritage – they declare they have never been slaves even though they have been commanded, notably in Deuteronomy 6, to remember, recite, and teach that God has liberated them from slavery in Egypt. (Their final renunciation comes when they declare to Pilate that they have no king but Caesar (John 19:6).) The ironic narrative of the man born blind immediately follows this discourse. Here, it is the blind man, ultimately cast out of the synagogue, who truly sees Jesus while "the Jews," who think they are protecting God's rule, are declared to be blind. Blindness is a strong echo of Old Testament and Second Temple depictions of Israel's apostasy. This second instance of the 'lifting up' motif reinforces the idea that those who believe in Jesus are the faithful people of God as opposed to those who reject him and become identified as children of the devil. John's voice drips with irony, perhaps akin to the moment in Mark's Gospel when it is a Roman centurion who recognizes that the crucified Jesus is truly God's son, for Jesus, by naming himself as God, tells "the Jews" and the reader/hearer that the moment of his crucifixion, the event that is also his exaltation and return to the Father, is the moment of God's revelation.

Into Glory (John 11-12)

The Book of Signs concludes with the narrative of Jesus' triumphant entry into Jerusalem and the request of some Greeks to see him, a request that indicates to Jesus that his hour to be glorified has arrived (John 12:23). A summary of Jesus' teaching closes this major section of the Gospel (John 12:44-50).

The third time Jesus refers to his being "lifted up" (12:32-34) is part of this dramatic transition from the Book of Signs to the Book of Glory. "'Now is the judgment of this world; now the ruler of this world will be driven out. And I, when I am lifted up from the earth, will draw all people to myself.' He said this to indicate the kind of death he was to die." This third "lifted up" statement follows closely on Jesus' declaration that the hour has come for the Incarnate One to be glorified (John 12:23). It is his third depiction of his death using the type of the upraised serpent and this time John makes it explicit that the crucifixion is indicated by the figure. This third declaration is followed by a commentary on unbelief from the narrator of the Gospel who uses a paraphrase of Isaiah 6 to say that God has blinded Israel, deepening the complexity of John's understanding of belief and unbelief and indicating that God has a purpose behind human blindness. Here John also says that Isaiah saw Jesus' glory, implying that Jesus was the Lord of Hosts in Isaiah's throne room vision (Isaiah 6:1-13). Also interesting is that seraphs are prominent in Isaiah's vision and it is the mediation of a seraph that allows Isaiah to see the Lord without perishing. (The story of Moses in Numbers 21, in the Hebrew, conflates the bronze serpent with a seraph.) Jesus' hour – his crucifixion, resurrection and ascension – returns Jesus to his place on the throne of the universe and accomplishes God's purpose, the salvation of the world. The current ruler of the world is driven out and all people are drawn into the life of God. For John, seeing Jesus allows one to move beyond blindness and see God in a way that not only preserves life, but leads to abundant life.

Literary Analysis of the 'lifting up' of the Incarnate One

John 3:1-21

As noted above, the first occurrence of the theme of the 'lifting up' of the Incarnate One occurs in John 3:14. What follows is a close reading of the passage that includes this verse. The literary unit to be examined is John 3:1-21 and it is chosen because it contains Jesus' conversation with Nicodemus and the Johannine discourse that follows.

Again as noted above, leading up to this unit, John 2:23-25 provides a transition from the narration of Jesus' sign in the temple to this passage, a transition that signals to the reader/hearer that there are issues with human responses to Jesus: even positive responses may not be what they seem. Jesus knows whom not to trust. The reader/hearer must be discerning as well.

John 3:1 introduces the next narrative section; the scene is set and the next important character introduced. It is night, a warning sign. For John, night is when people stumble and cannot work (John 9:4, 11:10), night is when Judas betrays Jesus (John 13:30), and the disciples catch no fish (John 21:3). Darkness signals opposition to God. The prologue depicts a struggle between light and darkness (John 1:5). Darkness also can signal the absence of Jesus. The disciples in the boat are in darkness before Jesus comes to them (John 6:17), Mary Magdalene is in the dark on the first day of the week until Jesus comes to her and reveals himself (John 20:1). Jesus' purpose is to lead people out of darkness and into light (John 3:30; 8:12; 12:35, 46) out of judgment and into communion with God.

Nicodemus is introduced as someone who should, on the surface of things, be trustworthy. He is a Pharisee and a leader (ἄρχων) of 'the Jews.' Up to this point in John's story of Jesus, "the Jews" have questioned both John and Jesus, but they have not been openly hostile. Nicodemus continues that role here, questioning, but the reader/hearer has been warned not to trust everyone who expresses belief and the warning is reinforced when it is revealed that Nicodemus comes at night. There is something unexpected, perhaps secret, to be discovered in what follows.

Nicodemus begins the conversation with an expression of belief, or at least of knowledge. His "we know" indicates the group he represents, the Pharisees as part of "the Jews." Their conclusion, based on unspecified signs, is that Jesus is a teacher sent from God. Jesus' reply seems a bit of a non sequitur. He says nothing about himself, instead raising questions about the basis of Nicodemus' knowledge. In contrast to Nicodemus' "no one is able do these signs that you do if God is not with them (author's translation)," Jesus replies, that "if one is not born from above one is not able to see the kingdom of God" (author's translation). Both of these statements are fifth class or present general conditions indicating, not a probable event, but a principle.[168] What is interesting here is the ironic contrast created by their juxtaposition. Nicodemus' statement is literally quite true. *No one* (οὐδεις, placed in the Greek in an emphatic position at the beginning of the clause) can do the signs that Jesus does except Jesus himself, who, as the readers/hearers have known since the beginning of John's Gospel, is "with" God and "is" God (John 1:1). The problem is that Nicodemus doesn't understand what he is saying. Jesus moves the conversation forward by responding, not to Nicodemus' words, but to his difficulty: Nicodemus cannot see who Jesus really is and what God is really doing without the birth from above, birth by water and the Spirit. John re-emphasizes Nicodemus' plight when Nicodemus misunderstands ἄνωθεν to mean "again", rather than "from above", and inquires how one can re-enter the mother's womb. Nicodemus is focused on the flesh, the earthly, and so misses the heavenly.[169] Nicodemus' part of the conversation is buttoned off with another comparison; the teacher of Israel, in ironic contrast to the teacher come from God, does not understand the work of the Spirit (John 3:10).

---

168 Daniel B. Wallace, *Greek Grammar Beyond the Basics: An Exegetical Syntax of the New Testament* (Grand Rapids: Zondervan, 1996), p. 696-698.

169 This conversation introduces John's mixed opinion of signs. Signs can be understood on two levels, earthly and heavenly. They can truly reveal Jesus, but they can also be misunderstood.

Jesus then speaks with the post-resurrection perspective of the people of the kingdom (the church); his "we know" stands in contrast to the knowing of "the Jews," and what the church has seen stands in contrast to the seeing of the signs.[170] For they have seen the risen Lord, the descended and ascended Incarnate One. Though John's Gospel does not present an ascension narrative, it is presupposed throughout: (1) introduced in John 1:51, when Jesus' tells Nathaniel that he will see heaven opened and angels ascending and descending on the Incarnate One (a reference to the story of Jacob); (2) here in John 3:13 ("No one has ascended (here in the perfect tense in Greek, indicating completed past action with ongoing significance) into heaven except the one who descended from heaven, the Son of Man."); (3) as a question in John 6:62 when the disciples are complaining about Jesus' teaching that they must eat the bread that is his body and Jesus asks "what if you were to see the Son of Man ascend to where he was before?"; and (4) as an expectation in John 20:17 where Jesus tells Mary not to hold on to his resurrected body because he will be ascending soon. The Gospel implies that the disciples do see Jesus ascend, even though that event is not narrated.

Thus the cross, the physical 'lifting up' of the Incarnate One, as described in John 3:14, is integral to the ascension of the Incarnate One. Here is the center from which the irony in John radiates – in the double meaning of ὑψόω. The physical 'lifting up' of Jesus on the cross; that violent, shameful, cursed (Deuteronomy 21:23) execution; is juxtaposed with Jesus' exaltation and glorification (the crucifixion is Jesus' hour to be glorified [John 12:23]). This event, in all its duality, is what is necessary so that humans may truly be born from above and thus have eternal life.

Necessity is a strong, if somewhat ambiguous, concept in John.[171] The Greek word δεῖ occurs repeatedly. It is necessary that one be born ἄνωθεν (John 3:7) and necessary that the Incarnate One be "lifted up" (John 3:14; 12:34). It is necessary (but is it a geographic necessity?) that Jesus go through Samaria (John 4:4). The Samaritan

---

170 O'Day, "John," p. 551.

171 O'Day asserts that δει is almost always used to indicate a theological necessity in John. O'Day, *Revelation in the Fourth Gospel*, 55.

woman claims that "the Jews" say that it is necessary to worship God in Jerusalem (John 4:20), but Jesus disputes this necessity; instead one must worship God in spirit and truth (4:24). It is necessary that the works of God be done in the day (9:4) and that Jesus must bring his sheep from outside "this" fold (10:16). It is necessary that Jesus rise from the dead (20:9). The necessity in John 3:14, that Jesus must be lifted up as was the serpent, is related to the salvation of the cosmos, that God loves οὕως, in this way); thus the Christ event is a definitive expression of God's love for the world, and understanding this is part of true faith.

It is here that John draws the story of Moses, the people, and the serpents into his narrative. The story, told briefly in Numbers 21:4-9, is that the Israelites grow impatient on their journey, having had to turn back along the way they had come in order to go around the land of Edom. So they speak against (κατελάλει) both God and Moses, bemoaning that God has led them out of Egypt into the wilderness, a place of "no food and no water," though they immediately contradict this statement by saying that they detest (ἡ δέ ψυχή ἡμῶν προσώχθισεν ἐν τῷ ἄρτῳ τῷ διακένῳ, i.e., their souls are angry[172] with the miserable bread) the manna that they are being given. God's response is to send deadly (θανατοῦντας) serpents which bite and kill many of the people. Then the people come to Moses confessing their sin ('Ημάρτομεν) and asking him to pray to the Lord to take the serpents away. Moses prays for the people and God replies by instructing Moses to make a serpent (ὄφιν) and set it on a signpost (σημείου), promising that all the bitten ones (πᾶς ὁ δεδηγμένος) seeing (ἰδών) it will live. So Moses makes a serpent out of bronze and puts it on a signpost and whenever a person who is bitten gazes (ἐπέβλεψεν) at the serpent, they live.

This story, as told in Numbers 21, will be revisited in more detail in Chapter 3; but for now, three features of the narrative that may have resonated in important ways within John's story of Jesus will be lifted up (pun intended).

---

172 It is interesting that this is the word used elsewhere to indicate God's feelings toward the unfaithful generation in the wilderness (Psalm 94:10, Hebrews 3:17).

First, the story represents a turning point for the people in the wilderness. It appears as the last of the stories where the people turn away from God and/or Moses. After this incident, the people move successfully, both geographically and in battle, to the Jordan river and their subsequent entry into the Promised Land. The implication is that this story describes the end of the unfaithful generation that refused to enter the land back in Numbers 14 and whom God swore would never enter it. In John's Gospel, then, the 'lifting up' of the Incarnate One represents a turning point in humanity's story. Humans now can find healing of their relationship with God and thus with one another and enter into the communion with God that is eternal life.

Second, this is the first time that an individual response is provided to a corporate problem. Up to this point (after the covenant at Sinai) when the people rebel, God's response affects the whole nation of Israel. When the people tell Aaron to make the golden calf (Exodus 32), God intends to destroy them all (until Moses changes God's mind). When the people complain in Numbers 11, the fire of the Lord consumes the outskirts of the camp and the people are struck with a great plague. When the people refuse to enter the land in Numbers 14, the Lord again intends to destroy them, and then when they change their mind and try to enter in Numbers 15, the Lord does not support them and they are struck down by their enemies. When Korah, Dathan, and Abiram revolt (Numbers 16:1-31), their families are destroyed, and when the people again rebel in Numbers 16:41-49 another plague breaks out. But here, though the snakes come against all of Israel, individuals are given the ability to respond in a way that provides individual healing. The whole event is a complex blend of individual and corporate action. Moses, as an individual, is an important mediator – the work of the one does benefit all. The mediation of Moses provides both communication with God and the fashioning of the bronze snake and thus makes the healing of the people possible, but his actions do not bring about a resolution of the problem on their own – the snakes are not removed – instead individuals are given the chance to respond. The healing is universally available – there is no restriction on who can look and be healed – but an individual response prompts it. John's

Gospel explores a conflict within a community, those who see God's faithfulness to Israel in the Christ event and those who do not. The story in Numbers 21 tells John's readers/hearers that they need to turn to Christ even if not all in their community choose to do so.

Third, there is something ironic or offensive about the solution God offers. The making of images was prohibited for Israel, so in Numbers 21 an act of disobedience becomes an act of obedience. The people are healed by something that they would have found doubly disturbing. Not only could looking to the serpent be considered idolatry, but they also had to look toward something that mirrored their troubles, the serpent represented not only the serpents that were causing their death but also reminded them of their rebellion and may well have (as has been discussed briefly in Chapter 1 and will be discussed again in Chapters 3 and 4) reminded them of the rebellion of their first ancestors. The first followers of Jesus had to deal with the question of how God could be found in one crucified. The offense of the serpent in the Numbers 21 provides strong support for the idea that a bad thing can indeed be a good thing.

So, the typology comparing Jesus and the serpent at this point in the narrative allows John to say: first, that Jesus' incarnation, death, resurrection and ascension are a turning point on humanity's journey toward God; second, that humanity stands before God as the Israelites did when they were in the wilderness – that they are beloved and led by God and that they need to respond as individuals to God's leadership, turning away from a herd mentality of corporate complaining and turning away from false leaders; and third, that the offense of the crucifixion, the Incarnate One's excruciating and humiliating death is not inconsistent with the actions of a God who has always entered into humanity's story to heal and save.

In what follows in John 3:17-21 the contrast presented is between being saved (σῴζω) and being judged (κρίνω). The Greek word κρίνω is another important, if ambiguous word in the Fourth Gospel. The theme of judging and judgment is introduced here and this theme will be developed throughout the rest of the book. In John 3, *judging* is contrasting with *saving*. Those who believe (ὁ πιστεύων) in the Incarnate One are not judged; those who do not believe are already under judgment on the basis of their unbelief. People who love darkness because it hides their deeds are under judgment (John 3:19); people who love the light because it shows that their deeds are done in God, are saved (John 3:21). What *judging* means to John will be explicated further as the narrative proceeds.

In John 3:1-21, the reader/hearer is reminded of the contrast between day and night, light and darkness. One is led to connect the presence of God with the kingdom (the people) of God, to identify entry into the kingdom of God as a new birth, and to recognize that being born of the flesh is a limited condition when compared to being born from the Spirit. The seeing of signs is contrasted to seeing Jesus and the necessity of seeing God's exalting and glorifying action in the crucifixion of Jesus as a means of being moved out of judgment into salvation is stated for the first time.

The irony of Nicodemus, as a Pharisee and leader of the Jews, being one who is (at least for the time being) unable to enter the kingdom of God recalls the irony of the prologue – that God came to God's own people and they did not receive him – and sets up a greater surprise and irony – that a woman of Samaria will.

John 8:12-30

This passage is part of a scene within John's narration of Jesus at the Feast of Tabernacles. The section begins at the start of chapter 7 and continues up through chapter 10 with its Good Shepherd discourse. This whole section of John's Gospel, beginning with the introduction to the Feast of Tabernacles (John 7:1), is interlaced with questions about revealing, judging, and testifying. Jesus is moving about in Galilee, but doesn't wish to travel in Judea because of the plot against his life. His brothers, a rather undefined group in John, urge him to go up to the feast and make himself known to the world, saying that no one who wishes to be known works in secret. John tells us that Jesus' brothers do not believe in him, an indication that Jesus should not follow their advice, and Jesus does not do so, saying that his hour has not yet come. Yet Jesus later goes to the feast, arriving secretly, but then teaching openly in the Temple area at the halfway point of the festival. This prompts a dialogue that continues to display the confusion among "the Jews" and the crowds as to who Jesus is.

The section under consideration here is a continuation from John 7:37-38 of Jesus' speech on the last and greatest day of the Feast of Tabernacles. There are a couple of asides that intervene (a report of the divisions of opinion about Jesus among the crowds that follow him, the guards' return to the Chief Priests without having arrested Jesus, and the [later inserted] story of the woman caught in adultery), but verse 8:12 returns the reader/hearer to the scene in the Temple where Jesus addresses the second prominent theme of Tabernacles. He has previously offered to provide a source of living water to all who thirst (John 7:37-38). Now he declares himself to be the light of the world.

The Festival of Tabernacles (or Booths) was a harvest festival that had become, by the First Century CE, a commemoration of Israel's journey through the wilderness. John's first readers/hearers would have known it as an eight-day celebration, centered in the Temple, that commemorated the light of God and the giving of water.[173]

When, on the last great day of the festival, Jesus declares himself to be the light of the world – giving the light of life to those who follow him so that they will no longer walk in darkness but have the light of life – he is recapitulating themes from both the Prologue (John 1:3b-5) and John 3:1-21 (implied by the nocturnal setting and made explicit in 3:19-21). Jesus shines the light of life so that no one who follows him will be in darkness and it can be seen (φανερωθῇ. of those who follow him that their deeds are true and are done in God. In response, the Pharisees present him with a legal challenge. Their claim is that because Jesus testifies about himself, his testimony (μαρτυρία) is not true (ἀληθής) (John 8:13). Jesus presents three arguments for why he can be believed over against the Pharisees.

First, he knows where he comes from and where he is going (John 8:14), a response to the questions (begun in John 7:27-29 and continued in 7:47-42) about where the Messiah is to come from. John is not interested here in resolving the tension reflected in the Gospels attributed to Matthew and Luke: between Jesus' origins in Nazareth or Bethlehem. It ultimately doesn't matter to John where Jesus began his earthly life or ministry; what matters is that he came

173 O'Day. "John", 542.

from God and will return to God.[174] The contrast between the Pharisees, who assume that Jesus' testimony is false because he is not following proper legal procedures; and Jesus, whom the reader/hearer has been told came from God and has returned to God and is therefore true (John 1:14,18, 3:13), exemplifies the dichotomy noted by Parsenios:[175] that Jesus makes himself known to those who seek God earnestly, while "the Jews" seek God in a prosecutorial way. "The Jews" want to render a verdict, based on legal proceedings and their own prejudices, but Jesus doesn't need to accept their suppositions or engage in these proceedings. Jesus emphasizes that it is the Pharisees' law (ἐν τῷ νόμῳ δέ τῷ ὑμετέρῳ) that requires two witnesses, implying that it is not God's law. Jesus also stresses that he is sent[176] by his father. This is patron/client language and it is a particularly striking feature of the Gospel of John.[177] Patronage was the machinery that kept the Greco-Roman society of the First Century functioning. Everyone related to others as either a client or a patron. Caesar would have been the ultimate patron for everyone under Roman rule. John's use of this language fits in with his above/below and flesh/Spirit dichotomies. The household of God is controlled by the patron of all patrons, God's own self. Any other patron is inferior. The treatment that Jesus receives at the hands of "the Jews" is both disgraceful and ironic. Disgraceful because the way one treats the client of another reflects one's attitude toward their patron. "The Jews" fail to show any consideration to one who, judging by his works, is worthy of consideration and honor. They have long since decided that Jesus cannot be who he claims to be. The irony is that in their attempts to honor God and administer the institutions of Israel, they reject the God of Israel by rejecting the one sent from God and acting on his Father's behalf. "The Jews" continually want to put Jesus on trial, but Jesus comes as a messenger

174 O'Day. "John", 633.

175 See the discussion in Chapter 1 p. 19ff.

176 "the Father who sent," (ὁ πέμψας με πατήρ) or "the one who sent" (ὁ πέμψας) could almost be considered titles in John and appear particularly frequently in Jesus' disputes with his opponents in John 5, 6, and 7-8.

177 Malina and Rohrbaugh, *Social Science Commentary on the Gospel of John*, 117-119.

and a message; a trial is not appropriate, a welcome is. Those who welcome him become part of the family of God; those who refuse to welcome him leave themselves to be judged in their own court.

Here John has interwoven the second thread of his judgment motif. "The Jews" judge falsely because they judge according to the flesh (John 8:15). This brings us to the climax of the theme begun in the prologue, that those who are only in the flesh cannot receive the word (John 1:13). Nicodemus also struggles with this issue (John 3:6). He is told that he needs to be born of the Spirit in order to understand heavenly things. The reader/hearer has been taught by Jesus that what is born of flesh is flesh and what is born of the Spirit is Spirit (John 3:6) and that the flesh is useless; it is the Spirit that gives life and Jesus' words are Spirit and life (John 6:63). That the Pharisees judge according to the flesh demonstrates conclusively that they, the keepers and protectors of the law, are standing on the wrong side of it. The ironic narrative of the healing of the man born blind and the Pharisee's farcical investigation of it leads to the same conclusion given here – those who do not see, see; and those who see, become blind (John 9:39).

Finally, Jesus claims that he doesn't judge, though he could judge because he is *not* alone (John 8:16). This is the third reason that Jesus gives to demonstrate that his testimony is valid. He does not, despite appearances, testify alone. Judgment is to be based on the testimony of two witnesses (see, for example, Deuteronomy 17:6, though there it is in reference to a murder trial, not a case of identity). Here Jesus declares that his Father also testifies on his behalf, indicating that somehow God is with him, a presence also suggested by his declarations in the Temple at Tabernacles. Jesus is a stand-in for God, providing water and light in Israel's current desert wanderings. Jesus has previously, in arguing with "the Jews," supported his testimony with four witnesses: John the Baptizer, Jesus' works, the Father's testimony, and the testimony of scripture (John 5:31-40).[178] This is another interplay of judgment and testimony, which again appears to be a legal argument. "The Jews" pass judgment against Jesus because they claim he testifies to himself. But they short circuit the process,

178 O'Day. "John", 586-7, 633.

unwilling to consider any other evidence that what he says might be true, they are not seeking to know who Jesus is, they are seeking to prosecute one whom they have already rejected out of hand. (Nicodemus has already pointed this out to them in John 7:51.) Jesus here claims that he judges no one, though he could, but instead provides testimony. This theme of whether or not Jesus judges will need to be examined further below, but the difficulty highlighted by the dialogue in John 8:12-19 is the one that confronts all would-be followers of Christ. There is no way to prove who Jesus is; one must see with the eyes of faith, the eyes of those born from above.

Again there is a break in the flow of the text here. John reminds us that Jesus is still in the Temple, now in the Treasury. Thus the reader/hearer knows that the context is still the Festival of Tabernacles. One is also reminded that even though "the Jews" are growing more angry with Jesus, as John says for the second time, no one can arrest him, because his hour has not yet come (John 7:30, 8:20).

Now Jesus begins to teach for the second time about his coming death. Jesus will be going to a place where "the Jews" cannot come, but they instead will die in their sins. Again the problem is that they are from below and Jesus is from above. They are from below because they do not believe that Jesus ἐγώ εἰμι (I am). This is a very strange sentence until one recognizes that ἐγώ εἰμι is referring back to the name God gave in answer to Moses' request at the burning bush. The name is used five times here in the context of Tabernacles, as it was also used five times in describing the miraculous feeding during the passover feast in John 6 and as it is used 12 other times throughout the Gospel of John (4:26; 10:7,9,14; 11:25; 13:9; 14:6, 15:1,5; 18:5,6,8).

When Jesus teaches here, in his second passion prediction, that he will be going away where "the Jews" will not be able to come even though they seek him, but will die in their sins, they seem to realize that "going away" means his death; but they misunderstand, wondering if he is going to kill himself. After the "from below/from above, of the world/not of the world" contrast is recapitulated, Jesus reemphasizes that they will die in their sins unless they believe that "I am" (ἐγώ εἰμι). Finally they ask the crucial question: "Who are you?" His reply is well translated: "What have I been saying to you from the beginning?" This answer causes the reader/hearer to recall all that has been said about Jesus from the beginning: that he is the Word that is with God and is God. Jesus' next statement reinforces this and refers back to the previous argument. Jesus has much to say and judge about the "the Jews" but he is not speaking on his own, "the one who sent" (ὁ πέμψας) him is true and Jesus speaks to the world what he has heard. John reemphasizes that "the Jews" do not know that when he speaks of "the one who sent" him, he is speaking of the Father, even though, ironically, he has twice before explicitly said "my father who sent me (ὁ πέμψας με πατήρ).

It is in response to the failure to recognize Jesus' relationship to the father that the second reference to the 'lifting up' of the Incarnate One occurs. "When you lift up the Son of Man, then you will know that *I am* (ἐγώ εἰμι), and I do nothing of myself, but just as the Father taught me these things, so I speak. And the one who sent (ὁ πέμψας) me is with me, [he] has not left me alone, because I always do what is pleasing to [him]" (author's translation). Jesus says this in direct response to "the Jews" lack of comprehension of the relationship between Jesus and his Father. The irony of John 3:14 resurfaces here. It is in the death, the moment that Jesus seems most abandoned and cursed, followed by the resurrection and ascension, that one knows the unity of the Father and the Son; that what Jesus says and does are taught to him by the Father and are pleasing to the Father. Again, Jesus' dialogue partners, "the Jews," cannot be expected to understand the statement about 'lifting up,' but John presupposes that the reader/hearer does. This conversation is buttoned off with the statement that as he was speaking many believed in him, a statement similar to the one made in John 2:23 about those who believed at the first Passover, another warning against belief on a human level. The conversation that follows between Jesus and "the Jews who had believed in him" continues the underlying confusion about the relationship between Jesus and his Father. Jesus invites those who believe to continue in his words, know truth, and be free. They show a certain confusion and forgetfulness: confusion by assuming that the Father whom Jesus refers to is Abraham; and forgetfulness in that they say that they have never been slaves (a forgetfulness of something that they have been commanded to remember: that they were slaves in Egypt and that God led them out with mighty acts of power [Deuteronomy 6:20-21]). Jesus addresses their confusion about which Father he is referring to: yes, they are descended from Abraham, yet they do not do what Abraham did, instead they are doing the works of their father. In response, they declare Jesus to be illegitimate and declare themselves to be children of God. But Jesus responds saying if they were indeed children of God they would love him because he has not come on his own, but has been sent by God. They are not able to hear his words because their father is the devil and they do what the devil desires. They say he is a Samaritan and has a demon. He denies this and then points out that though he is from God they dishonor (ἀτιμάζετέ) him. The problem is again related to the issues of above and below, of heaven or of the earth. Jesus does not seek glory for himself - there is another who seeks his glory and who judges. If they will only keep Jesus' words they will never see death. At this they say that they "know" that he has a demon because Abraham and the prophets died and he is therefore declaring himself to be greater than Abraham. They ask again, "Who are you making yourself (John 8:53b)?" Jesus answers again that he is not seeking his own glory, but the Father glorifies him and his Father is the one they claim as their God. He will not make himself a liar as they are and that Abraham rejoiced to see his day. When "the Jews" question this he says, "Before Abraham was I am" (ἐγώ εἰμι). It is then that they take up stones against him.

This section of John shows a pattern similar to that found in John 6. First there is a dialogue about the ability to know God and become children of God, being in God. This dialogue is followed up with an explanation in which those who have some level of belief are pushed beyond their comfort zone by Jesus; pushed to a point where they can no longer accept what he is saying and reject him. In John 6 all leave except the disciples; here they take up stones to kill him.

The dialogues and discourse of John 7 and 8 bring up the questions that those readers/hearers not yet convinced to follow Christ might have and address them rhetorically and through irony to move the reader/hearer in the proper direction. Those who oppose Jesus do so, ironically, on the basis of appearance and misunderstanding. As God's own people, "the Jews" should recognize him and yet they do not. But those who see truly will know that Jesus speaks the truth because he is the only one who has descended from and ascended back to heaven. He is the one who speaks with the voice of the Father.

At this point in John's Gospel three classes of responders to Jesus have been illustrated: (1) those who authentically accept and follow Jesus (John the baptizer, the disciples, the Samaritans); (2) those who believe, yet only on a human level (the crowds at the first Passover [John 2:23]; at the miraculous feeding [John 6:60]; Nicodemus; and the crowd at the third Passover when Jesus enters Jerusalem [John 12:42-43]); and (3) "the Jews" whose opposition to Jesus has hardened to the point where they seek to kill him. John's strategy throughout has been to confirm the faith of those readers/hearers who are in this first group and move those from the second group into the first. The third group become a caricature and, to later history, a harmful stereotype, but the way is also left open to them. They are Israel grumbling in the wilderness, but still receivers of God's providence and correction. They are under judgment, yes, but never finally condemned. The witness of John's Gospel is open to them as it is to all.

John 12:20-50

The final allusion to the 'lifting up' of the Incarnate One comes in John 12:32. The narrative material in Chapter 12 transitions the reader/hearer from the Book of Signs into the Book of Glory. It begins with a dinner for Jesus at the home of Lazarus, Martha, and Mary. When Mary anoints Jesus' feet, the house is filled with fragrance, but Judas' heart is filled with deceit and rejection. Jesus refers to anointing for his burial. The great crowd who have come to see not only Jesus, but also Lazarus, prompts the chief priests to plan to put both Lazarus and Jesus to death. Next Jesus enters Jerusalem amid the shouts of the crowd, who acclaim him as the king of Israel, the one coming in the name of the Lord; and the reader/hearer gets another retrospective from the disciples' point of view. At the time they did not realize the truth of what the crowds were saying, but from the post-ascension (glorified) perspective they remember the ironic truth of that day.

The accolades of the crowd, who had also seen Lazarus raised, cause the Pharisees to comment in despair, "You see, you can do nothing. Look, the whole world has gone after him!" The ironic truth of this statement is reinforced when some Greeks (῞Ελληνές) come to Philip and ask to see Jesus. (This ironic truth is also confirmed by Jesus third "lifted up" statement in John 12:31-32). There is a brief scene that recapitulates the first gathering of the disciples and then Jesus announces that the hour has come for the Incarnate One to be glorified; the grain of wheat must fall into the ground and die in order to bear fruit; and that he must hate his life in this world in order to keep it for eternal life. Jesus' servants must follow him, and they will be with him and will be honored by his Father (John 12:23-26).

John 12:27 continues with "Now my soul is troubled" (ἡ ψυχή μου τετάρακται); what is likely to be a reference to Habbakuk 3:2, "when my soul is troubled" (τῷ ταραχθῆναι τήν ψυχήν μου). The reference to Habbakuk draws into this context the revelation of God, at the right time, and God remembering God's mercy when the soul is troubled in wrath. Jesus then prays not to be rescued from what is to come, but to glorify God's name through it. The sign of the voice is given to confirm God's approval. But as with all of the signs in John, those who hear it have varying understandings. The reader/hearer is given the correct interpretation, but the crowd is all over the map: some think it is thunder, some think the voice of an angel. Jesus teaches, again, that the sign is not for his benefit but for theirs. Then Jesus announces the judgment of the world. In the hour in which he is glorified the ruler of the world will be driven out and when the Incarnated One is "lifted up" he will draw all people to himself (John 12:31-32).

The narrator informs the reader/hearer that Jesus is making explicit the manner of his death as crucifixion, but this confuses the crowd. They understand that death by crucifixion is intended, but they cannot reconcile the idea of crucifixion with the idea of the Messiah (χριστός) and of the "Son of Man," though they have no trouble equating these two ideas. Their expectation is that the Messiah/"Son of Man," once he has come, will remain forever. Jesus replies cryptically to their confusion by referring to himself again as light. The implication, again, is that by having faith (πιστεύω) in Jesus, one can see what God is doing; one can walk in the light. Those who do not believe will be overtaken by darkness and do not know where they are going, but those who walk in the light become children of God. The judgment of the world occurs when the Incarnate One is lifted up, the ruler of the world is driven out, and those who walk in the light are divided from those who are lost in the darkness. Yet it is not God or Jesus who does the dividing: the individuals see or do not see, trust (πιστεύω) or do not trust, are children of God or are children of Satan. Again, there is ambiguity here. Jesus has just said that he will draw all people (or perhaps all things to himself).[179] What does this "drawing" mean? The reader/hearer is reminded again of John 6, where Jesus says, "no one is able to come to me unless the Father, the one who sent me, draws [him] and I will raise [him] in the last day" (author's translation). The text implies that by the cross, resurrection, and ascension God enables everyone to come to Christ.

The narrator goes on to discuss this in John 12:36b-50, the summing up of the Book of Signs. Although, Jesus performed so many signs, they, the crowd (ὁ ὄχλος), did not believe in him, but this result fulfilled a prophecy of Isaiah. John quotes Isaiah 53:1 directly from the Septuagint "Lord, who has believed our message, and to whom has the arm of the Lord been revealed?" (κύριε τίς ἐπίστευσεν τῇ ἀκοῇ ἡμῶν; καί ὁ βραχίων κυρίου τίνι ἀπεκαλύφθη;) and then answers this question by paraphrasing Isaiah 6:9: "He has blinded their eyes and hardened their heart, so that they might not look with their eyes, and understand with their heart and turn – and I would heal them." John's understanding is that the crowds were not able to believe, because God did not intend that they should (John 12:39). John then declares that Isaiah saw Jesus' glory and spoke about him. Isaiah 6:1-9 describes the throne room theophany in which Isaiah is called to prophesy the word of God that will make the minds of the people dull, will stop their ears and shut their eyes so that they might not look, listen and turn to be healed, until the Lord has brought

179 Bruce G. Metzger, *A Textual Commentary on the Greek New Testament*, 2nd Ed, (Stuttgart: Deutsche Bibelgesellschaft, 2001), 202.

about the intended consequences. The implication here then is that Isaiah saw Jesus enthroned in the heavenly temple amid seraphs; and that he was prevented from dying at the sight by being cleansed by a coal from the altar. The echo of this scene here in John further implies that the eyes of Israel are blinded, their ears stopped and their minds dulled in order that 'the lifting up' of the Incarnate One can take place so that God can save the world by making God seeable for sinful limited human eyes.

But John does not let Israel off the hook entirely, telling the reader/hearer that many really did believe in Jesus, but did not confess it because of their fear of the Pharisees, who would expel them from the synagogues, and because of their love of human glory above the glory of God.

John 12:44-50 then presents Jesus crying out a teaching that summarizes and closes the Book of Signs. This discourse recalls many of the Gospel's major themes: 1) the connection of Jesus with the Father, 2) that having faith in (πιστεύω) and thus seeing Jesus is having faith in and seeing the one who sent him (τόν πέμψαντά με), 3) that Jesus comes as light to the world so that those who believe (πιστεύω) will not walk in darkness, 4) that Jesus does not come to judge rather to save, but that the word that he has spoken will judge on the last day, because he has said what his Father has given him to say.

This speech also begins a new thread, hinted at in John 10:18, of God's commandment. In John 10, Jesus' good shepherd discourse, Jesus says that he will lay down his life in order to take it up again and that he has the power to do this because he is obeying his Father's command. Here in John 12:49-50, Jesus says that the word he has spoken will judge because it was not spoken by Jesus on his own but was spoken as commanded by his Father and that God's commandment is eternal life. This sets the reader/hearer up to hear the new commandment that Jesus will give to his disciples as he washes their feet and goes willingly to the cross in John's Book of Glory to follow.

The 'lifting up' of the Incarnate One in John's Rhetorical Strategy

Overall John's rhetorical strategy is one of presenting a drama of contrasts, always moving his reader/hearer to recognition of Jesus and thus to side with God and God's representatives against the world and those who are enslaved to it. Following the prologue which sets the stage, the readers/hearers walk through a series of vignettes where they meet various characters, some with whom they are drawn to identify, others of whom they are warned against. We are told in the prologue that the first character we will meet, John the baptizer, is trustworthy, sent from God. The disciples begin as followers of John and so they can be considered trustworthy, but we are warned against Nicodemus, who at first stands with "the Jews." The woman at the well would normally be suspect, but the meeting at a well (as an echo of the Old Testament stories of Jacob and Isaac) softens the reader/hearer to listen with expectant ears; and on it goes throughout the narrative.

The figure of the 'lifting up' of the Incarnate One is central to the controversy that all these characters represent. It is presented to the reader/hearer initially in the context of a non-hostile dialogue. Nicodemus appears curious, feeling about for truth in the darkness, and he is left at the end of John 3 still groping in the dark. When the 'lifting up' thread resurfaces again in John 8, the context is distinctly adversarial. "The Jews" are arguing their case against the Incarnate One, and the way forward that he offers them is unacceptable with their limited, fleshly sight. The final 'lifting up' reference declares what God is about to do in Jesus' hour: 1) judge the world to save it, 2) drive out the ruler of the world and draw all people (things) to God, 3) glorify the Father and the Son, 4) return Jesus to the glory he had with the Father from the beginning (John 17:5) and 5) bring all of humanity with him into glory (John 17:22). The context of all three 'lifted up' sayings, within narratives that recall Israel in the wilderness (Passover and Tabernacles), reinforces the image that the people who encounter Jesus are like the people in the wilderness and the Christ event is the turning point in their journey toward God. When they see beyond the offense of the cross, they become the ones who enter into God's kingdom. The readers/hearers will learn in the farewell discourse that this entrance into the kingdom is actually entrance into the family and into the very being of God (John 17:21-22).

The backward look so distinctive to John's Gospel aids in this strategy by keeping the readers/hearers "in the know" so that John's irony can function.[180] It begins with the prologue, where the readers/hearers is told that the eternal Word became flesh and lived among humanity and that "we," his followers, saw the glory of God. In John 2, with Jesus' sign in the Temple, the reader/hearer is told that, though the disciples did not understand at the time, they later remembered and were able to connect the dots between Jesus' words and actions and the scriptures (John 2:17, 22). In John 3, in addition to the "we" perspective of the followers of Jesus, Jesus' ascension is referred to as a past event (John 3:13). The reader/hearer is told in John 6:71 that Judas will be the betrayer of Jesus. Again in John 7:39 the reader/hearer is told that the Spirit will be given after Jesus is glorified. At Jesus' triumphal entry into Jerusalem (John 12:16), the reader/hearer is again reminded that, from the perspective of the end of the story, the events as they occur make sense.

Irony then can draw the reader in and thus become a powerful rhetorical tool. Because the readers/hearers see the events of Jesus' life through the post-resurrection perspective and "get" who Jesus is, they identify strongly with those characters in the narrative who also get it and reject the views of those characters that do not. Because the readers/hearers have been given enough clues to be "in the know" about Jesus, they are in a position of superior knowledge over all the characters in the story except Jesus, John the baptizer, and the sending Father. Through irony, the reader/hearer is given the tools to interpret the events narrated in the Gospel correctly, *because* the characters within the narrative are unable to. The central irony of the Gospel is that in order to see and know God one must look to the crucified Messiah; to the flesh of a bloodied and broken failure,

180 Culpepper presents a detailed discussion of these "analepses." R. Allen Culpepper, *Anatomy of the Fourth Gospel: A Study in Literary Design* (Philadelphia: Fortress Press, 1983), 56-61.

executed publicly on a Roman instrument of torture; the image of an unclean, sinful, cursed creature. This is the crisis, the moment of judgment to which all of humanity is brought. Only those who are born from above, united to God through Christ by the Spirit, can see in this event the depth of the love of God for the creation. Everyone else sees disgrace and filth, something to be rejected and utterly avoided and yet, ironically, it is this very judgment and rejection that brings about the saving of the world. It appears that use of the story of the serpent on the pole is ironic in at least two ways: the equating of crucifixion, that most shameful method of execution, with exaltation and glorification; and the equating of the snake, the bringer of sin and death into the world with God.[181]

The 'lifting up' of the Incarnate One Amidst Other Johannine Themes

As can be seen from the literary analysis conducted above, the typology of the serpent on the pole contributes to a great number of closely related motifs that run throughout John's Gospel: 1) birth from above, 2) ascending and descending, 3) knowing and seeing, 4) flesh or spirit, 5) testimony and belief, 6) judging and saving, 7) light or darkness, 8) truth or lies, 9) necessity, 10) glory, 11) "ἐγώ εἰμι," 12) the sent and sending one, 13) the presence of God, 14) Temple festivals (Passover and Tabernacles), 15) and the identity of Jesus, at a minimum. The following section explores what some of these contributions and combinations might say about the meaning of the serpent/Jesus typology.

Above and Below/Flesh or Spirit

The motif that contrasts above or below, flesh or spirit is introduced in the prologue. Those who are born, not of flesh, but of God are those who received the Word and believed in his name. These are the ones given power to become the children of God (John 1:13). This motif surfaces again in John 3 where Nicodemus is told that unless one is born from above, by water and Spirit, one can neither see nor enter the kingdom of God; that what is born of flesh is flesh

181 The rational for this statement will be discussed in detail in Chapter 4.

and what is born of Spirit is spirit. In John 6, when Jesus feeds the multitude, he declares that flesh is useless, it is the Spirit that gives life. In Chapter 8 the problem that the Pharisees have, according to Jesus, is that they judge according to the flesh (John 8:15). "The Jews" are from below, Jesus is from above (John 8:23). On their own they cannot go where he is going, but instead will die in their sins. The reader/hearer has been warned already that those who are born of flesh cannot see or enter the kingdom of God, so the judgment of the Pharisees is a human judgment not a heavenly one. In John 17:2 we learn that Jesus has been given authority over all flesh. In John 19:11 we learn that Pilate's human authority has come from above. John uses this thematic thread to teach that life comes from being part of the kingdom of God, being children of God, while death comes from remaining only in the flesh. The dichotomy between flesh and spirit, below and above is stark and thus God's solution to this separation is both ironic and astonishing. The reader/hearer is told in the prologue the the Word became flesh (1:14) and that Jesus will give his own flesh as the bread of life for the life of the world (John 6:51,52). Those who eat Jesus' flesh and drink his blood have eternal life. The Spirit abides in them and they abide in Jesus as Jesus abides in his Father (John 6:54,56; 14:17; 15:9-10). God's solution to humanity's inability to see and enter the kingdom of God is to join humanity on the fleshy side of the divide. The humans who see and know God there – God in the flesh in Jesus; Jesus in the serpent on the pole, that is, Christ on the cross; and Jesus in the bread and wine – are drawn into God on the Spirit side.

Ascending/Descending of the Incarnate One

The motif of above or below, flesh or spirit, moves the reader/hearer into the motif of the ascending/descending of the Incarnate One. This theme is introduced when Jesus promises Nathaniel of Cana that he will "see heaven opened and the angels of God ascending and descending upon the Son of Man" (John 1:51). This image, recalling as it does the story of Jacob at Bethel (Genesis 28:10-17), conveys into the narrative the ideas that Jesus connects heaven and earth, that the presence of Jesus is the presence of God, and that Jesus is the Temple and the gate of heaven. The next time ascending and descending comes up, it is Jesus who has both descended and ascended. (John 3:13). Jesus is the only one who can know and speak of heavenly things because he is the one who has been in heaven, come down to earth, and (from the church's post-Easter perspective) has returned to his Father. John 3:14 tells the reader/hearer that the cross, resurrection, and ascension – the 'lifting up' of the Incarnate One – is the mechanism by which Jesus returns to his Father in heaven. Jesus again refers to ascending to heaven during the dispute with those of his disciples who are offended by his teaching that he is the bread come down from heaven that gives eternal life. Jesus then speaks ironically of the greater offense of his return to God via the cross (John 6:62). John speaks again of Jesus' ascension when he records the conversation between Mary and Jesus on the first day of the week. Jesus tells Mary not to hold on to him (ἅπτω) because he has not yet ascended, but instead to go and tell his "brothers" that he is ascending to his Father and their father, his God and their God (John 20:17). John leaves the time of Jesus' ascension ambiguous; the fulfillment of the promise to Nathaniel is not narrated. Thus it is left unclear if the Jesus that the disciples see twice in the room behind locked doors or meet on the shore of the Sea of Tiberias is the ascended Jesus. What John does make clear is that upon the ascension of Jesus the relationship between Jesus and his Father becomes the same as the relationship between his siblings and the Father; as Jesus ascends they become children of God. Thus it is implied that John sees his gospel as also 'lifting up' Jesus. The stated purpose of the writing of the testimony of the beloved disciple is that the reader/hearer will see, come to believe, and thus have life in Jesus' name (John 20:31, 21:24, 25).

The Exodus and Glory

Another cluster of motifs closely associated with the 'lifting up' of the Incarnate One are the Exodus and the glory of God, themes that are also introduced in the prologue. When the Word became flesh and "tented" (σκηνόω) among humans, "we," those who are part of John's community, the church, saw his glory (δόξα) a glory unique to the Son, full of grace and truth. Thus from the very beginning images drawn from Israel's wandering in the wilderness are woven throughout the fabric of John's Gospel, images such as God dwelling among the people in the Tabernacle, as evidenced by the "glory" (כָּבוֹד) descending upon it, and God leading them in a pillar of cloud by day and fire by night. The recurring event of Passover in John (three of them: John 2:13- 3:21, John 6, and finally John 12-19) sets the narrative of Jesus' life in the context of God's liberation of the people from slavery in Egypt. The signs (σημεῖον) which are such a prominent feature of John's Gospel, while they do not parallel the signs performed in Egypt in a direct way, are given, as the plagues were, in order to demonstrate the power of God in opposition to the powers that oppressed the people of God; slavery in Egypt and bondage to sin and death in first century Palestine.[182] Thus glory represents for John not only honor, praise, and renown, but also the visible, powerful, presence of God with God's people throughout the Gospel narrative. It is used in this way, as already mentioned, (1) in the prologue (John 1:14); (2) at the eschatologically colored wedding at Cana, where Jesus turns water into wine (John 2:11); (3) at the death and raising of Lazarus (John 11:4, 40); and (4) with the reference to Isaiah (John 12:41). Glorifying (δοξάζω) in John's Gospel – again in addition to praising, revering, and worshipping – also has a strong sense of revelation. When Jesus is glorified, God is revealed in him.

Isaiah 52:13 establishes a connection between exaltation (ὑψόω) and glorification (δοξάζω), as was mentioned in Chapter 1, in the final of Isaiah's servant poems ('Ιδοὺ συνήσει ὁ παῖς μου καὶ ὑψωθήσεται καὶ δοξασθήσεται σφόδρα. Behold my servant will understand and will be exalted and highly glorified. (Author's translation)). This is a fascinating passage. Christopher Seitz describes the servant introduced in Isaiah 49, identity unknown, as one who is successful as a prophet, by God's design, in a way that his predecessor, Isaiah of Jerusalem could not be.[183] This servant is shown to be a prophet like Moses (referred to in Deuteronomy

182 The same word, σημεῖον, is used in the Septuagint to indicate the signs performed in Exodus, 3-12.

183 Christopher R. Seitz, "The Book of Isaiah 40 - 66: Introduction, Commentary, and Reflections" in *The New Interpreters Bible: A Commentary in Twelve Volumes, Volume VI* (Nashville: Abingdon Press, 1994), 320.

18:15) and his legacy – his oracles – are preserved by the servants who follow him after his death described in Isaiah 52:13-53:12. This passage speaks of the continuing of God's liberation of God's people and the passing on of the teachings of one revered by his followers to the next generation of followers. It also speaks of revelation to the nations surrounding Israel. There is much here to suggest Jesus to the author of John's Gospel and much here that would fit the situation of Jesus' followers when the Gospel was written.

This is the great and ironic sense of Jesus' "hour" to be glorified (John 2:4; 4:21,23; 5:25,28; 7:30; 8:20; 12:16,23,27; 13:1; 16:25,32; 17:1; 19:14). It is 1) when some Greeks seek Jesus just before the Festival of Passover (John 12:23, 27), 2) when Judas has gone out into the night (John 13:1), 3) when Jesus' followers have left him alone (though his Father has not left him alone [John 16:32]), 4) when Pilate hands him over to be crucified, 5) when Jesus is lifted up on the cross, 6) when the soldiers cast lots for his clothes, 7) when he gives his mother into the care of the disciple whom he loved, and 8) when he receives the sour wine from the hyssop branch and gives up his spirit (19:14-30), 9) when Jesus is resurrected and 10) when Jesus' ascends, that Jesus is glorified – that is, revealed as the Incarnate One. Jesus' "hour" is also the hour when 1) people begin to worship in Spirit and in truth (John 4:21,23); 2) the dead, all in their graves, hear the voice of the Son of God and live (John 5:25,28); and 3) when Jesus no longer speaks in figures but plainly (John 16:25). It is in his "hour" that Jesus is revealed as one with the God of Exodus liberation. It is also this hour, series of events and actions, that allows the giving of the Spirit to humanity (John 7:39).

There is another sense in which glory and glorifying are used in John. They become part of the dichotomy between flesh and spirit, above and below. Jesus describes the difficulty that "the Jews" have in receiving him in terms of their seeking or receiving glory from humans rather than from God. Whom one seeks to honor, praise, and worship reveals to whom one belongs, one's patron. Is it God or the ruler of the the world as it stands in need of salvation? This is the sense used in the dialogues following the sabbath healing of the man at the pool of Bethzatha (John 5:41,44) and when Jesus' teaching is questioned at the Festival of Tabernacles (John 7:18; 8:50,54).

Judging and Saving

The 'lifting up' of the Incarnate One is also closely tied to the motifs of judging and saving, knowing and seeing. Judging (κρίνω) is expressed as the opposite of saving (σώζω) in the two passages in John where those activities are most closely linked to the 'lifting up' of the Incarnate One. In both John 3:17 and John 12:47 the reader/hearer is told that Jesus has come not to judge the world but to save it. In both of these places the 'lifting up' of the Incarnate One and its purpose has just been described. In John 3:14 Jesus says he will be "lifted up," just as Moses lifted up the serpent, so that the ones who believe (trust, have faith in, or are faithful in him (ὁ πιστεύων ἐν αὐςτῷ.) might have eternal life (ἔχῃ ζωὴν αἰώνιον).[184] In John 12:47, as part of the summary that closes the Book of Signs, Jesus has just declared that he has come to his "hour" so that his Father's name will be glorified (John 12:27,28) and that his "hour" now brings the judgment (κρίσις) of the world in which the ruler of the world will be driven out and Jesus, in his being "lifted up," will draw all people to himself (John 12:32). Thus the 'lifting up' of the Incarnate One is the mechanism which provides the eternal life referred to in John 3, and the implication is that eternal life is associated with being drawn to Jesus (John 12:32). These things – having eternal life and being with or in Jesus – are what it means to be saved. Jesus himself defines eternal life as knowing the only true God and Jesus as the one whom God has sent (John 17:3). Therefore, by the contrasts given in John, being judged implies the failure to know God; being away from or apart from Jesus; and, rather than having eternal life, being on the way to death.

Knowing and Seeing

Knowing and seeing in the Gospel of John are subjects that are much too complex to be addressed in detail here, but the serpent on the pole is a central strand in the complex web of knowing and seeing/not knowing and blindness that has been woven throughout the Gospel. If the human problem narrated in John's Gospel is the

184 The use of the subjunctive indicates not possibility, but purpose and result. Wallace, *Greek Grammar Beyond the Basics,* 473-474.

difficulty of truly knowing and seeing God and the consequences of knowing and seeing God in the wrong way, then the solution to that problem is ultimately the Incarnate One "lifted up" through the cross, resurrection, and ascension. The figure of Jesus "lifted up" just as the serpent was lifted up by Moses is introduced in John 3 as part of a conversation that contrasts what the "we" of "the Jews," represented by Nicodemus, know versus what the "we" of the church, represented by Jesus, know. Nicodemus' knowledge is earthbound and flesh bound. He knows that Jesus is somehow from God because of the signs Jesus does, but he thinks that rebirth means returning to a mother's womb. The knowledge of the church is Spirit born. It comes from above and cannot be seen with earthly sight. It is they who believe in (trust, have faith in, are faithful in) the "lifted up" Incarnate One who are reborn into the life that comes from the Spirit. The recurring controversy throughout John's story of Jesus concerns what is known about Jesus versus what is known about the expected Messiah or Prophet. People claim to know where Jesus comes from and the Pharisees challenge his testimony because they believe he testifies to himself alone. They do not understand (γινώσκω) that he is speaking to them of the Father (John 8:27). Jesus' response is that when they have "lifted up" the Incarnate One they will realize (γινώσκω) that "I am" (ἐγώ εἰμι). With the final reference to the 'lifting up' of the Incarnate One, after Jesus has told them that his 'lifting up' will drive out the ruler of this world and he will draw all people to himself, they question the manner of his death. In their understanding the Messiah remains for ever. If he is to be "lifted up," he must be someone else. Jesus calls them to walk while they have the light, for when the light is gone they will not see where they are going. John then explains their lack of response by referring to the prophecies of Isaiah, that their eyes had been blinded so that they would not see and turn and be healed, actions very much connected to the narrative of Numbers 21. John closes the Book of Signs with Jesus teaching that whoever believes in him believes in the one who sent him and whoever sees him sees the one who sent him; that Jesus knows that God's commandment is eternal life and that he speaks what his Father has given him to speak.

Judgment

Judgment is a theme throughout the disputes between Jesus and "the Jews" in John 5, 7, 8 and 12. When "the Jews" persecute Jesus for healing the man at the pool of Bethzatha on the Sabbath and making himself equal to God by calling God his father, Jesus declares that the one who hears Jesus' word and believes in the one who sent him (τῷ πέμψαντί) has eternal life and does not come (ἔρχομαι) into judgment (John 5:24). Here it is Jesus who is the judge, having received all judgment from the Father who does not judge (John 5:22, 27, 30). Those who recognize the relationship between Jesus and the Father are those who honor the Father appropriately. In John 5:29, Jesus declares that those who have died prior to the hour of the Incarnate One, when they hear his voice, will come out of their graves; those who have done good (ὰ ἀγαθὰ ποιήσαντες) into resurrection life, those who have done poorly (τὰ φαῦλα πράξαντες) into resurrection judgment. This implies that judgment or life are states that can be entered into after physical death, because of Jesus' hour. There is some ambiguity in terms of what good (ἀγαθα) and poorly (φαῦλα) mean here, but the context and the use of φαῦλα rather than πονηρός implies again, that good means recognition of Jesus as the Incarnate One, rather than conforming to a moral tradition. What John declares as evil (πονηρός) are the deeds of those who love darkness rather light (John 3:19) and the work of the world (John 7:7) and thus John implies that the ruler of the world (John 12:31) is the evil one (John 17:15).

At the Festival of Tabernacles, John questions the ability of "the Jews" to judge rightly. First, Jesus questions their interpretation of the Law of Moses by comparing the appropriateness of initiating a man into the nation of Israel through circumcision on the Sabbath to making a man well on the Sabbath (John 7:24). Nicodemus questions their judging practices in John 7:51, when he says, "Our law does not judge people without first giving them a hearing to find out what they are doing, does it?" Jesus continues his critique when he declares that "the Jews" judge by human standards while he reflects what the Father says, thus judging by heavenly standards. (John 8:15, 26, 50). In John 12 before Jesus' final Passover, he declares his hour to be the time of the judgment of the world (John 12:31) and that not he, but his word, is the judge, again because his words come from the Father (John 12:48). The idea of the inability of "the Jews" to judge rightly, or even at all, is restated ironically when Pilate tells them to judge Jesus themselves and they reply that they are not permitted to put anyone to death (John 18:31). Jesus speaks again about judgment in his farewell discourse, this time in terms of the Spirit (ὁ παράκλητος). It is the Spirit that will prove the world wrong about sin and righteousness and judgment. Here *sin* is not believing in Jesus, *righteousness* is associated with Jesus' vindication as he returns to the Father, and *judgment* is that the ruler of this world has been judged. Judgment is a state of being for John and there is considerable ambiguity about its permanence. The ones who believe (trust, have faith, or are faithful) in the Incarnate One (ὁ πιστεὺων ἐν αὐτῷ) are not judged, but pass from death to life. The implication is that everyone else is still in some way belonging to the world and the ruler of the world and are thus being judged. Yet the ruler of this world has been cast out (ἐκβάλλω) by the events of Jesus' hour. The dual-time perspective of the narrative leaves the reader/hearer in the ambiguity of John's realized yet not realized eschatology with a feeling of urgency for action still to be taken, but also with the reassurance that what was needful has already been done.

Conclusion

The structural, rhetorical, and thematic investigations into the use of the typology between Moses' bronze serpent and Jesus on the cross conducted in this chapter have indicated some important meanings that arise as it is read/heard. First, the figure is central to the Gospel narrative, occurring three times, each in sections of the narrative that have a well defined theme and purpose. In John 3, part of the section of the Gospel that explores authentic responses to Jesus, the typology indicates that those who look to Christ on the cross, by virtue of birth from above, are those who respond to God with authentic faith and thus have eternal life. In John 8, as part of the section of the Gospel that explores Jesus as the antitype of the Tabernacle/Temple, the typology between him and the serpent deepens the irony of the events narrated in the Gospel by emphasizing that God is present and known in the crucified One. The final reference in John 12 as part of the transition into the narration of Jesus' "hour" to be glorified emphasizes that the scandal of the 'lifting up' of the Incarnate One contributes to the blinding of Israel, leading to the rejection of Jesus that, ironically, saves the world.

The typology between Jesus and the serpent also contributes to one of the controlling metaphors of the Gospel of John, that of the Passover/Exodus from Egypt and God's provision for Israel in the wilderness. If Jesus is like the serpent on the pole, the people who encounter him are like the children of Israel, the cross is the turning point in their history that makes entry into the kingdom of God possible and they enter into eternal life when they overcome the offense of the cross and look to him.

Thus the serpent on the pole becomes a testimony to the word becoming flesh and the salvation that that event offers. The one who hears about the Incarnate One crucified, must judge whether God is present in Jesus or not. The witness to the resurrection and ascension help one to judge rightly. The one who judges rightly - that Jesus is indeed God – will be saved, will have life.The one who judges wrongly - that God is not with and in him - is still in darkness and does not have the light of life. The Christ event confronts each person with the question of their acceptance or rejection of God as revealed in the Incarnate One whom God has sent.

Given the ironic nature of the use of this typology in John's Gospel, it seems likely that the image of the serpent is a negative one, adding shock value to the idea that the Word became flesh, entering into the sin and uncleanness of humanity in its captivity to sin and death. The nature of serpents in the Old Testament, particularly in Numbers 21 will be considered in the next chapter.[185]

185 Raymond Brown includes an interesting exploration of whether Nicodemus could have understood Jesus' sayings here in light of Old Testament prophecy (Brown, *The Gospel of John* i-xii, 1966, 140-141), but I believe John's point is that Jesus' teaching cannot be understood except from a post resurrection perspective.

Chapter 3

Serpents in the Old Testament

Introduction

It was said in the last chapter that the typology between Jesus and the bronze serpent seemed to draw together several ideas about Jesus' death in John's Gospel: that those who look to Christ on the cross, by virtue of birth from above, are those who respond to God with authentic faith and thus have eternal life; that God is present and known in the Crucified, Risen and Ascended One; and that the scandal of the 'lifting up' of the Incarnate One contributes to the blinding of Israel, leading to the rejection of Jesus that, ironically, saves the world.

In this chapter the nature of serpents in the Old Testament will be considered in their own right. The hope is to provide some sense of the tradition that John might have been acquainted with in order to discern whether the reading detailed in Chapter 2 is responsible; that is, is one that recovers part of the range of possibilities for reading the Old Testament witness. The goal of this research is to suggest how John's use of the serpent might resonate with the narrative world of the Septuagint and thus provide direction as to how it might inform this author's current context. This chapter then is an attempt to demonstrate that the reading given in the previous chapter is consistent with the witness of Scripture, perhaps as John might have understood it, but more importantly as one might understand it now.

The discussion will begin with a survey of the scholarship on Numbers 21. Next, other important references to serpents in the Old Testament will be considered, beginning with the remark about the bronze serpent in 2 Kings 18:4 since it speaks directly of the serpent that Moses made. Deuteronomy 8:15 will be considered next, as it may refer in a general way to the incident narrated in Numbers 21. A brief look at the serpents in Jeremiah 8:17 and the serpent in Genesis 3 will follow. The results of this survey will show that there are indeed features of the snake references in the Old Testament that bear out the objectives for the typology used in John as explored in the previous chapter: the cross is the new turning point in the journey of God's people towards God's kingdom; in Christ on the cross, humanity is confronted with its failure and rebellion; and the image of the serpent on the pole is a rhetorical call to see in Christ, the healing and providing God of the Exodus – and in seeing, receive that healing and life.

Numbers 21

A great many of the scholarly investigations of Numbers 21 follow primarily text-critical avenues; their purpose being either to contest, affirm, or refine the documentary hypothesis. Other scholars have been intrigued by the mention of the serpent that Moses made in 2 Kings 18:4 and seek to discover if a relationship between the two texts proves or disproves the historicity of either account. Such studies, by their nature, focus on discontinuities in the text, the history of its production, or the world behind the text, rather than its narrative shape. The author of the Gospel of John would not, in all likelihood, have questioned whether or not the events recounted in Numbers 21 actually happened or what sources were redacted to make up the story as it had been preserved as scripture and passed down. Such studies are aimed at a different purpose then that of this work, so while this author would like to acknowledge a very great debt to these scholars, very little of the discussion of the historical and textual critical work on Numbers 21 will be included here.

Most commentators also deal with the Hebrew text of Numbers 21 and its many striking features; but as it appears that the author of John's Gospel worked with the Greek text,[186] aspects of the text that occur in the Hebrew but not in the Greek will not be discussed here. This means that the reference to "seraph" serpents and any connection to Isaiah's throne room theophany (Isaiah 6:1-13), suggestive though it might be, will not considered. There doesn't seem to be any reliable linguistic connection between Isaiah 6 and the Greek text of Numbers 21.

The book of Numbers has been described as "a collection of a great variety of genres, literary styles, and subject matters."[187] Scholars have tried to organize the book based on a variety of principles. The following discussion will focus on literary readings of Numbers 21 and seek to identify a theological core for the story based on its placement within Numbers and the Hexateuch.

For Dennis Olson, the major structural elements on which the book as a whole rests are the two census lists in Numbers 1 and 26.[188] An outline based on these two features convinces Olson that the unifying theme for the Book of Numbers is the death of the old generation and the birth of the new.[189] Olson arrives at this idea by examining the differing organizing principles that past scholarship posited for Numbers (chronology, geography, tradition-historical themes and detection of sources).[190] None of these organizing principles explain, to Olson's satisfaction, the current text of the book of Numbers as a narrative unit, separate yet attached to the

186 Köstenberger includes a detailed survey of references to the Old Testament in John's Gospel. He concludes that its author primarily draws on the Septuagint though he occasionally adapts it. Köstenberger believes that the author of John may have known the Hebrew and also had another source such as a *testimonium* since in John 19:37 he deviates from the LXX because it misconstrues the Hebrew. Köstenberger, "John", 418.

187 Dennis T. Olson, *The Death of the Old and the Birth of the New: The Framework of the Book of Numbers and the Pentateuch*, Brown Judaic Studies 71 (Chico California: Scholars Press, 1985), 9.

188 Olson, *The Death of the Old and the Birth of the New*, 55.

189 Olson, *The Death of the Old and the Birth of the New*, 2.

190 Olson, *The Death of the Old and the Birth of the New*, 33.

rest of the Pentateuch and moving into the Hexateuch. For Olson, what makes sense is to understand that the book is structured as two units demarcated by the two genealogies presented in Numbers 1:19-43 and Numbers 26:4-65. The census in Numbers 26 expands on the census in Numbers 1 indicating the multiplication of the new generation of Israel after the death of the old and indicating progress toward the realization of the divine promises made to Abraham, Isaac and Jacob of a great number of descendants and a great nation.[191] Numbers 1-25 then, in Olson's proposed structure, recounts the death of the first generation to be led out of Egypt. This was the generation that failed to enter the land from Kadesh (Numbers 14:22). Numbers 26-36 presents a new generation, counted on the plains of Moab and left, at the end of the book, poised on the verge of entering the land of promise.[192] Olson also sees throughout the book of Numbers, in the repeated phrase "a perpetual statute throughout your generations," a concern for the movement from one generation on to the next and the maintenance of the integrity of God's law into the future. But this is coupled with an openness to change under new circumstances and in answer to new questions (as evidenced by the inheritance given to the daughters of Zelophehad (Numbers 27:1-11), flexibility in the passover laws (Numbers 9:9-14), and by allowing the tribes of Gad and Reuben to settle in the Transjordan (Numbers 32)).[193] For Olson, the theology that Numbers expresses is that God overcomes all obstacles that stand in the way of keeping the promises given and that God replaces the rebellion and death of each generation with the hope and promise of a new one.[194] The book of Numbers is, for Olson, "the story of God's uncompromising justice and mercy which condemns prideful rebellions but gives life and hope to 'little ones' who trust in God and [God's] faithfulness to [God's] promises."[195] Most importantly for this present work is how Olson's structure shapes the context for the

191 Olson, *The Death of the Old and the Birth of the New*, 80.

192 Olson, *The Death of the Old and the Birth of the New*, 83.

193 Olson, *The Death of the Old and the Birth of the New*, 97.

194 Olson, *The Death of the Old and the Birth of the New*, 95.

195 Olson, *The Death of the Old and the Birth of the New*, 180.

story of Moses and the bronze serpent. Numbers 21:4-9, in Olson's scheme, while it is not the end of the first generation (which occurs when the people of Israel yoke themselves to the Baal of Peor and Phinehas ends the resulting plague) might be considered at or near the lowest point in this generation's history. There is a brief glimmer of victory at Numbers 21:1, when the Israelites utterly defeat the King of Arad, but the Israelites immediately again grow impatient. It is this impatience that moves God to send the snakes, as recounted in Numbers 21:6. What follows directly on the snake episode is two military victories and the Balaam oracles which pronounce blessing on future generations.[196] So, the story of the snake plague narrates an important corner in Israel's wilderness journey. The story in Numbers 21:4-9 expresses Olson's theology of God's uncompromising justice and faithfulness in a nutshell, for God both calls Israel to account for its lack of trust, but at the same times gives them a way to turn back to God and move forward.

Baruch Levine expresses that Numbers 21 has a more complex historical and literary history than any other single chapter in the Hebrew Bible because it presents a historiographic link between the wilderness wanderings and the Transjordian phase of Israel's journey from Egypt to the land of promise.[197] Levine puts the death of the first generation in Numbers 21 between verse 12 and 13, but without any explicit reference to this critical moment.[198] He believes that this account in Numbers parallels the account in Deuteronomy 2:13-15 with its description of the death of the first generation of warriors between Kadesh-barnea and the Wadi Sered. For Levine, the setting of Numbers 21:4-9 as part of the dramatic account of Israel's wars with the Amorites, prevents it from becoming simply a horrendous tale of divine wrath tempered with divine providence. The interest of the final editor of Numbers is the encounters with the nations of the Transjordan.[199] Levine believes that the healing accomplished

196 Olson, *The Death of the Old and the Birth of the New*, 89.

197 Baruch A. Levine, *Numbers 21-36: A New Translation with Introduction and Commentary* (New York: Doubleday, 2000), 110.

198 Levine, *Numbers 21-36*, 79.

199 Levine, *Numbers 21-36*, 128.

by the bronze serpent is a case of sympathetic magic employing "an empowered snake capable of destroying the inimical one."[200] Levine, then, considers the snakes to be instruments of God's wrath and hostile to the Israelites, but also a necessary element of the transition between the first generation of Israel and the second.

Klaus Koenen sees a parallel in narrative shape and purpose between the story of Moses and the bronze serpent and that of the golden calf of Exodus 32.[201] Koenen sees in the story told in Numbers 21:4-9 a complex interplay between a story about Yahweh as a healing God and an etiology for the Nehuschtan of 2 Kings 18 that gets turned on its head.[202] He notes the irony that the thing that the Israelites complain against God and Moses about – dying in the wilderness – is the thing that comes about through the snakes in response to their complaining.[203] Koenen believes that the story is preserved in its present literary form because worship of the Nehuschtan in the Temple achieved a legitimacy in the cult of Yahweh which was later lost; as was also the case with the golden calf that Jeroboam set up at Bethel.[204] The story's final form results from the tension between the blessing intended in the construction of the bronze serpent as a command from God to Moses and its destruction by Hezekiah as an idol that leads the people of Israel astray. Thus, while the story teaches that God brings life out of death, the bronze serpent is to be considered a dangerous object.[205]

Jacob Milgrom believes that Numbers 21:4-9 is the last of the complaining stories of Israel's wilderness journey and one that follows the typological structure of the other wilderness complaints (Numbers 11:4-35 and Numbers 12:1-15). It is also the most serious, because here the people are in open defiance of the Lord God and

---

200 Levine, *Numbers 21-36*, 88.

201 Klaus Koenen, "Eherne Schlange un goldenes Kalb: Ein Vergleich der Überlieferungen," *ZAW* 111. Bd. S. 353-372.

202 Koenen, "Eherne Schlange un goldenes Kalb," 353-354.

203 Koenen, "Eherne Schlange un goldenes Kalb," 357.

204 Koenen, "Eherne Schlange un goldenes Kalb," 360, 364.

205 Koenen, "Eherne Schlange un goldenes Kalb," 361.

not just God's intermediaries: Moses, Aaron, and Miriam.[206] (By this time in the wilderness narrative, Aaron and Miriam have died leaving Moses as the only intermediary.) Milgrom notes that the peoples' complaints entirely reverse the divine promise: they attribute evil to God and represent Egypt as good.[207] He understands that God's grace toward Israel is marked by progress toward the promised land while God's punishment is marked by delays in that progress.[208] Milgrom also notes that despite the continual murmuring of the Israelites, God continues to provide for all their needs. This is, for Milgrom, the main thrust of the story of Moses and the bronze snake; that God heals those whom God has afflicted, provides them with what they need, and gives them victory.[209] Milgrom notes many important features of the story. The problem for the Israelites is the journey itself; they have grown restive in their wandering and so, in their worst complaining yet, they speak out against the very idea of divine authority. Their attitude is the polar opposite of the trust they had when they crossed the Red Sea. Milgrom observes that the Israelites contradict themselves when they complain that there is no food and yet detest the bread they are given and he points out that Numbers 21:17-18 disproves their claim that there is no water.[210] Milgrom affirms that ancient sources testify to the danger of poisonous snakes in the Sinai and draws on Targum Jonathan and the Wisdom of Solomon to explain that the snakes are not removed as a threat because God uses them to continue to test the obedience of Israel. Only those who follow God's command recover.[211] But Milgrom, in disagreement with Levine, emphasizes that the healing that comes through the bronze serpent is not sympathetic magic. Moses, appointed by God to be the leader who teaches this ragtag group of former Egyptian slaves to rely on God alone, has to distinguish himself from being a practitioner of Egyptian magic.

---

206 Jacob Milgrom, *The JPS Torah Commentary: Numbers* (Philadelphia: The Jewish Publication Society, 1990), 376.

207 Milgrom, *The JPS Torah Commentary: Numbers*, 379.

208 Milgrom, *The JPS Torah Commentary: Numbers*, 380.

209 Milgrom, *The JPS Torah Commentary: Numbers*, 464.

210 Milgrom, *The JPS Torah Commentary: Numbers*, 173.

211 Milgrom, *The JPS Torah Commentary: Numbers*, 174.

Moses repeatedly "describes the miracle in advance" and designates the precise moment of its occurrence though a specific manual act."[212] Then Moses completes the described action in silence. The power that performs the miracle is God's power and it is intended for the saving of the people. It does not come from manipulating the natural world through magical incantations or gestures that are automatically effective.[213]

At this point the reader may be thinking of Genesis 3; the story of the serpent and Eve. There are some striking resonances: there is an issue with food, serpents bring death, the deeper underlying problem is human denial of God's authority. Genesis 3 will be discussed below.

To Christoph Berner, the story in Numbers 21 is a theologically elaborate variation on the first murmuring story in Numbers 11:1-3. The story told in Numbers 21 is filled with material from Numbers 11-20 so that it can create a conclusion to the murmuring sequence.[214] In this way the murmuring stories create, according to Berner, a healing theme illustrated by a cycle of complaint back to faith that begins in Exodus 15:24-25, the first murmuring story, and ends in Numbers 21 with the bronze snake. This gives an emphasis on God as Israel's healer during the entire time in the desert.[215]

Frederick Gaiser also sees Numbers 21:4-9 as a healing story. For Gaiser, "God's statement, that to continue to complain against God will bring death, is not just a threat; it is a theological fact. God is the source of life, so rebellion against God is rebellion against life itself; death will naturally ensue."[216] Gaiser sees an *inclusio* encompassing the first murmuring story in Exodus 15 and Numbers 21:4-9. In Numbers 21 God fulfills the promise given in Exodus 15:26: "I am the Lord who heals you." For Gaiser, "God will not allow death to

---

212 Milgrom, *The JPS Torah Commentary: Numbers*, 453.

213 Milgrom, *The JPS Torah Commentary: Numbers*, 452.

214 Christoph Berner, "Die Eherne Schlange: Zum literaischen Ursprang eines mosaischen Artfakts," *ZAW* 124 (2012), 346.

215 Berner, "Die Eherne Schlange," 348.

216 Frederick J. Gaiser, *Healing in the Bible* (Grand Rapids: Baker Academic, 2010), 38.

have the last word."[217] When the people are embarked on a course of death, judgment is in some sense a gift meant to turn them around.[218] Gaiser, like Levine, sees this as an instance of sympathetic magic, "that in response to a diagnosis of serpents, Yahweh prescribes a serpent."[219] For Gaiser this use of magic illustrates that God enters the world and makes use of the things experienced by its people. Moses acts as a Shaman here and "God uses the means available to the world at hand." But God also transforms the real world so that what happens is not technically magic. What occurs here is a dialogue between God and God's people with Moses as mediator. On the people's part, this dialogue involves repentance and faith. God's response is to give a symbol of healing that confirms God's forgiveness and promise.[220] Gaiser also notes the interplay in the Numbers 21 story between communal and individual action. Up to this point in the narrative of Israel's wilderness journey, isolation is a cause of suffering and suffering produces isolation while healing is communal. Here it is the behavior of the community that causes the suffering while health and healing come from an individual response. The community had mistaken death for life, so health demanded turning away from the disease of the community.[221] The people speak and are bitten, but the "one" who looks lives. In Numbers 21, for Gaiser, "Healing is neither automatic or communal; it is deliberate and individual."[222] Gaiser understands that within the story itself, this same point is made by the fact that God does not respond directly to the people's request; the serpents are not removed. The prayer that there be no death, no consequences, is an unfaithful and impossible one because it asks God to be other than God covenanted to be. But at the same time, God makes it possible for an individual to withdraw from the network of death by faith in God's promise

217 Gaiser, *Healing in the Bible,* 39.

218 Gaiser, *Healing in the Bible*, 40.

219 Gaiser, *Healing in the Bible*, 40.

220 Gaiser, *Healing in the Bible*, 41- 42.

221 Gaiser, *Healing in the Bible*, 42.

222 Gaiser, *Healing in the Bible*, 43.

to heal.[223] For Gaiser, "Healing involves grace and faith. It is neither the automatic reward for sufficient appeasement nor the necessary consequence of deterministic behavior. God heals because God is love. Humans open themselves to healing through an expectant attitude of faith in a gracious God."[224]

Andre Wenin examines the story in Numbers 21 and then explores connections between this story and the serpent in Genesis 3.[225] Wenin is among those who see the story in Numbers 21 as the last of the stories of rebellion in the desert. He notes that Israel's complaint is the same as it had been in earlier murmuring stories – that God has led them out of Egypt not to give them life, but for death.[226] The people's evidence for this conclusion in Numbers 21 is the lack of food and water, but here in reality there is no lack of provisions: the peoples' problem lies elsewhere, in their mental state. They are discouraged at having to turn back and tired of nothing to eat but manna. Wenin notes, as did Gaiser, that God does not remove the serpents nor deprive their bite of its venom, instead God gives a sign to be seen. The seeing, which represents trust in God and Moses, gives life.[227] For Wenin, everything happens as it does because God complies with the image of God that the people have. When they believe that God wants to kill them, they are killed by the snakes that God releases. When they believe that God can save them they are saved.[228] Wenin compares the story told in Numbers 21 with the other murmuring stories and detects a pattern. In the earlier murmuring stories, the thing that kills the Israelites is directly related to their offense. It is the meat that they craved that kills them

---

223 Gaiser, *Healing in the Bible*, 43.

224 Gaiser, *Healing in the Bible*, 46.

225 Andre Wenin. "Le serpent de Nb 21,4-9 et de Gn 3,1. Intertextualité et élaboration du sens" in *The Books of Leviticus and Numbers,* ed. Thomas Römer, (Leuven: Peeters, 2008), 545-554.

226 Wenin. "Le serpent de Nb 21,4-9 et de Gn 3,1. Intertextualité et élaboration du sens," 546.

227 Wenin. "Le serpent de Nb 21,4-9 et de Gn 3,1. Intertextualité et élaboration du sens," 550.

228 Wenin. "Le serpent de Nb 21,4-9 et de Gn 3,1. Intertextualité et élaboration du sens," 550.

in Numbers 11. When they refuse to enter the promised land in Numbers 14, it is God's decree that their generation will indeed die in the desert and not enter into the promised inheritance.[229] With this pattern in mind, Wenin notes the gaps in Numbers 21:4-9. Why do the people immediately repent when the serpents come? Is there an intrinsic relationship between serpents and the peoples' complaint that God desires their death? Wenin believes that there is an intertextual link between the story in Genesis 3:1-14 that establishes just this connection. In both Numbers 21:4-9 and Genesis 3:1-14 a snake is frequently referenced. Additionally, the issue in both texts is around the food that God has provided. In Genesis 3, the serpent draws attention not to what God has provided, but to what God has restricted. The serpent casts doubt on God's gift of all the trees but the one. On the lips of the serpent, God becomes a malicious being who prevents eating so as to live.[230] This pattern is repeated, for Wenin, when the people obscure the gift of manna, given so that they might live in the wilderness and on this basis suspect God of wanting them to die. When God releases the snakes against Israel their deadly logic is revealed. Just as God had taken their first ancestors at their word and removed them from proximity to the tree that gives life, so God here removes his protection from them and they are destroyed by snakes. When viewed in this way, the peoples' immediate repentance makes sense to Wenin because the serpents have opened their eyes and allowed them to see that the snake kills but God gives life. Their request to remove the snake (singular here in both the Hebrew and the Greek) is really, according to Wenin, a request for God to remove the snake within them that drives them to evil. God's response is a direct answer to this prayer, for the serpent that Moses puts on the pole is a symbol both of what brings death – their insatiable lust and their suspicion of God – and a symbol of God's will to give them life. A look directed at the bronze serpent is a look that is clear-sighted as to both the peoples' failure and God's faithfulness. God removes the inner serpent from the people by making sure that each person

229 Wenin. "Le serpent de Nb 21,4-9 et de Gn 3,1. Intertextualité et élaboration du sens," 550.

230 Wenin. "Le serpent de Nb 21,4-9 et de Gn 3,1. Intertextualité et élaboration du sens," 551-552.

knows internally the power of the serpent. Wenin believes that this reading also sheds light on the variation between the use of Yahweh and Elohim throughout this brief narrative and in the Genesis 3 account. Elohim represents an anonymous God who deprives of life, while Yahweh is the personal God who gives his name to Moses and responds to the people's cries. The people speak against Elohim, but it is Yahweh who responds. Ultimately for Wenin, in the story told in Numbers 21:4-9, God sends the serpents to save the people by showing them a symbol of their offense and its consequence, a symbol that allows them to turn back to God.[231]

James Charlesworth believes that the big problem in the story told in Numbers 21 is the open defiance of the people for God and for God's chosen intermediary, Moses. The people have forgotten the wonders performed by God through Moses. Charlsesworth understands that Numbers 21:4-9 describes the people's final complaint.[232] For him, whether or not this account describes an actual historical occurrence, the primary importance of the story is to report how God heard the cries of the Israelites and provided a means by which those bitten could, through faith, look to the copper serpent and continue to live. The story would have brought comfort to those plagued by snakes and would have celebrated Yahweh as the bringer of health and life.[233] Charlesworth discusses the symbolism of the copper serpent itself in the context of archeological finds at Timna on the Sinai peninsula. It is from this find that Charlesworth determines that the serpent that Moses made was copper. He believes that all the symbolism associated with this serpent would have been positive since it was an idol found in a cultic setting. For him the serpent most probably represented wisdom, divinity, power, healing, and rejuvenation; all of which were possible because of God's intervention in the lives of God's people.[234] Charlesworth also believes that this story is the first time in salvation history that "God

231 Wenin. "Le serpent de Nb 21,4-9 et de Gn 3,1. Intertextualité et élaboration du sens," 553.

232 James H. Charlesworth, *The Good and Evil Serpent: How a Universal Symbol became Christianized* (New Haven: Yale University Press, 2010), 324.

233 Charlesworth, *The Good and Evil Serpent*, 326.

234 Charlesworth, *The Good and Evil Serpent*, 329.

will not do everything for God's people."[235] This time God requires their participation. He concludes that the ancient Hebrews must have been aware of the association between snakes and healing in ancient Palestine, because in the story, whatever else it may be about, Moses crafts the serpent with the intent of healing the people bitten by snakes.[236] For Charlesworth there is a reverse correspondence between the story told in Numbers 21 and the one told in Genesis 3. In Genesis 3 disobedience led to death, while in Numbers 21 obedience to God's command through the mediation of Moses leads to life.[237] This helps Charlesworth reach the conclusion that Israel's journey through the wilderness was not a time or place for punishment, but for preparation.[238]

Shawn Aster presents the interesting argument that the Israelites' complaint against the "miserable" bread in Numbers 21:5 indicates that the people see God's providence as unreliable. The miserable bread relates to grain that has to be gathered from amongst refuse rather than grain that is produced through agriculture. For Aster the complaints in Exodus 16 and Numbers 11 look back to the peoples' lives in Egypt, but the complaints in Numbers 20 (the episode at Meribah) and Numbers 21:4-9 are comparing the wilderness to life in the promised land.[239] The people are fed up with the journey and have come to doubt the reliability of their food supply, the bread from heaven given by God. Upon hearing their latest complaint, God removes his protection, releasing the dangers of the journey, in this case deadly snakes. But death from snake bite renews Israel's awareness of their reliance on God for both providence and protection.[240]

The brief survey conducted above has uncovered some important features of the story of Moses and the bronze serpent told in Numbers 21. The snake plague represents an important point in

---

235 Charlesworth, *The Good and Evil Serpent*, 331.

236 Charlesworth, *The Good and Evil Serpent*, 329.

237 Charlesworth, *The Good and Evil Serpent*, 331.

238 Charlesworth, *The Good and Evil Serpent*, 329.

239 Shawn Zelig Aster, "'Bread of the Dungheap': Light on Num. 21:5 from the Tell Fekherye Inscription," *Vestus Testamentum* 61 (2011), 353.

240 Aster, "Bread of the Dungheap," 354.

the transition between the generation of the people who left slavery in Egypt but were not allowed to enter the promised land because of their lack of trust in God's promise and the next generation who did enter and inherit it. It is the conclusion of the murmuring stories and closes that theme in the Pentateuch. It is primarily a healing story, and healing comes when the people are confronted with their illness and then shown that the way to the cure is trust in God. Though Wenin's argument is complex, it is likely that the snakes in Numbers 21 are not only a deadly threat, they are also a reminder of something that happened in the garden in the beginning, a reminder of the human failure to believe that God has humanity's best interest at heart. Context makes it apparent that the snake plague is a step along the way in God's faithful fashioning of Israel as a people; a way which maintains continuity, but is also open to change; a way that involves both God's justice and God's mercy. It both recapitulates and furthers the theme that God is Israel's healer. Lastly, it introduces the idea that individual faith-full participation is an integral part of God's healing work.

Other Snake References

What follows next is a brief summary of other references to snakes in the Old Testament that may have been connected in an ancient reader's mind to the story told in Numbers 21. The hope is that this survey will provide a composite picture of serpents in scripture, possibly known by the author of John's Gospel, and thus a window onto how one might view serpents in general and the bronze serpent in particular.

2 Kings 18:4

The two texts 2 Kings 18:4 ("He removed the high places, broke down the pillars, and cut down the sacred pole. He broke in pieces the bronze serpent that Moses had made, for until those days the people of Israel had made offerings to it; it was called Nehuschtan.") and Numbers 21:4-9 are certainly related, since they both refer to Moses making a bronze snake, but the nature and direction of that relationship is the subject of scholarly debate.

The general consensus is that the description of the destruction of the Nehuschtan was written first; and the story in Numbers, whether or not its origin as an oral tradition is older, was written down later.[241] John Sturdy is one scholar who represents the view that the story of Moses and the bronze serpent in Numbers 21 was told to explain the presence of the Nehuschtan in the Temple of Hezekiah's time.[242] Baruch Levine points out that the account in 2 Kings is polemical, expressing the zealously monotheistic belief that any iconic symbol was "susceptible to degeneration."[243] Bernd Schipper notes the ambivalence connected with this object in 2 Kings, of all the things destroyed by Hezekiah, only the bronze serpent receives mention as something that Moses made.[244]

Unlike any of his predecessors, King Hezekiah receives a positive appraisal – in fact the most positive of any of the kings of Israel and Judah – greater than David, greater than Josiah.[245] Hezekiah "trusted" and "clung" to God.[246] He may even be subtly commended above Moses because, while he kept the commands given by Moses (2 Kings 18:6), he removed the bronze serpent that Moses had made but which had become an idolatrous cultic object.[247] Hezekiah undertakes sweeping cultic reforms and rebels against the King of Assyria and the Lord is with him in everything he does (2 Kings 18:7). But the tide turns against Hezekiah. When the towns of Judah are attacked by Assyria he capitulates and pays tribute, raiding the Temple and his palace in order to do so (2 Kings 18:13-16). When

241 Christoph Berner disagrees on literary grounds, since the story in 2 Kings appears to be aware of the tradition that Moses made the bronze serpent, while the Numbers story gives no indication that the object later becomes an object of worship. (Berner, "Die Eherne Schlange," 342).

242 John Sturdy, *Numbers* (New York: Cambridge, 1976), 140.

243 Levine, *Numbers 21-36*, 90.

244 Bernd U. Schipper, "Die Eherne Schlange: Zur Religiongeschicte und Theologie von Num 21, 4-9" *ZAW* 121 (2009), 370.

245 Terence E. Fretheim, *First and Second Kings* (Louisville: Westminster John Knox, 1999), 197.

246 Robert L. Cohn, *2 Kings* (Collegeville: The Liturgical Press, 2000), 125.

247 Choon-Leong Seow, "The First and Second Book of Kings" in *The New Interpreter's Bible in Twelve Volumes*, ed. Leander E. Keck, Volume III (Nashville: Abingdon Press, 1999), 260.

Sennacherib sends a representative to threaten Hezekiah and the people of Jerusalem, the people remain silent at Hezekiah's command (2 Kings 18:36) and Hezekiah goes into the Temple in sackcloth and sends for the prophet Isaiah son of Amos. Hezekiah is told that the threat of the Assyrians will be turned aside (2 Kings 19:5-7). This does indeed occur. Hezekiah's life is prolonged by God an additional fifteen years after a grave illness (2 Kings 20:1-11), but his reign ends under the long shadow cast by the Babylonian empire (2 Kings 20:16-19). Hezekiah, in the final episode of his life appears to be weakening in his reliance on God and catering to the envoys from Babylon, and God decrees that all he has will be taken there.[248]

From the perspective of a reader with both narratives available, the impression of the bronze serpent is that it is an ambivalent, dangerous object. An object created, at God's command, by God's chosen mediator, to bring about the healing of a difficult and rebellious people. But it is also an object that the descendants of that people tragically turn into an idol that turns them away from God. An idol that, despite its destruction by Hezekiah, contributed to the ultimate crisis in the history of Judah, the conquest of Jerusalem by the Babylonians and the destruction of the Temple itself. Thus Milgrom's explanation of the healing that the snake provides, as described above, rings more true than the idea of sympathetic magic. The danger of creating an image, even when it is commanded by God, is felt in both the story told in Numbers 21 and the reference in 2 Kings. The healing is not achieved by magic resident in an object, nor is it achieved by a manipulation of the natural world. It comes from God in the form of an image that confronts Israel's disobedience and provides life only in their repentant response to that confrontation.

Deuteronomy 8:15

It seems likely that there is a literary connection between Numbers 21:4-9 and Deuteronomy 8:15, though there is a mismatch in the chronology. As Baruch Levine points out, the incident recorded in Numbers 21 would have most likely fit chronologically into

248 Cohn. *2 Kings*, 125.

the narrative of Deuteronomy at 2:13-15. But linguistically the references to wilderness (ἔρημος), snakes (ὄφις), bites (δάκνω), the scarcity of water, and the necessity of gathering bread/manna, as well as the reference to God's leading, (ἐξάγω in Numbers 21 and ἄγω in Deuteronomy 8) makes a connection between these two texts probable.

Again there is debate among scholars as to the direction in which the influence flows, depending on how each one dates the stories and the texts. Christoph Berner believes that the author of Numbers 21:4-9 was inspired by both Jeremiah 8:17 and Deuteronomy 8:15 to include snakes as the divine penalty in his story.[249]

Deuteronomy 8 is an exhortation to remember the commands of God and how God led the people through the wilderness. It is sandwiched between the ruthless injunctions to root out the religious practices of the previous inhabitants of the promised land in Deuteronomy 7 and the beginnings of the preparation for the people to enter that land in Deuteronomy 9. For Ronald Clements, Deuteronomy 8 has had far reaching influence on the interpretation of the experience of Israel in the wilderness, influence that includes the interpretation of Jesus' temptation in the wilderness in the Gospel of Matthew.[250] Deuteronomy 8 presents a set of contrasts between the difficulties of the wilderness and the blessings of the promised land. The people of Israel are instructed to enjoy the blessings (Deuteronomy 8:10) but not to forget the source of those blessings, the God who brought them out of slavery in Egypt and led them "through the great and terrible wilderness... with poisonous snakes..." (Deuteronomy 8:15). The purpose of the dangers and privations of the wilderness is described throughout Deuteronomy 8 as 'to humble you, testing you to know what is in your heart, whether or not you would keep [his] commandments" (8:2); "as a parent disciplines a child so the Lord your God disciplines you" (8: 5); "to humble you and test you, and in the end to do you good (8:16)." So, the image of the snakes in the wilderness, from the

249 Berner, "Die Eherne Schlange," 349.

250 Ronald E. Clements, "The Book of Deuteronomy" in *The New Interpreter's Bible in Twelve Volumes*, ed. Leander E. Keck, Volume II (Nashville: Abingdon Press, 1998), 356.

perspective of Deuteronomy 8 is not retributive punishment, a harsh response to bad behavior; it is corrective, restorative justice, a way for the people to learn from their faults and move forward into their promised future.

Jeremiah 8:17

The connection between Numbers 21:4-9 and the reference to snakes in Jeremiah seems less certain than that found in either 2 Kings 18 or Deuteronomy 8, but the linguistic connection, particularly in the Septuagint, is fairly strong. God sent or will send (forms of ἀποστέλλω) deadly snakes (ὄφεις θανατοῦντας) which bite or will bite (δάκνω) the people.

Jeremiah 8:17 ("Therefore, behold I am sending out among you deadly snakes, that cannot be charmed, and they will bite you."(Author's translation.)) is part of a collection of oracles that may begin as early as Jeremiah Chapter 2 and extend through Chapter 10, but that is interrupted by a sermon in the Temple (Jeremiah 7:1-8:3). Within this set of oracles is a persistent movement from sin to judgment to lament in which "a sinful people evoke God's judgment and end up in lamentation, a lament that is shared by God."[251] Repeated themes among these oracles are references to the enemy from the north, a concern for turning away and repentance, false prophets of peace, and the divine action of testing and correcting.[252]

The text itself presents interesting similarities and yet a striking contrast to the story told in Numbers 21. The concern in both stories is the people turning away from God and the need for them to repent and return. The provocation is a bit different in each case; in Numbers 21 the people grow tired on the journey and doubt God's promised providence, while in Jeremiah the people are convinced that their way is right – they listen to false prophets of peace (Jeremiah 8:11) and the wisdom of the lying pen of false scribes (Jeremiah 8:8). They are, as Jeremiah says, like a horse charging into battle (Jeremiah 8:6). In both cases deadly snakes are part of God's remedy.

251 Patrick D. Miller, "The Book of Jeremiah: Introduction, Commentary, and Reflections" in *The New Interpreter's Bible in Twelve Volumes*, ed. Leander E. Keck, Volume VI (Nashville: Abingdon Press, 1995), 642.

252 Miller, "The Book of Jeremiah," 643.

Here is where the starkest difference occurs: in Numbers 21, the people immediately repent when the snakes come. They turn back to God and Moses, their leader. God provides, through Moses, for their healing. This allows them to move forward into God's promised future. But in Jeremiah 8 the people never repent or turn back to God at all. They pursue their course even though they know that it leads to their destruction. The people hear the threat coming and retreat to their fortified cities, but only to perish there (Jeremiah 8:14). They know that God has doomed them to die because of their sin, but they accept that doom rather than repent. God announces the sending of the snakes and Jeremiah laments over the people, but the people will not be turned. In this case the health of the people is not restored and ultimately the nation collapses and the people go into exile (Jeremiah 8:22).

Bernd Schipper believes that the story told in Numbers 21 grew from seeds planted by Jeremiah 8:17. There may be a polemic element in Jeremiah 8:17 against the healing practices of the nations around Judah when God indicates that these snakes cannot be charmed. Healing will not come for these people unless it comes from God. Their own false practices cannot save them. There is also perhaps an echo here of what Patrick Miller calls the sentence parable of the prophet Amos (Amos 5:19). There the theme also is retreating to a place of safety (in this case a house) only to find the danger of biting snakes there as well.[253] In Numbers 21, Moses, the mediator, replaces the snake charmer, a religious specialist. Thus for Schipper and those who follow his thinking, the story in Numbers 21 is speaking against other religious practices of the time.[254]

Christoph Berner believes that snakes as a divine penalty in both Deuteronomy 8 and Jeremiah 8:17 may have suggested snakes as the means of causing the change from complaint back to faith in the narrative from Numbers 21. He believes that the story told in Numbers 21 is a literary construct that is intended to cap off the murmuring stories and express that Yahweh is a healing God. Berner believes that the story of the serpent on the pole was written in a time

253 Miller, "The Book of Jeremiah," 648.

254 Shipper, "Die Eherne Schlange," 386.

when the serpent as a symbol of Asclepius was known and one aspect of the Numbers 21 story is to demonstrate that Yahweh is greater than Asclepius.[255]

Stefan Beyerle notes that one can see that the author of Numbers 21 would have known that Yahweh can send snakes from reading Jeremiah 8:17.[256]

So, Jeremiah 8:17 presents another instance of snakes as God's instruments sent to bring about repentance, a turning of God's people away from their own doubts or waywardness back toward trust and following God's ways. But here in Jeremiah the threat of snakes fails utterly and the sound of the Babylonian army grows ever nearer.

Genesis 3

Finally, it will be important to consider the snake in Genesis 3. While there is a massive amount of literature written on this subject, this discussion will be necessarily brief. Many scholars perceive a connection between the ambiguous serpent in Numbers 21:7 and that craftiest of animals that encountered Eve and Adam in the Garden. It is likely that any Old Testament writer or reader would also have made this connection. As Michael Fishbane notes, "it is not by virtue of objective criteria that one may identify aggadic exegesis, but rather by a close comparison of the language of a given text with other, earlier Scriptural dicta or topoi."[257] The lexical connection here would be snakes (ὄφις or נָחָשׁ). A thematic association might be snakes as bringers of death. These connections have already been explored above in the discussion of Andre Wenin's work on Numbers 21.

James Charlesworth begins his examination of the story told in Genesis 3 with the supposition, derived from symbology and ancient Canaanite, Mesopotamian, and Egyptian mythology, that serpents were positive symbols. He asks that the Genesis account be

255 Berner, "Die Eherne Schlange," 354.

256 Stefan Beyerle, "Die Eherne Schlange: Numbers 21, 4-9: synchron und diachron gelesen" ZAW 111Bd., S 34.

257 Michael Fishbane, *Biblical Interpretation in Ancient Israel* (New York: Oxford, 1985), 285.

read with this in mind.[258] For Charlesworth the serpent is a divine figure possessing supernatural power and the knowledge of life and death. The serpent is described as the wisest of all the creatures that God had made because the serpent knows what God knows. Charlesworth wants to push back against Christian interpreters who equate the serpent with Satan and evil. He reads the story against a backdrop of other ancient literature, such as the Gilgamesh epic.[259] For Charlesworth, the serpent is not a trickster nor does it lie. Charlesworth does not believe that the serpent was originally a reptile.[260] It was swift and elusive, not horrible or ugly. It probably went upright and had feet. Charlesworth seems to read the story in Genesis 3 not as a fall story, but as more of a coming of age story. He assumes that the humans and the serpent are punished, but notes that the humans are not cursed. For Charlesworth, one should not imagine that the serpent alone is responsible for the entrance of sin into creation.[261]

Karen Joines also reads Genesis 3 in light of the Babylonian Epic of Gilgamesh, but reaches a very different result than Charlesworth. She too recognizes the multivalence of the serpent in the ancient world as a strange combination of positive and negative symbols: life, wisdom, and chaos. But for Joines, the serpent in Genesis 3 sets out to deceive and destroy humankind and thus here symbolizes chaos.[262] In light of ancient near-eastern myths, Joines understands that the serpent embodies what the author of Genesis 3 sees as humanity's flaw – the desire to become a god. In her reading of the narrative, the serpent calculates that if the humans achieve godlike wisdom, the next step will be to demand immortality. If the serpent's plan had succeeded, the result would have been the destruction of a monotheistic cosmos (there would have been more than one divine being) and the destruction of mortals (humans would have become divine). God foils the serpent's plan by driving the first humans away

258 Charlesworth, *The Good and Evil Serpent*, 279.

259 Charlesworth, *The Good and Evil Serpent*, 296.

260 Charlesworth, *The Good and Evil Serpent*, 312.

261 Charlesworth, *The Good and Evil Serpent*, 320.

262 Karen Randolph Joines, "The Serpent in Gen 3" *Zeitschrift für die alttestamentliche Wissenschaft*, 87 1 (1975), 9.

from the tree of life.[263] For Joines despite the ability to have resurgent life (as seen by its shedding of its skin) and its great wisdom (knowing what God knows), the serpent is a crafty and evil agent seeking to despoil God's good creation.

Terence Fretheim, however, is reluctant to see the serpent as evil and he does not go so far as to see it as possessing supernatural powers or a divine nature. To him, it is a creature like any other in the Genesis account, created by God and named by Adam. The serpent appears to the reader of Genesis 3, according to Fretheim, initially as a neutral observer of the God-human relationship and a conversation partner positively disposed toward the woman.[264] The reader's understanding of the serpent changes as the conversation continues. The serpent's question pertains to the amount of freedom God has given the humans, but it appears to be a tactic that sets an agenda centering on God. The serpent appears to assume that the woman knows more than it does, but its question paints her into a box; it is impossible to answer with a simple yes or no, so the woman is drawn in deeper. The woman's answer seems to indicate that she, perhaps along with the man, has reflected on God's prohibition of the tree of the knowledge of good and evil and that she is anxious about death; determined to avoid it at any cost. The serpent picks up on this "point of exaggeration and vulnerability" with the promise that the humans will not die.[265] It is not clear to Fretheim whether the serpent's intent is to contradict God or if the serpent's claim is true in the unstated event that the humans eat from both trees. Either way, the element of being like gods is new; God has said nothing about this. The serpent is subtle, however, and has not spelled out all the possibilities. The serpent does not lie, the humans do not die (at least not immediately), and God admits that they have indeed become godlike, knowing good and evil (Genesis 3:22). But the serpent implicitly makes the claim that God has withheld something from the humans and implies that God has done this for selfish

263 Joines, "The Serpent in Gen 3," 10.

264 Terence E. Fretheim, "The Book of Genesis: Introduction, Commentary, and Reflections" in *The New Interpreter's Bible in Twelve Volumes*, ed. Leander E. Keck, Volume I (Nashville: Abingdon Press, 1995), 360.

265 Fretheim, "The Book of Genesis," 361.

reasons. The issue then, for Fretheim, comes down to trust. Can the woman believe that God has her best interests at heart in giving the prohibition, even if she has not been told everything? Despite the fact that the serpent has called the word of God into question, the serpent does not entice or coerce the woman. She makes her own decision, and she makes it without any further conversation with the serpent or with the man, who has been her silent companion all along. She does not weigh the prohibition or complain about it. She takes the fruit and eats it based on its desirability as food and, believing the serpent's claim, its ability to make one wise. Her male companion silently follows suit. For Fretheim then, the serpent becomes a metaphor representing "anything in God's good creation that could present options to human beings."[266] The tree of the knowledge of good and evil becomes the temptation as the serpent unveils the options it presents. It is a temptation not because obtaining its knowledge is a bad thing, but because that knowledge is gained apart from God. For Fretheim, if the fear of the Lord is the beginning of wisdom, then the knowledge that the pair have acquired by eating of the fruit is not wisdom. God can see the whole of creation; the humans as yet cannot. The fourfold result of eating the fruit: (1) that their eyes are opened, (2) that they realize they are naked, (3) that they make clothing, and (4) that they hide – all indicate that the man and the woman were not ready for their new knowledge.[267] When God comes and declares judgment upon them, it becomes clear that their actions have disrupted every conceivable relationship within the creation: humanity's relationship with other creatures, with the ground, with each other, with God, and within their own selfhood. God's relationship with the earth and with the creatures of it has been shattered. Disharmony reigns.[268] As God passes down judgement, Fretheim notes that the serpent is not interrogated. God does not ask it why it entered into conversation with the woman, but God does seem to recognize some responsibility on the serpent's part for what happened. The serpent receives a curse that sets it apart from

266 Fretheim, "The Book of Genesis," 360.

267 Fretheim, "The Book of Genesis," 362.

268 Fretheim, "The Book of Genesis," 363.

other animals. For Fretheim this is a moral order correspondence in which the punishment fits the crime. Fretheim sees crawling on its belly and eating dust in this context as humiliation and shame, rather than a change in the serpent's physique. God's curse makes the serpent into a symbol that reminds all who encounter it of the subtleties of temptation and the humiliating and conflict-producing consequences.[269]

Nicholas Ansell approaches the serpent in Genesis 3 in a similar fashion to Fretheim, but with an even stronger conviction that the serpent is not responsible for the entry of evil into God's good creation. Ansell wants to pin that responsibility squarely on humanity. Ansell is pushing back against dualistic views that locate the power of evil beyond humanity and have it stemming from the primordial fall of Satan.[270] His reading links the origin of evil to idolatry – religious allegiance given to created realities – which he sees as the primary category for understanding the nature of evil in the Old Testament. Ansell reads the story canonically, choosing the Protestant canon. He sees Genesis as an introduction to a whole biblical drama, which is carried on throughout the rest of the Bible. This allows him to draw insights from all parts of the biblical narrative including the New Testament, and to exclude extra-canonical sources such as the Wisdom of Solomon. For Ansell, as for Fretheim, the serpent is a wild animal created by God and named by Adam. Ansell chooses to call it the wisest, rather than the craftiest.[271] He understands that human wisdom can be gained from the creation, as long as it is obtained in the right way. For him, what went wrong in the garden was that Eve set the word of the serpent above the word of God. Adam and Eve failed to rule over the serpent as they had been created to do. They had been blessed by God at their creation to continue God's work of filling and subduing the earth. They were, as creatures in the image of God, "to let the earth be filled with God."[272] Now the creation, that

269 Fretheim, "The Book of Genesis," 363.

270 Nicholas John Ansell, "The Call of Wisdom, The Voice of the Serpent: A Canonical Approach to the Tree of Knowlege," Christian Scholars Review 31 1 (2001), 34.

271 Ansell, "The Call of Wisdom, The Voice of the Serpent," 37.

272 Ansell, "The Call of Wisdom, The Voice of the Serpent," 38.

should have been blessed by humanity, is cursed. Now it is impossible for a creature to occupy its place in creation without violence and suffering.[273] For Ansell, the serpent is right, the wisdom gained from eating of the tree of the knowledge of good and evil does make Adam and Eve like God. This might even have been appropriate for those made in the image of God. The deadly consequences have come from the disobedience of "treating something that is only God's to give as a possession, as ours by right." Adam and Eve fail to respect the covenantal nature of their being and thus violate a potential gift of great wisdom by grasping it autonomously.[274] The words of the serpent are indeed wisdom; until Adam and Eve trust them in a way that turns them from God, only then in Ansell's view do its words become misleading and deceptive.[275]

Andre Wenin's viewpoint was discussed earlier but it is worth summarizing here. For Wenin, the narrative in Genesis 3 displays the same "deadly logic" as the Exodus and wilderness narratives. When the humans listen to the serpent and see God as a malicious being who prevents eating so as to live, death becomes the ultimate result.[276] The serpent becomes a symbol of humanity's failure to believe that God wants to give them life.

For R.W. L. Moberly the crux of the story told in Genesis 3 is the apparent truthfulness of the snake.[277] At the narrative level everything that the snake says comes true, implying that God has somehow been false – the humans' eyes are opened and they do not die. Moberly helpfully suggests that the solution to the disconnect that the story creates lies in the interpretation of the word 'die.' If it is interpreted in a non-literal, metaphorical way, as is consistent with other uses of death and life throughout the Old Testament (one example being life as set before Israel in Deuteronomy 30:15, 19) it can refer to quality of life and distinguish between a good and

273 Ansell, "The Call of Wisdom, The Voice of the Serpent," 39.

274 Ansell, "The Call of Wisdom, The Voice of the Serpent," 42.

275 Ansell, "The Call of Wisdom, The Voice of the Serpent," 43.

276 Wenin, "Le serpent de Nb 21,4-9 et de Gn 3,1. Intertextualité et élaboration du sens," 551.

277 R. W. L. Moberly, "Did the Serpent Get it Right?" *The Journal of Theological Studies* 39 1 (1988), 9.

blessed life lived in relationship with God or an evil and cursed life lived in opposition or apart from God. Physical death does fit in to this wider metaphorical picture, just as physical death does become a reality for the human pair once they are driven away from the tree of life.[278]

A close and careful reading of the story told in Genesis 3 rules out both such a positive assessment of the serpent as Charlesworth assumes and one as negative as that provided by Joines. Also, in the context of a literature that is so strongly focused on rejecting foreign influences, it seems unlikely that the authors would have imported foreign symbolism wholesale. It is much more likely that for them the symbols would take on rather the opposite meanings than those implied by the Gilgamesh epic. The truth of the serpent as a symbol lies elsewhere. But Charlesworth, like Ansell, is correct in his rejection of the interpretation, popular now, that equates the serpent with Satan. Such an extensive importation of ideas from later extra-canonical literature and the New Testament, as read through more modern eyes, distorts the Genesis account also. In the context of the Old Testament, the serpent is a good creation of God. It is wise (φρόνιμος) in some sense, though in the Greek this word carries the nuances of prudent or perhaps wary. But the results of its interaction with the woman are indisputably negative, a disruption of all the relationships established by God in creation. The snake's motives are not explored at all in this story, but we see enough of the woman's to know that she choses to trust the word of the serpent over the word of God and she chooses to do what is good in her own eyes, rather than obey the command of God, thus displaying a fundamental lack of trust that what God has in mind for her is the highest good. Reflection on the serpent in the narrative of Genesis 3 leads one inevitably back to reflection on the nature and response of the human pair to it, a response that dooms all of God's good creation to some measure of suffering and ultimately death.

278 Moberly, "Did the Serpent Get it Right?" 16.

Conclusion

If Christian Frevel is correct in his assessment that the narrative of the snake plague in Numbers 21 is part of a very late redaction aimed at "clamping the numerous murmuring stories with a last and new one,"[279] then regardless of his source material, which is no longer recoverable, the redactor most likely inserted this story against the backdrop of all the other snake references discussed above. Even if this is not true, it is more than likely that all these references to snakes were available to the author of the Gospel of John as he composed his own story of Jesus in the light of his scripture.[280] What might John have taken away from all these snake references? Why might they have made the image of Moses' bronze serpent on the pole a fitting illustration of Christ's death, resurrection, and ascension? What might modern interpreters of Scripture take away from this discussion?

First, it seems safe to say that the picture of serpents in the Old Testament is in general negative. The possible positive connotations, life, rebirth, protection, healing, while not entirely absent, are only indirectly implied. Serpents in all the cases that have been discussed here bring with them risk, suffering, and in many cases death. This does not necessarily make them evil, in fact in the case of Jeremiah 8:17 and Numbers 21 the reader is told that the snakes are sent by God. The purpose of this sending is corrective, restorative. This is made explicit in Deuteronomy, where the purposes of the privations of the wilderness are to test and discipline God's people; to do them good by preparing them to enter the land of promise. The intent of the snakes in Numbers 21 and Jeremiah 8:17 is to turn God's wayward people back to God. During the wilderness wanderings,

---

279 Christian Frevel, "Understanding the Pentateuch by Structuring the Desert: Numbers 21 as a Compositional Joint," in *The Land of Israel in Bible, History, and Theology: Studies in Honor of Ed Noort.* ed. Jacques van Ruiten and J. Cornelis de Vos (Leiden: Brill, 2009), 130.

280 It is impossible to know exactly what scriptural resources were available to John. Kostenberger's survey shows that John quotes explicitly from Isaiah, the Psalms, Exodus, Numbers and Zechariah, probably from the Septuagint and includes allusions that range over virtually the entire Old Testament. (Köstenberger, "John," 416-421).

the snakes are sent only after more positive teaching methods have been applied – the signs and wonders of Egypt; the providing of manna, quail, and water; the giving of the law; the sign of Moses' and Aaron's staffs; even victory in battle – only when all these other means have failed do the snakes come. In Jeremiah 8:17 the threat of snakes comes after many calls to repentance and under the threat of the advancing armies of Babylon. In Jeremiah 8:17 the sending of snakes, if it ever happens, fails. The people never turn aside from their own way and Jerusalem and the Temple are destroyed. In Numbers 21 however, the remedy works, the people repent and return to Moses and God. The bronze serpent, set up by Moses at God's command to heal them is effective and the people are poised from then on to receive blessing and victoriously enter the land that they had refused to enter and possess before.

In light of this, the reference to Nehuschtan in 2 Kings becomes ironic. The thing that was made by Moses' obedience in response to the people's repentance; the thing that allowed the people to turn back to God, later became the cause of their turning away. Its destruction, in turn, becomes an instance of obedience for Hezekiah, the king of Israel perhaps portrayed as the most beloved by God, but its destruction does not ultimately halt the people's slide into idolatry, their seeking their own way, or their following their own prophets of peace.

There are numerous indications in the Gospel of John that the controlling metaphor for the Gospel is Israel's journey through the wilderness: (1) Jesus as the passover lamb, (2) Jesus taking on himself the functions of the Tabernacle (or Temple) at the wilderness festivals, (3) Jesus both providing and being the miracle bread of life from heaven, (4) water flowing from Jesus' side as from the rock. In this context, the typological relationship between Jesus and the bronze serpent indicates a number of things. First, that the cross is the turning point in humanity's journey toward becoming the people of God; those who see God in Christ are those who enter into the family of God. Second, in Christ on the cross, humanity comes face to face with its ultimate fault: its failure to trust that God has humanity's best interest at heart through the belief that God desires to withhold life rather than give it. This distrust leads humans to take matters into their own hands in order to gain life and prosperity.

Perhaps John chooses the comparison between the serpent and Jesus to remind his people of three important things. The failure of the first human pair to trust God, as related in Genesis 3. The failure of Judah to listen to God in the face of the threat of Babylon in Jeremiah 8, and by extension the threat of Rome. But also the success of Israel in learning to become the people of God in Deuteronomy 8 and Numbers 21. This story is a reminder of both God's discipline and God's willingness to do whatever it takes to be Israel's healer.

A closer reading of snakes in the Old Testament does nothing to contradict the possible resonances identified in Chapter 2. Instead it adds depth to John's portrait of Jesus and his rhetorical strategy of helping people respond to Christ with authentic faith through the witness of his Gospel. The next chapter will entail a survey of references to the story of Moses and the bronze serpent in literature of around the turn of the era to see if the same themes may be detected there.

Chapter 4

The Serpent that Moses Lifted up in the Biblical Tradition

Introduction

This chapter is an exploration of how the story of Moses and the bronze serpent, told in Numbers 21, is interpreted by the nearest contemporaries of the author of the Gospel of John. It is hoped that by examining texts from the periods just prior to and immediately following the Gospel's composition, some insight can be gained into what interpretations of the story are possible. Five authors will be considered: Philo of Alexandria, Pseudo-Solomon, Paul, Barnabas, and Justin Martyr.[281] The contexts of *Allegory on Genesis*, *The Wisdom of Solomon*, *The First Letter to the Corinthians*, *The Epistle of Barnabas*, and Justin Martyr's *First Apology* and *Dialogue with Trypho* will be explored based on a close reading of each text. Then each passage that interprets the Numbers story will be read in light of its context within each work and its author's interpretation. A brief look at the Targums, the Cult of Asclepius, and some early patristic exegesis will round out the discussion.

281 The names Pseudo-Solomon and Barnabas are used for convenience, since the authors of these works are unknown.

It needs to be said that in describing this time period it becomes very difficult to find appropriate language. Judaism and Christianity did not exist then as they do now. What we understand as Judaism in all its diversity has developed over the centuries in division and dialogue with what we now know as Christianity, which is also quite different from the infant church and very diverse in its historic and current expressions across the globe. The boundaries between the two were quite fluid in the First Century and today scholars are still searching for "the parting of the ways." Philo and the author of the Wisdom of Solomon will be described as Jewish for lack of a better term; Barnabas and Justin will be described primarily as followers of Christ and occasionally as Christian, but they must be understood to be authors whose relationship to the religion of the people in the first and second centuries whose ancestry, religion, and culture originated in Judea, i.e., "the Jews," was quite complex. Paul is more ambiguous than any of the above; the degree to which he retained his Jewish beliefs and practices in light of his conversion to Christ is still under debate. The 'religion' of the author of the Gospel of John may be as ambiguous as Paul's, for it seems likely that he would have called himself a member of the same faith as Philo, Pseudo-Solomon, Paul and Jesus himself, and yet the conflict depicted in his Gospel indicates that already at the time of his writing there was tension – a tension that is well reflected in the writings of Paul – between those Jews who in some way saw Jesus as the promised one from God and those who did not.

The discussion in this chapter will show that a comparison of the Gospel of John with the five texts listed above raises more questions than it answers, but that it is a useful exercise nonetheless because it adds to the current understanding of the ways that the gospel puts the story of Moses and the bronze serpent to theological use.

Philo of Alexandria

Both Philo's own writings and the writings about Philo are quite extensive and can only be touched on briefly here, but current scholarship is, again, rediscovering how important Philo's thought was both within the Greco-Roman world of the First Century and also within early Christianity.[282]

Philo of Alexandria (15 BCE – 50 CE) was a prominent, wealthy, well-educated, and cosmopolitan Jewish man who had substantial knowledge of Greco-Roman culture and philosophy and a deep respect for Jewish scriptures. Many of his writings, about 40 works, have been preserved, mostly in Christian circles. Almost all of these are exegetical and concerned with the Pentateuch in some way.[283] It is thought that Philo may have had a school in Alexandria that taught his philosophical exegetical method, since many of his writings are the types of writings that would have been produced in an educational setting.[284] While Philo is known for his allegorical interpretations of the Torah, he was also very interested in its literal meaning.

Philo was a strictly observant Jew throughout his life. His explorations of the deeper meaning of scripture through allegory did not lead to a dismissal of what he felt were the explicit requirements of the Law. Not only was Philo interested in observance of the law, his commentaries were also deeply concerned with ethical issues. In addition to commentaries, Philo wrote on other philosophical topics that contributed to contemporary dialogue.[285]

Philo's allegorical interpretations of the story told in Numbers 21 have been dealt with in some detail in Chapter 1 of this study. As was noted there, Philo interprets a Jewish text using both Hellenistic and Jewish techniques. He makes sweeping connections between his text of interest and other scriptural texts. In this instance he uses the

---

282 Gregory E. Sterling, "The Place of Philo of Alexandria in the Study of Christian Origins," in *Philo und das Neue Testament: Wechselseitige Wahrnehmungen*. ed. Roland Deines and Karl-Wilhelm Niebuhr (Tübingen: Mohr Siebeck, 2004), 40.

283 William Yarchin, *History of Biblical Interpretation: A Reader* (Peabody: Hendrickson, 2004), 18.

284 Sterling, "The Place of Philo of Alexandria in the Study of Christian Origins," 29.

285 George W. E. Nickelsburg, "Philo among Greeks, Jews and Christians," in *Philo und das Neue Testament: Wechselseitige Wahrnehmungen*. ed. Roland Deines and Karl-Wilhelm Niebuhr (Tübingen: Mohr Siebeck, 2004), 55-56.

story told in Numbers 21 to aid in his exegesis of the story told in Genesis 3.

Philo sees the serpent in Genesis 3 as part of God's good creation, but one that has led to negative consequences for humanity. It is his understanding that in the story told in Numbers 21 God uses a serpent, a symbol of humanity's original problem, to provide humanity with a solution to that problem. Those who see both the serpent of temperance and God are able to overcome the overindulgence in pleasure that leads to death.

Wisdom of Solomon

The *Wisdom of Solomon* was most probably written somewhere between the late third century BCE and the middle of the first century CE. The book is full of Hellenistic philosophical thought and tinged with animosity against Egypt, which makes Alexandria, the known seat of a vibrant Jewish Community and a seat of Hellenistic learning and culture under the Ptolemies, its most likely place of origin.[286] The time frame for the creation of the work can be narrowed by considering the circumstances that might have prompted its writing. The book appears to be written to comfort and encourage a community experiencing an eroding social status. Under the Ptolemies, the Jewish community in Alexandria had enjoyed special privileges as compared to their native Egyptian neighbors, but with the annexation of Egypt by Rome, this changed. The Jewish people went from being identified with the Hellenists to being identified with other non-Roman citizens. This resulted in a loss of self-government and increased taxation. The trouble reached its peak during the reign of Caligula, which inaugurated open persecution of the Jews, thus 38 – 41 CE is a likely time frame for the writing of this work.[287] The learned nature of the Jewish community in Alexandria is reflected in the Wisdom elements of this work. The atmosphere of persecution and doubt helps to clarify the presence of its apocalyptic elements. The attribution to Solomon post-dates the actual writing –

286 Andrew T. Glickman, *The Wisdom of Solomon 10: a Jewish Hellenistic Reinterpretation of Early Israelite History through Sapiential Lenses* (Boston: de Gruyter, 2011), 12-13.

287 Glickman, *The Wisdom of Solomon 10*, 16-17.

there is no direct claim to his authorship – but there is enough detail linking the narrator to the biblical king to explain the book's title.

Scholars generally divide the book into two sections. The first section is addressed to the rulers of the earth. It contrasts the thoughts and destiny of the ungodly to those of the righteous and describes the nature of Lady Wisdom. The second section begins in Chapter 10 and comprises the remainder of the book. This section recapitulates the story of Israel in the Wilderness.

The passage of interest to the current discussion is the third of seven diptychs[288] that contrast the situation of the Israelites to that of the Egyptians at the time of the Exodus. These diptychs support the theme of this entire section, which is that while God corrects all people through punishment, God has a special regard for Israel, limits her punishment, and follows judgment with mercy. Wisdom 16:5-14 deals with the story of the bronze serpent as follows:

> For when the terrible anger of wild animals came upon them so that they were being destroyed by the bites of crooked serpents, your wrath did not remain up to the end; but as a warning, they were troubled for a little, having a symbol (σύμβολον) of salvation for a reminder of the commandment of your law. For the one turning to it was not saved because of the thing seen, but because of you the Savior of all. And by this also you convinced our enemies that you are the one who delivers from all evil; for they, on the one hand were killed by the bites of locusts and flies, and no healing was found for their soul, because they were worthy to be punished by such things. On the other hand your children were not even conquered by the venomous teeth of dragons, for your mercy came upon them and healed them. For

288 A diptych was originally a hinged tablet with writing on both sides that could be closed to protect the writing. By extension it has come to mean a work made up of two matching parts (Merriam-Webster Online Dictionary, http://www.merriam-webster.com/dictionary/diptych (Accessed on August 19, 2016)). In this context it refers to a narrative that is told twice from differing perspectives. Here the sufferings of the Egyptians as God dealt with them through Moses are contrasted with God's treatment of the Israelites during the Exodus and wilderness wandering.

> as a reminder of your words they were being stung and quickly delivered, so that they might not, falling into deep forgetfulness, become un-noticing of your act of kindness. For neither herb nor plaster healed them, rather your word, Lord, that heals all. For you have authority over life and death and you lead down to the gates of Hades and raise up. Indeed a man kills in his wickedness but cannot return the spirit that has gone out nor set free the taken soul (Author's translation).[289]

The intent of this passage is both to reassure the persecuted Jewish community of God's power and mercy towards them as God's people and to exhort them to remember God's commands. The passage uses the story of Moses in Numbers 21 as part of a broader reinterpretation of Deuteronomy 8, an important passage in Israel's self understanding, harking back to the description of the wilderness in 8:15, and reminding the people of the promise of God to give them a good land and the prohibition of God against forgetting the commandments by following other gods. It would appear that under persecution in Pseudo-Solomon's context, some Jews were leaning toward practicing Roman religion on some level. Of interest here, the snake on the pole is described as a symbol (σύμβολον) and is never mentioned directly – perhaps understandable when the context within *The Wisdom of Solomon* is a passage forbidding worship of false gods. The author is not particularly interested in the flow or details of the Numbers 21 narrative so there is no way to determine his source. The order of his diptychs[290] also indicates that he is not

---

289 The Greek text is from *Septuaginta*, Alfred Rahlfs, ed. Editio altera by Robert Hanhart, Deutsche Bibelgesellschaft, Stuttgart, 2006, Bernard A. Taylor and Dale M. Wheeler, Kraft/Taylor/Wheeler Septuagint Morphology Database v. 4.7, 2012, Accordance 9 Bible Software Version 9.6.6, Oak Tree Software, 2012.

290 The first diptych compares the thirst of the Egyptians, when their water was turned to blood, with the quenching of the Israelites thirst with water from the rock. The second compares the hunger of the Egyptians when their appetites were destroyed, presumably by frogs, to the feasting of the Israelites on quail. The third is Wisdom 16:5-14 in which the Egyptians succumb to the bites of locusts and flies while the Israelites survive the bites of poisonous serpents. This

particularly interested in the chronology of the Exodus narrative per se.

Though it is difficult to prove any exact connection between Pseudo-Solomon and Philo, and despite the different purposes evidenced in their writing, one can find similarities. Both are intensely interested in Jewish writings and practices, but both are perfectly willing to express this interest in the vocabulary of their Greco-Roman world. Both recognize both God's grace and mercy while at the same time reenforcing the need for responsible behavior.

Paul

Paul, writing around 55-57 CE[291] to the church he founded in Corinth, alludes to the story told in Numbers 21 in 1 Corinthians 10:9. This is part of a larger section (1 Corinthians 8:1-11:1) that addresses eating meat offered to idols and the relationship between strong and weak believers. Several scholars note that in 1 Corinthians 10:1-22 Paul is expressly forbidding eating pagan food at pagan temples in the presence of idols.[292] Such meals in pagan temples were social occasions for the citizens of Corinth, events that they would have attended and enjoyed regularly before their commitment to Christ.[293]

According to Gordon Fee, Paul has to address three concerns here: 1) that Paul has the apostolic authority to command obedience from the Corinthians, 2) that being present at the worship of idols is in reality worshipping demons, and 3) that the basis for any

---

is followed by a comparison of the destruction of the crops of the Egyptians by hail while the Israelites feast on bread from heaven. The fifth contrasts the darkness that covered Egypt with the light that shone on Israel in the pillar of fire and the light of the Law. The sixth is the contrast between the Egyptians killing of the children of Israel and the deaths of the first-born sons of Egypt. The seventh contrasts the righteous action of one man who prevents a plague from destroying Israel with the destruction of the Egyptians at the Red Sea.

291 Magnus Zetterholm, *Approaches to Paul: A Student's Guide to Recent Scholarship* (Minneapolis: Fortress Press, 2009), 29.

292 Gordon D. Fee, *The First Epistle to the Corinthians* (Grand Rapids: Eerdmans, 1987), 357.

293 Anthony C. Thiselton, *The First Epistle to the Corinthians: A Commentary on the Greek Text* (Grand Rapids: Eerdmans, 2000), 7.

Christian action is not knowledge, but love. Paul uses a snapshot of Israel's history in an attempt to convince the Corinthians that just as the chosenness of Israel did not protect them from God's wrath when they were disobedient, neither will the chosenness of the Corinthians, as shown by the giving of the Spirit and performance of the sacraments, protect them from the consequences of their disobedience.[294] If the Israelites, despite being given the advantages of being under God's guiding and protecting cloud, being baptized into Moses through the sea, and being given spiritual food and drink, could still displease God to the point of their destruction and thus the failure to gain the prize of the promised land; so also might the Corinthians fail to attain the prize of being in Christ. Paul is working to shake the sense of security that the Corinthians have in their spiritual superiority, a sense of superiority that allows them to compromise themselves by participating in rituals in pagan temples in the belief that idols are not real gods.[295] For Fee, in 1 Corinthians 10:7-10 Paul gives four examples of how "privileged Israel lusted after evil things" which led to the destruction of most of them.[296] Paul chooses examples that fit the situation in Corinth. That Israel ate and then rose up to dance before the golden calf fashioned by Aaron addresses the issue of idolatry, i.e., celebrating in a pagan temple in front of an idol. The example of sexual immorality appears to refer to the incident recounted in Numbers 25:1-9 where the men of Israel had relations with the women of Moab and yoked themselves to the Baal of Peor and Phinehas' action of impaling an Israelite man and a Moabite woman in the act stopped the punishing plague. The issue in Corinth may perhaps have been temple prostitution. Paul's third example is the Numbers 21:4-9 story, which Paul refers to as putting Christ to the test. Fee sees a parallel between the Israelites complaints against eating manna instead of food of their preference and the Corinthians insisting on their right to eat in pagan temples.[297] While "test" is not a word used in the Numbers 21 passage, Fee believes

294 Fee, *The First Epistle to the Corinthians*, 363.

295 Fee, *The First Epistle to the Corinthians*, 442-443.

296 Fee, *The First Epistle to the Corinthians*, 453.

297 Fee, *The First Epistle to the Corinthians*, 456.

that Paul arrives at this interpretation by connecting the Numbers story with Psalm 78, also a retelling of Israel's wilderness wanderings (though one that does not refer directly to the snake incident) and Deuteronomy 6:16, "Do not put the Lord your God to the test, as you tested [God] at Massah." It is interesting to note that, reading with his christological lens, Paul has no difficulty declaring that the one tested in the wilderness was Christ.[298] The final example of the people grumbling refers in a fairly general way to the grumbling stories of Numbers 14 or 16, though Paul's use of "destroyed by the destroyer" (1 Corinthians 10:10) as punishment is a bit puzzling. Paul opens and closes this discussion by stating that these incidents occurred in Israel's history as examples and were written down as warnings for the Corinthians so that they might avoid these same errors. For Fee this illustrates that Paul understands that the events recorded in the scriptural narrative are not simply history or isolated scriptural texts, but a recounting of the eternal purposes of the living God, who has woven prefigurement into the earlier story to benefit those at the end. This is true for Paul because he sees the Christ event as marking the turning of the age.[299]

Anthony Thiselton believes that Paul is addressing "the incompatibility between commitment to Christ pledged in the Lord's supper and the possible participation in more explicitly cultic sacrificial meals of ceremonies in pagan temples, especially if put under pressure by colleagues, patrons, or civic duties." Paul continually rejects "knowing my rights" in favor of "foregoing my rights," which is the way of Christ on the cross and the way that Paul himself models."[300] For Thiselton, 1 Corinthians 10:1-13 might be titled "All Shared, Many fell."[301] Thiselton understands that Paul is insisting on exclusive "loyalty to Christ as a definitive revelation of God."[302] Paul's argument suggests that in first-century Corinth, Christ followers who had come to believe that idols were

298 Fee, *The First Epistle to the Corinthians*, 457.

299 Fee, *The First Epistle to the Corinthians*, 459.

300 Anthony C. Thiselton, *The First Epistle to the Corinthians: A Commentary on the Greek Text* (Grand Rapids: Eerdmans, 2000), 607.

301 Thiselton, *The First Epistle to the Corinthians*, 724.

302 Thiselton, *The First Epistle to the Corinthians*, 18.

nothing, may have also come to feel that either participating in the cultic worship that was so prevalent and popular in their society was not harmful, or that since there is one God, any form of worship honored God. Paul's "no" to both these ideas is emphatic. Paul's strategy to combat the church's buy-in to the cultural values of Corinth is to accomplish a "reversal of value systems" by "placing the community as a whole under the criterion and identity of the cross of Christ."[303] He uses scripture as his central means of doing so.[304] According to Thiselton, 1 Corinthians 10:1-13 demonstrates that for Paul at least three things are true of scripture: 1) it is definitive for a mixed congregation of Jews and Gentiles, 2) it can be read in a Christ-centered way, and 3) it shows that salvation is anchored in a history that encompasses both Israel and the Christ event.[305] Paul's emphasis is on God's generous grace to all (both the Israelites and the Corinthians), but Paul points out that not everyone appropriates God's gifts or exercises the self-discipline necessary to achieve the goal of being in Christ.[306] For Thiselton, "craving represents a general stance from which the specific four failures of vv. 7-13 flow."[307] Paul uses examples from the Old Testament for spiritual and ethical formation to accomplish transformation.[308] Thiselton sees Paul's use of typology here as flowing from Paul's belief that both the Israelites and the Corinthians are part of a story that stretches from beginning to end with Christ's life, death, resurrection, and ascension at the center. Events in Israel's history are linked to events in Paul's and the Corinthian's present "because they share in the common purpose of God."[309] Thiselton believes that Paul uses his four typologies to warn that "absolute self-willing" alienates one from God. It is misdirected desire that lies behind all four Old Testament examples: self-indulgence and

303 Thiselton, *The First Epistle to the Corinthians*, 33.

304 Thiselton, *The First Epistle to the Corinthians*, 718-719.

305 Thiselton, *The First Epistle to the Corinthians*, 719-720.

306 Thiselton, *The First Epistle to the Corinthians*, 725.

307 Thiselton, *The First Epistle to the Corinthians*, 731.

308 Thiselton, *The First Epistle to the Corinthians*, 731.

309 Thiselton, *The First Epistle to the Corinthians*, 732.

sensuality lead to idolatry and immorality while unbelief, leading to doubt, results in grumbling and putting the Lord to the test.[310] The Corinthians, in assuming that they are spiritually powerful (and thus can participate without harm in pagan feasts) are putting God's love and promise to the test and "presume to force God's hand to preserve them."[311] To counteract this thinking Paul calls "attention to the eschatological situation of continuity and contrast between Israel and Christian believers."[312]

J. Paul Sampley agrees with Fee and Thiselton that it is Paul's strong conviction that individual rights are secondary to the well-being of others in the community, though Sampley believes that Paul never denigrates the importance of individuality.[313] For Sampley, the example and cautionary tale of the Exodus (1 Corinthians 10:1-13), follows on Paul's use of himself (1 Corinthians 9) as an example of how the Corinthians should be behaving.[314] Sustaining the note of judgment with which Paul's own example ends, "so that after proclaiming to others I myself should not be disqualified" (1 Corinthians 9:27b), Paul tells "a cautionary version of Israel's exodus from Egypt."[315] Sampley understands that Paul tells the Exodus story twice: once in a general way 1 Corinthians 10:1-4, ending with a warning in 10:5, and then again in 10:6-13 with more detail to show how Israel provides an example for the Corinthians.[316] This example is a negative one. Paul asks his readers/hearers to focus on the doers of evil with an eye to not being like them. The retelling focuses, according to Sampley, on God's judgment: thousands fell in one day, snakes killed some, others were destroyed by the destroyer.[317] For Sampley, Paul is saying "Fair warning." Apparently there were

---

310 Thiselton, *The First Epistle to the Corinthians*, 733.

311 Thiselton, *The First Epistle to the Corinthians*, 741.

312 Thiselton, *The First Epistle to the Corinthians*, 745.

313 J. Paul Sampley, "The First Letter to the Corinthians" in *The New Interpreter's Bible in Twelve Volumes*, ed. Leander E. Keck, Volume X (Nashville: Abingdon Press, 2002), 787.

314 Sampley, "The First Letter to the Corinthians," 912.

315 Sampley, "The First Letter to the Corinthians," 913.

316 Sampley, "The First Letter to the Corinthians," 913.

317 Sampley, "The First Letter to the Corinthians," 913.

persons in Corinth who Paul considered in danger of judgment and Paul makes the point strongly that God's people – though chosen, baptized, and fed – are still accountable for their behavior. Their special status does not shield them from God's judgment and their failings are not God's fault.[318] Paul's retelling of the story of Israel warns that being included in God's story does not remove the responsibility to act in ways that show love to others and are pleasing to God. Paul is nuancing the Corinthians' understanding of their freedom in Christ. His personal example of the athlete who might be disqualified and his example of those of Israel who did not achieve the land of promise are intended to awaken the Corinthians to the peril of their situation and actions.[319]

As Fee, Thiselton, and Sampley demonstrate, Paul thinks through four important pieces of the Exodus story in ways that are both old and new. New because his focus is not on the biblical text, but on the Christ given to him through revelation. Paul sets scripture in a new horizon of meaning that transforms both the biblical text and the heritage of the Hellenistic synagogue.[320] But Paul also reflects older Jewish exegetical methods: allegory, typology, midrash, pesher, and the middot of Hillel. His "manner of biblical interpretation is at home in contemporary Jewish exegesis and documents the apostle's background of Hellenistic Diaspora Judaism in the area of Asia Minor and Syria."[321] In his allusion to Numbers 21, while the overall focus of his argument is as always the cross and the Christ revealed to him at Damascus, his specific read of this story is one that Philo or Pseudo-Solomon could have produced. He agrees with them that God's judgment, harsh as it seems in the wilderness context, is intended to teach God's people and turn them back to God's purposes.

But even though Paul does not see in the uplifted serpent a type of Christ, there are at least two aspects of Paul's thought that are

---

318 Sampley, "The First Letter to the Corinthians," 914.

319 Sampley, "The First Letter to the Corinthians," 915.

320 Udo Schnelle, *Apostle Paul: His Life and Theology*, trans M. Eugene Boring (Grand Rapids: Baker Academic, 2005), 109.

321 Schnelle, *Apostle Paul: His Life and Theology*, 110.

interesting in the context of the current study. First, Paul defends his apostleship based on his claim to have seen the risen Lord (1 Corinthians 9:1, 1 Corinthians 15:8, Galatians 1:12-16). For Paul "seeing" (ὁράω) takes on a christological/soteriological meaning.[322] Paul himself is the type of Christ that he sets before his churches. This is why Paul uses himself as a positive example in 1 Corinthians 9, to be followed by the negative examples of 1 Corinthians 10:1-13. This is also the basis for Paul's arguments in 2 Corinthians 11, where he speaks of humbling himself, deprecates his ability as a speaker, reminds them of his need and weakness, and gives a litany of his sufferings. (And, additionally, uses the serpent that tempted Eve as a figure for those who oppose him (2 Corinthians 11:3)). For Paul, "seeing" Christ, by grace, leads to faith and incorporation in the body of Christ. Paul wants his churches in Galatia and Corinth to return to faith in Christ in part by seeing Christ in him. Second, Paul has the central theological problem of understanding a crucified criminal as the Messiah.[323] As Paul rereads his scripture in light of his encounter with Christ, he comes to see that the cross overturns the curse that has come upon humanity because of human failure to keep the law. As he says in Galatians 3:13, reworking Deuteronomy 21:23, "Christ redeemed us from the curse of the law by becoming a curse for us—for it is written, 'Cursed is everyone who hangs on a tree.'" Paul alludes again to Christ's transformative assumption of humanity's failing in 2 Corinthians 5:21 where he says of God's reconciling work through Christ, "For our sake he made him to be sin who knew no sin, so that in him we might become the righteousness of God."

Thus three things can be noted from Paul, the earliest extant writer of the followers of Christ. First, the story told in Numbers 21:4-9 continued to be used as an example of God's teaching and molding of Israel into God's people through suffering. Second, seeing God in Christ was the pivotal experience that led to faith and ultimately inclusion in the Jesus movement. Third, the transformative process of finding God in a crucified Messiah was accomplished, at

322 Schnelle, *Apostle Paul: His Life and Theology*, 89.

323 Thiselton, *The First Epistle to the Corinthians*, 21.

least in part, by seeing Christ as embodying evil in some way. For Paul, Jesus took on humanity's curse and became sin on the cross to save humanity and this was, paradoxically, a demonstration of God's righteousness.

Epistle of Barnabas

The Epistle of Barnabas is a document ascribed to Barnabas, the one time companion of Paul. This authorship is a subject of debate, but the ascription is likely secondary. The pseudonym Barnabas, who was known to be a Levite (Acts 4:36), was likely chosen, both because a large portion of the material in the so-called Epistle is cultic and legal and because of the traditional association between Barnabas and Alexandria in Egypt.[324] Alexandria is thought to be the place of writing for the epistle because the earliest witness to the book is Clement of Alexandria and other witnesses are associated with Alexandria.[325] There are also useful parallels between The *Epistle of Barnabas* and Jewish-Alexandrian authors, particularly Philo, including the reference to the serpent on the pole.[326] The author of the epistle will be referred to as Barnabas in this discussion for the sake of convenience.

There is an apparent reference to the destruction of the Jerusalem Temple in 70 CE at verse 16.4, perhaps the first explicit mention of this event in writing,[327] but no mention of the Bar Kochba revolt (130 CE), which in such an anti-Jewish document as this epistle, would certainly have warranted attention; as its negative effects on Judaism were at least as dramatic as the loss of the Second Temple. The date range can be narrowed further, using the content of the letter, most probably to the reign of the Emperor Nerva. Nerva's rise to power may fit with Barnabas' variant quotes from Daniel.[328] Also Barnabas appears to be writing in response to a hope for the physical rebuilding of the Temple in Jerusalem in the very near future, a situation that

324 James Carleton Paget, *The Epistle of Barnabas: Outlook and Background* (Tubingen: Mohr Siebeck, 1994), 7.

325 Paget, *The Epistle of Barnabas*, 36.

326 Paget, *The Epistle of Barnabas*, 37.

327 Paget, *The Epistle of Barnabas*, 9.

328 Paget, *The Epistle of Barnabas*, 16.

fits with the circumstances of Domitian's fall from power in 96 CE and Nerva's more tolerant attitude toward the Jews.[329]

This context appears to be a fitting one for *The Epistle of Barnabas*. Barnabas was writing to Christians in Alexandria. There was a large educated Jewish community there. This Jewish community had been under a good deal of pressure; their legal status had suffered under Roman rule. The events in Palestine, leading to the destruction of the Temple had made them look recalcitrant. But things were looking up, a more favorable outlook by the new Emperor had resulted in expectation that the Temple would again be rebuilt and the Jewish community was again talking of God's faithfulness to Israel. In this context, Barnabas sought to reinforce his own teaching that Christianity had replaced Judaism and that the church should not be tempted to see Judaism and Jewish practice as an increasingly attractive alternative.[330]

The Epistle of Barnabas is nominally a letter in form. It begins with a greeting, but does not name its addressees or refer directly to their personal circumstances. A lot of the focus is on 'Barnabas' himself. He appears to use the device of self-deprecation to build up the character of his readers (Barn 1:5). At 1:6 Barnabas launches into his teaching. The setting for this teaching and the tone of it indicate that there is personal investment behind it; it is perhaps a homily. It is not a scholarly exercise.[331]

The epistle can be divided roughly into three main parts. There is a framework, Chapters 1 and 18 – 21, which emphasizes the exegesis of scripture and ethics. This framework stands in tension with the main body of the document, Chapters 2-16, which sets forth Barnabas' Christian interpretation of sacrifice, fasting, the covenant, circumcision, food laws, the Sabbath, and the Temple.[332] The entire epistle is concerned with knowledge. The main body (Ch. 2-16) is exegetical in orientation, while 18-20 is more practical. Barnabas uses

329 Paget, *The Epistle of Barnabas*, 27.

330 Paget, *The Epistle of Barnabas,* 64. S. Lowry, "The Confutation of Judaism in the Epistle of Barnabas," in *Studies in Early Christianity: A Collection of Scholarly Essays*, ed. Everett Ferguson (New York: Garland, 1993), 334.

331 Paget, *The Epistle of Barnabas*, 44.

332 Paget, *The Epistle of Barnabas*, 51.

a mixture of exegetical methods: allegorical, typological, and literal. He wants to express an entirely Christocentric sense of scripture and uses whichever method serves his purpose. His exegesis is entirely of Old Testament texts; no New Testament writings are mentioned.[333] Barnabas ends his specific teaching at Chapter 16, but follows it up with 'Two Ways' material, a tradition also found in the *Didache*, and some practical applications of the knowledge he has previously imparted.[334]

The epistle, paradoxically, is strongly Jewish in character, but also has a distinctly anti-Jewish perspective. Barnabas is conservative, he does not want to dismiss Israel's scripture, instead he wants to interpret it 'properly.' Barnabas believes that the law should never have been interpreted literally. He thinks that the Jews lost the only true covenant at Sinai when they worshipped the golden calf. Christians have gained this covenant through Christ's saving work and the commands of the covenant, rightly understood – that is spiritually – are what should direct Christian behavior.[335]

Source critics have investigated *The Epistle of Barnabas* thoroughly, noting its choppy flow and rough Greek. It seems likely that Barnabas, like Justin Martyr and perhaps other early Christian authors, was relying, at least in part, on a testimony document – an early Christian production, now lost, that summarized Christological interpretations of Septuagint texts.[336]

The passage of interest to this work comes in Chapter 12. It is the part of Barnabas' main discussion that seeks to demonstrate that Christian baptism and the cross are both foretold in Scripture. Baptism is dealt with in Chapter 11, while Chapter 12 focuses on the cross. The first citation (12:1) is from an unknown source, perhaps 4 Ezra, a Jewish eschatological source, or an already Christianized passage.[337] Next comes the story, told in Exodus 17, of Moses holding

333 Paget, *The Epistle of Barnabas*, 49.

334 Paget, *The Epistle of Barnabas*, 51.

335 Paget, *The Epistle of Barnabas*, 52.

336 Oskar Skarsaune, *The Proof From Prophecy: A Study in Justin Martyr's Proof-Text Tradition: Text-Type, Provenance, Theological Profile* (Leiden: Brill, 1987), 425. Paget, *The Epistle of Barnabas*, 103-104.

337 Paget, *The Epistle of Barnabas*, 158.

up his hands so that the Israelites could prevail over the Amalekites, though the account is very different in Barnabas, perhaps again indicating a lost Christian source. Moses appears here to be a type of Christ. It is Moses' hands that are stretched out so that the people's hope might be placed in him in order to be saved – in Barnabas from the perpetual war that is the result of being handed over to death because of their sins. The account of Moses and the bronze serpent comes in 12:5-7. It is followed by a discussion of the name of Jesus.

Barnabas retells the account of Moses and the bronze serpent thus:

> Again Moses makes a type (τύπον) of Jesus, because it is necessary that he suffer, and he will make alive the one they think has been destroyed, when Israel was falling, with a sign (σημείῳ). The Lord made every serpent bite them, and they were dying because of the disobedience that was born through the serpent with Eve, so that he might convict them, for because of their disobedience they will be handed over into the affliction of death. Furthermore, though truly Moses himself commanded, "there will not be with you either a molten cast or carved thing as a God for you," he made one so that it might show a type of Jesus. Therefore, Moses made a bronze snake and put it in a place of honor and, with a proclamation, called the people. Thus coming to him, they begged Moses that he might offer up a prayer for them concerning their healing. And Moses said to them, "Whenever," he said, "one of you is bitten, come to the snake, the one placed on the tree, and hope, believing that he (or it) being dead is able to make alive, and immediately he will be saved. And so they did. Again you have in these things the glory of Jesus, because in him and for him are all things (Author's translation)."[338]

---

338 *The Epistle of Barnabas*, Apostolic Fathers, 3rd ed: Greek Texts and English Translations edited and translated by Michael W. Holmes, Grand Rapids: Baker Books, 1992, 1999, 2007, Accordance 9 Bible Software Version 9.6.6, Oak Tree Software, 2012.

There are many things to note about this passage. The serpent on the tree that Moses made is twice declared to be a type of Jesus. The biting serpents are, as in Philo, connected directly with the serpent that brought about the disobedience of Eve in Genesis 3, disobedience that resulted in death. The word sign (σημείῳ) is used to refer to an event that sounds like the resurrection. The passage is not a strict retelling of the story from Numbers 21, in fact, while Barnabas clearly references that event, there is almost no similarity in how the story is told. The people come to Moses after the serpent has been set up in *Barnabas*, where as in Numbers 21 the people come to Moses first, after the biting of the serpents makes them recognize their sin. The setting of the serpent in a place of honor is also an interesting interpretation of putting the snake on what appears in the Numbers account to be a staff that would ordinarily hold a flag. Here in *Barnabas* the Numbers story is directly preceded by the story of the battle with Amalek, a paring that will be repeated in many later interpretations, and it is followed by a reference to Joshua son of Nun spying out the Promised Land. Barnabas is either not concerned with or unaware of the correct sequence of events in the Biblical narrative.

Even though Barnabas is primarily concerned with demonstrating that the story of Moses and the bronze serpent shows the saving power of the cross for Christians, he retains a Jewish anti-idolatry perspective, choosing to point out the irony of an image being made for the express purpose of doing the work of healing even though it is believing hope in the one who died that brings salvation. Barnabas concludes his discussion with an interesting reference to the glory (δόξαν) of Jesus.

Justin Martyr

Justin was born in Roman Syria to pagan parents in around 110 CE. He describes a process of philosophical education that gradually led to his conversion to Christianity. Eventually he founded a school in Rome. He was martyred there around 165 CE. Justin's writings are apologetic writings – the *First* and *Second Apology* are addressed to the leadership of Rome and the *Dialogue with Trypho* disputes

Jewish thinking. Thus in his writings Justin is in conversation with the philosophies and traditions of the Greco- Roman world.[339]

Justin sees himself as passing on a received tradition. He quotes extensively from what he believes are Christ's post-resurrection teachings to the Apostles. For Justin, the meaning of the Old Testament texts was hidden until the resurrection. The risen Christ taught the apostles how to read the prophecies so that they could understand who he was. Then the Holy Spirit came to give the apostles power to proclaim what they had been taught. For Justin all later exegesis depends on this apostolic instruction.[340] He emphasizes both the rationality of his teaching and that it comes through being given "the grace to understand." The apostolic teaching and "the grace to understand" are synonyms because the apostolic teaching came directly from Christ to the apostles.[341]

It is interesting to explore Justin's sources. Justin appears to refer to the extant Septuagint as a Jewish source. He has another source that he calls the Seventy, which he regards as the real Septuagint. This text appears to have been a testimony source, a Christian compilation of Old Testament texts reinterpreted in light of the life, death and resurrection of Jesus – a hypothesized source that appears to have become so authoritative for Christians that it was used by later scribes to correct manuscripts of the Septuagint that have come down to us.[342] Many of the disputes that Justin composes in his *Dialogue with Trypho* concern the differences between his text and Jewish texts. The quotes that Justin takes from what is now considered the biblical manuscript, he brands as Jewish and claims that the Jews have corrupted them. The quotes taken from what Justin calls the Septuagint appear to be from his testimony source, now lost to us.[343] It is probable that in Justin's time the Jews had a scribal tradition while the Christians did not. Jewish scribes were adjusting the Greek text of the Septuagint to the emerging normative

339 Yarchin, *History of Biblical Interpretation*, 31.

340 Skarsaune, *The Proof from Prophecy*, 11.

341 Skarsaune, *The Proof from Prophecy*, 12.

342 Skarsaune, *The Proof from Prophecy*, 30.

343 Skarsaune, *The Proof from Prophecy*, 43.

Hebrew text. When Justin complains about Jewish alterations of the text of the Seventy, he may be responding to real changes that the Jewish scribes were making. It would be natural for Justin to assume that his Christian sources were correct, even if they differed from the Septuagint manuscripts.[344] This discussion is pertinent to the subject at hand because it might help in understanding the differences that appear in the story of Moses and the bronze serpent in Justin's accounts.

The story appears earliest in Justin's *First Apology* (60) where he is explaining that the phrase from Plato's *Timaeus*, "He placed him crosswise in the universe," was borrowed from Moses. Justin writes:

> For in Moses' writings it is recorded that at that time, when the Israelites came out from Egypt and were in the wilderness, venomous beasts, both vipers and asps and serpents of all kinds met them. They were putting the people to death. And according to the inspiration and energy from God's speech, Moses took bronze and made a type of the cross and put this in the holy tabernacle and said to the people, "If you gaze at this type, and you believe in him/it you will be saved." And this came to pass, it was recorded that indeed the serpents died; and thus it delivered and the people escaped death (Author's translation).[345]

This rather strange account seems to conflate Deuteronomy 8:15 with the reference to the Nechuschtan in 2 Kings 18:4. There is very little here that need necessarily come from Numbers 21, except the command to Moses to make the serpent and the people to look at it. What Justin takes away from his first acquaintance with the story is that the serpent on the pole is a type of the cross, it was placed in the tabernacle, and that it saved the people by killing the serpents. There is no suggestion that the grumbling of the Israelites caused the serpents to appear.

---

344 Skarsaune, *The Proof from Prophecy*, 45.

345 *The Christian Apologists; A Digital Version of Selected Works from Jacques-Paul Migne, Patrologiae Graecae* (Paris, 1866). Volume 6. Morphologically tagged by Rex A. Koivisto, Multnomah University, Portland, Oregon USA. Copyright © 2009 OakTree Software, Inc. Version 1.8.

A second and extended discourse on the story begins in paragraph 89 of the later *The Dialogue with Trypho* where Justin writes that Trypho, while agreeing with Justin that the Scriptures tell of the suffering of the Messiah, questions whether that suffering could possibly have been the shameful death of the crucifixion, "for the one who is crucified is said to be cursed in the law." Justin's response is a lengthy explanation that includes three "signs (σημείων) that Moses made." The first sign is Moses "stretching his hands to either side" as he prays to God while Jesus (Joshua) leads the fight. Aaron and Hur support Moses' hands so that they "might not be let down" when he grows tired. This story is clearly from Exodus 17, but Moses' staff is missing from the account. Instead the image is of Moses standing with arms outstretched as a type of the crucified Christ. The second sign, in *Dialogue* 91, is Moses' blessing of Joseph from Deuteronomy 33:13-17. In verse 17 Joseph is compared to a firstborn bull whose horns are, in the Septuagint, the horns of a unicorn. These horns are for Justin another type (τύπου) of the cross. Here the cross both pricks the hearts of idol and demon worshippers to turn them towards God and destroys and condemns unbelievers, just as Amalek was destroyed by Israel.

The "third type and sign,"

> set up against the serpents which were biting Israel, appeared, becoming the salvation of the ones who believe that soon, through the crucified one, death will come thereafter, as was preached beforehand, to the serpent; but salvation to the ones bitten by him and fleeing to the one who sent his crucified son into the world. For the prophetic spirit through Moses did not teach us to believe in the serpent, since it declares him to be cursed from the beginning by God, and in Isaiah indicates that he will be destroyed as an enemy through the great sword, which is Christ (Author's translation).

Justin wants to explain that through the cross, death would come to the serpent, but those bitten by the serpent who fled to the God who sent the Christ into the world to be crucified, would be saved. The biting serpents are equated with the serpent who was cursed by God after Eve and Adam ate the fruit of the forbidden tree in the garden in Genesis 3. The Isaiah reference appears to be 27:1: "On that day the LORD with his cruel and great and strong sword will punish Leviathan the fleeing serpent, Leviathan the twisting serpent, and he will kill the dragon that is in the sea." In the Old Testament this is a text about the victory of Judah and the return of Israel from exile in Assyria and Egypt. For Justin the sign of the serpent on the pole points to Christ's death on the cross in the same way that Moses' outstretched arms and Joseph's unicorn horns do. Gone are the references to the holy tabernacle but the association of the serpents with sin is stronger.

And once again Justin describes the bronze serpent in the following account, which appears in the *Dialogue with Trypho* (112):

> Since also Moses would ever be judged a wrongdoer in this way. He, having commanded that no image be created, neither of that in heaven or that on earth or in the sea, then made a bronze snake and putting it on a certain signpost (σημείου) commanded the bitten ones to look to it/him, and looking to it/him, they were saved. Will the snake be understood then as saving the people, which, as I said before, God cursed in the beginning and destroyed by the great sword as Isaiah said? And will we thus foolishly receive, as your teachers do, the saying of such things and not [receive them] as signs (σύμβολα)? But will we not bring up the signpost (σημεῖον) as pointing to (ἐπί) the image (εἰκόνα) of the crucifixion of Jesus, since also Moses, through the extending of his hands together with the one called by name Jesus worked victory for your people? For thus will we stop being at a loss concerning what the lawgiver did, for without forsaking God, he persuaded the people to hope on a beast through which transgression and disobedience received their beginning. And this was born of and was said, with great understanding and mystery through the blessed prophet; but there is nothing one has of the sayings or deeds by any one of the prophets, with which one can justly find

> fault, if you have the knowledge that is in them (Author's translation).

Again for Justin the bronze serpent on the pole is a type of the cross. But this time Justin discusses the contradiction between God's command against idols and Moses' making of an image and moves to a symbolic interpretation. This third account is the most detailed and seems more similar to the Numbers 21 account, though again many of the details are absent. Justin will continue and explain that Moses was blameless when he made the serpent, even though images were forbidden, because God had commanded it and just as God was blameless when God commanded that an image be made, so also Christ is blameless when he is crucified, even though the Law curses those crucified, because he is the Christ of God who saves those who are worthy of the Law's curse (94). The image of the cross as the saving event is what is of primary importance to Justin. But it seems that he does connect the serpent and Christ typologically, because, he says, the people were persuaded "to hope on a beast through which transgression and disobedience received their beginning." This Justin declares to be a great mystery.

Discussion

It is striking that the five different authors use the story for five different, yet perhaps related, purposes. Philo and Pseudo-Solomon, who write before the coming of Christ and write at very nearly the same time are vastly different in their use of the story, perhaps because, even within the Jewish community in Alexandria, their situations were quite different. The story is used later by Barnabas and Justin to demonstrate that Jesus was the one foretold by the scriptures of Israel and yet, ironically, they use it to some extent as polemics against the Jews whose scripture they find so important, but who have not become followers of Jesus. Paul who stands in the middle uses the story somewhat like Pseudo-Solomon does, but Paul also has to address the same concerns that Barnabas and Justin have, though he uses different means.

Philo is an exegete, interpreting scripture to teach his wealthy, urban, Hellenized kinsman to continue to keep the Law of Moses in their syncretistic setting. His concern is ethics and so he reads the story of Moses and the serpent allegorically. The serpent who came to Eve was pleasure and it had a purpose within God's creation – to unite Adam (mind) and Eve (external sense). But something went wrong with how Eve and Adam received it. Overindulgence in pleasure became an ethical problem for God's people and so God provided a solution. The bronze serpent here is an antidote. People who practice temperance while believing in God no longer suffer from death but have life. Philo draws a distinction between common death and the death of the soul. The death of the soul, which he sees as the combination of the body and soul, but with the body – the inferior part – having control (Allegory 1:105), is the death that temperance combined with belief in God can overcome.

Philo does not need to be concerned with the bronze serpent as an idol because he allegorizes it. To him it is a solution that God provides to a problem that God's people have. This solution is participatory – the bronze serpent provides a way for God's people to act in faith. The bronze serpent functions as a counterpart to the serpent who seduced Eve. Interestingly, Philo is the only one of our five authors who is using a Septuagint text that is very close to what is extant today, which he quotes extensively.

The author of the Wisdom of Solomon is writing to a community facing the crisis of persecution. Pseudo-Solomon uses the story to say that even though God punishes Israel when she sins, the punishment is short lived when compared with how God treats Israel's enemies – in this case Egypt. It is a message that encourages people to remain within the Jewish community and not give in to pressures to become part of the wider Greco-Roman world. Like Philo, Pseudo-Solomon sees the serpent on the pole as a way for Israel to look to God, and when they look to God they are saved from death – no other gods, of Egypt or Rome for that matter, could save – only Israel's God can lead down to Hades and back – others can kill, but they cannot make alive. But Pseudo-Solomon, unlike Philo, is concerned that the serpent on the pole not be considered an idol to be worshiped. He is at pains to say that God is the one who heals, not the bronze serpent. His readers/hearers are not a community that is being seduced by the pleasures of the wealthy Greco-Roman world. His is a community that is considering blending into the cultures around them to avoid persecution; blending in enough to lose their identity as God's people – to, in some form, worship the gods of Rome or Egypt. Pseudo-Solomon is urging them to persevere; promising them that God will not wait too long to deliver them. Pseudo-Solomon does not quote enough of his text for us to tell us what he is working with – presumably some form of the Septuagint or a form of the story that precedes it. He avoids giving any detail about the serpent or how he understands it, except that it is a symbol and not a false God.

Paul stands apart from all the other authors discussed here in his reinterpretation of the story told in Numbers 21, but in a way he is also a bridge between them. Paul's use of the story is in some ways similar to Philo and Pseudo-Solomon in that, to Paul, it speaks of how keeping the law matters to God. It also exemplifies how God teaches God's people: that suffering and death are God's instruments in spiritual formation. But Paul goes beyond his Jewish predecessors in that the revelation of Christ that he received on the road to Damascus tells Paul that Christ is the definitive answer to humanity's problem of not being able to keep the law. Keeping the law, as interpreted by love, becomes possible when one is in Christ. One is in Christ when, through faith, one sees God's righteous and redeeming action in the cross. Thus Paul shares the theological problem that Barnabas and Justin Martyr have to address: how can God's Messiah have suffered and died on the cursed instrument of shame and torture that the cross was in the Greco-Roman empire? While Paul does not use the serpent on the pole to address this question, it is a central concern of his writings.

Paul's source of Scripture appears to be the Septuagint, though not all of his quotes can be found there. Scholars postulate that he may have had access to a recension that was closer to the Hebrew text or he may have quoted from memory when his circumstances prevented direct access to a manuscript.[346] Paul's allusive reference to the incident in Numbers 21 is so brief that nothing can be gleaned about the text to which he had access.

346 Schnelle, *Apostle Paul: His Life and Theology*, 108.

Barnabas is most probably writing to some segment of the Alexandrian community, as did Philo and Pseudo-Solomon. He is notable for his intense interest in interpreting Jewish scripture combined with his extremely anti-Jewish stance. It is possible that Barnabas is using a Christian testimony source; his story seems to be a version of the story told in Numbers 21, but, like Pseudo-Solomon, he is short on detail. Like Philo, he associates the punishing serpents with the serpent of Eve. Barnabas is clear that the cause of the biting serpents was disobedience brought about by the serpent that persuaded Eve. Like Pseudo-Solomon he is concerned about the contradiction between God's command against graven images and Moses' making of the serpent. His conclusion is that the serpent on the pole is not an idol, but a type of Christ, put into history and scripture to show the Jews, who lost the covenant at Sinai, that they must look to Christ. Barnabas adds the nuance that the bronze serpent is placed on a tree.

Barnabas is the earliest writer of the five considered here to follow the interpretation of the story of Moses' hands raised over the battle with Amalek with the story of the bronze serpent. This interpretive coupling survives in Jewish interpretation in the *Mishnah* (Rosh HaShanah 3.8)[347] and the *Mekhilta According to Rabbi Ishmael.*[348] Philo also discusses the story of Moses' hands, but not in any proximity to his discussion of the bronze serpent. Pseudo-Solomon does not mention it nor does Paul.

For Barnabas the serpent on the pole demonstrates that the Messiah must suffer and will be brought back to life, even though Israel thinks they have destroyed him. The serpent is a sign pointing to the crucifixion and the crucifixion is the solution to the problem of the disobedience brought about by the serpent in the garden. Thus Barnabas expresses that turning to the crucified Christ is the solution to disobedience, rather than simply turning to God in the way that his pre-Christ predecessors did.

---

347 Herbert Danby, *The Mishnah* (Oxford: Clarendon Press, 1933), 192.

348 Jacob Neusner, *Mekhilta According to Rabbi Ishmael: An Analytical Translation, Volume Two* (Atlanta: Scholars Press, 1988), 10.

Justin Martyr's purpose in writing appears to be to commend his faith to those outside of it. He wants to demonstrate that the teachings of Christians contain wisdom and philosophy, better than, but also not entirely incompatible with, other philosophers.

In our first passage of interest, he wants to demonstrate that Plato also was speaking of Christ. His description of the Numbers 21 story from his *First Apology* is very different from the others. He has the snake set up in the tabernacle as well as the serpents dying. But when he works with the passage again in the *Dialogue with Trypho* we see more similarities with the other accounts. Like Pseudo-Solomon, Justin is troubled by the contradiction between the command against images and the making of an image. Like Barnabas, he interprets the bronze serpent on the pole as a type and sign of the crucifixion. Also like Barnabas he couples his interpretation with that of Moses' hands above the battle between Israel and Amalek. Unlike Pseudo-Solomon, but like Philo and Barnabas, Justin links the biting serpents with the serpent who came to Eve in the beginning.

The transformation that occurs when people begin to become followers of Christ is evident in the various interpretations of the story of Moses and the bronze serpent. For Philo and Pseudo-Solomon, life comes to the people when, by seeing the serpent, they turn back to God. For both of these authors turning to God involves continuing to keep God's law and remain part of the Jewish community. Paul uses the story, as Philo and Pseudo-Solomon do, to exhort a pattern of behavior that conforms to God's ways rather than the ways of the surrounding culture. Barnabas and Justin have the serpent point to the crucified Christ. Belief in him brings deliverance from death, death that was brought about by the other serpent, who tempted Eve in the beginning. Justin adds the further explanation that Jesus' death results in the death of that other serpent. Paul, Barnabas, and Justin have to explain the shameful death by crucifixion of the one they follow. While all three feel that it is important to explain that Christ's death is not incompatible with Jewish scripture. Paul reinterprets the faith of the Jews, while both Barnabas and Justin reject it. Barnabas and Justin Martyr are among the earliest writers to express clear supersessionism – the idea that the followers of Christ have replaced the Jewish nation in God's covenantal relationship.

Barnabas has this occurring when the Israelites worship the golden calf at Mt Sinai. Justin explains that it happened because the Jews did not recognize Jesus as God's Messiah.

Mark Turnage postulates a Jewish *theologoumenon* that interprets the story of Moses and the bronze serpent and that preexisted, but perhaps has its earliest written expression, in John's Gospel. Turnage emphasizes that the influence of Judaism on the formation of the theology of the early church is at least as important as that of Greco-Roman religion and culture.[349] The present study seems to support Turnage's conclusion, both as to the importance of Jewish thinking for Christian Theology and of the possibility that there is a tradition of interpretation that connects these five disparate writings with the Gospel of John. Yet while Turnage's discussion of the way texts are interpreted and reinterpreted in streams is useful, his discussion downplays the differences in the purposes for which these texts are interpreted and the uncertainty of the sources that the earlier writers may have used. The datings of these writings and the possible connections between them are quite tenuous. Turnage is interested in material from the Mishnah; the *Mekhilta de Rabbi Ishmael*, a commentary developed to supplement the Mishnah; and the Targums, Aramiac interpretations of the Hebrew Bible. These are all written much later than the writings discussed here. What the Mishnah and Targums tell us about John's Gospel is very vague indeed.

Paul Flesher and Bruce Chilton define a targum as "a translation that combines a highly literal rendering of the original text with material added into the translation in a seamless manner."[350] The targums developed over a long period of time out of the need for Aramaic speaking Jews to be able to comprehend the Hebrew Scriptures. According to Jewish tradition, targums have been used since the time of Ezra. Nehemiah 8:8 states that when Ezra read

349 Marc Turnage, "Is it the serpent that heals? An Ancient Jewish Theologoumenon and the Developing Faith in Jesus," in *Israel in the Wilderness: Interpretation of the Biblical Narratives in Jewish and Christian Traditions*. ed. Kenneth E Pomykala (Leiden: Brill, 2008), 71-72.

350 Paul V. M. Flesher and Bruce Chilton, *The Targums: A Critical Introduction* (Waco: Baylor University Press, 2011), 22.

from the book of the law of God, the sense was given so that the people could understand. The Babylonian Talmud understands this to refer to a targum.[351] There is no manuscript evidence to determine what these targums may have been like. Because of the difficulty of dating the extant targums, interest in their relationship to the New Testament has languished until recently. The targum that is of most interest in regards to the New Testament is the *Palestinian Targum to the Pentateuch*, which is preserved as a whole in *Targum Neofiti* and in part in the *Fragment Targum*. The *Palestinian Targum to the Pentateuch* is thought to have come from the same manuscript tradition that produced the Babylonian *Targum Onkelos to the Pentateuch* and was a source for *Targum Pseudo-Jonathan to the Pentateuch*.[352] The texts of these targums are from the third century CE, but many scholars think it likely that there were in Palestine, early, perhaps pre-Christian, targums and this tradition continued into the third century. Care must be taken to note that some paraphrases in the texts of these targums are later additions, but it is likely that there are individual passages that developed at the same time and in the same milieu as the New Testament.[353] Martin McNamara notes a number of strikingly similar theological concepts and linguistic expressions between the Palestinian Targum on the Pentateuch and the Gospel of John. These include the use of "glory" and "*Logos*" (Memra); Jesus' "hour" in John and the "Hour of Distress" in the Palestinian Targums; Abraham's Vision of the Christ, the Well of Jacob, Jacob's Ladder, the Second Death and the Brazen Serpent.[354] Targum Neofiti adds some significant interpretive elements to the story of the bronze serpent. The people speak against the *Memra* (Word) of the Lord and against Moses. There is also a *Bath Qol*, a heavenly voice, that tells the people

351 Martin McNamara, *Targum and Testament Revisited: Aramaic Paraphrases of the Hebrew Bible: A Light on the New Testament* (Grand Rapids: Eerdmans, 2010), 120.

352 Edward M. Cook, "The Interpretation of the Hebrew Bible in the Targums," in *A Companion to Biblical Interpretation in Early Judaism*, ed. Matthias Henze (Grand Rapids: Eerdmans, 2012), 96. Flesher and Chilton, *The Targums*, 156.

353 McNamara, *Targum and Testament Revisited*, 135.

354 These are discussed in detail in McNamara, *Targum and Testament Revisited*, 154-166, 213-227.

that the serpent, who was cursed from the beginning to eat dust, will come and rule over the people because the serpent does not murmur over eating dust while the Israelites murmur even though God has given them manna, well water, and quail. This Targum also specifies that the bronze serpent be put in an elevated place. Targum Pseudo-Jonathan also adds the *Bath Qol* but shortens its speech. It too includes putting the bronze serpent in "a place aloft" and adds that the person who looks at the bronze serpent and whose heart pays attention to the *Memra* of the Lord lives.

A brief survey of patristic interpretation of the story of Moses and the bronze serpent show that their interpretations tend to be a mix of allegory and typology. Many connect the serpents in the wilderness with the serpent of Genesis 3.They also particularly note that the bronze serpent had never been a living serpent. Some include aspects of serpents that were of interest in the ancient world. In general serpents are seen in a negative light. To Bede, the bites of the serpents are the enticement of the vices. The raising of the serpent prefigures Jesus' suffering on the cross. The sins that destroy human souls and bodies are represented by the serpents, both because they were deadly and because they recall the serpent that led the first parents into sin. Jesus is made known by the bronze serpent since he came in the likeness of sinful flesh. The bronze serpent had the likeness of a fiery serpent but without its poison. It cured those who had been stricken by being lifted up. Christ the Redeemer entered bodily into sinful flesh, and by suffering death on a cross freed those who believed in him.[355] Ephrem the Syrian directly equates the serpent of Genesis 3 with the serpent in Numbers 21. For him the eyes that saw the bronze serpent in the wilderness are bodily eyes, but the eyes that look to Christ are spiritual eyes and will live spiritually. For Ephrem, Moses' standard is also a cross and the bronze serpent which could not by nature suffer was analogous to the Christ who could not by nature die.[356] For Augustine, being made whole by the serpent

355 Joseph T. Lienhard S. J. ed. *Ancient Christian Commentary on Scripture: Old Testament III: Exodus, Leviticus, Numbers, Deuteronomy* (Downers Grove: InterVarsity Press, 2001), 241.

356 Lienhard. *Ancient Christian Commentary on Scripture: Old Testament III: Exodus, Leviticus, Numbers, Deuteronomy*, 242.

is a great sacrament because it is to be made whole from death by believing in one who is dead. The one who has been bitten by the snake of sin has only to gaze on Christ and will receive healing for the forgiveness of sins. The mortality that the Lord took on, the church must keep experiencing as his body. People owe death to the sin of the first persons, but will reach eternal life through Christ at the end of the world.[357] For Gregory of Nazianzus, the bronze serpent is not a type of Christ, but a contrast. It saved because it was killed and with it, and the powers subject to it, namely death were destroyed as they deserved.[358] Ambrose calls the brazen serpent a type of the cross. That a bronze serpent, not a real serpent was hung, corresponds to the fact the Lord took upon himself the likeness of a sinner though he was without sin. Thus he imitated a serpent in imitating human weakness, but he then laid aside the flesh and was able to destroy the cunning of the serpent.[359] Cyril of Alexandria describes the story of Moses and the serpent as a mystery of the incarnation. The serpent represents the deadly sin that was destroying the human race, biting human souls and infusing them with wickedness. But relief came from heaven. The Word of God was made in the likeness of sinful flesh "that he might condemn sin in the flesh" (Romans 8:3). He becomes the giver of salvation to those who understand divine doctrines and gaze on him with faith. The serpent was set on high, as Christ was clearly shown by his passion, so that none could fail to see him.[360]

Turnage argues for a strong connection between forgiveness of sins and healing,[361] but his connection seems forced and overstated. The bronze serpent as a way to turn back to God is the solution to

---

357 Joel C. Elowsky, ed. *Ancient Christian Commentary on Scripture: New Testament IVA: John 1-10* (Downers Grove: InterVarsity, 2006), 124.

358 Lienhard, ed. *Ancient Christian Commentary on Scripture: Old Testament III*, 242.

359 Elowsky, ed. *Ancient Christian Commentary on Scripture: New Testament IVA: John 1-10*, 123.

360 Elowsky, ed. *Ancient Christian Commentary on Scripture: New Testament IVA: John 1-10*, 123.

361 Marc Turnage, "Is it the serpent that heals? An Ancient Jewish Theologoumenon and the Developing Faith in Jesus," 77.

the problem of sin – not because it earns forgiveness – but because it returns one (or keeps one) within the covenant community, either that of the Jews or of the followers of Jesus depending on the author. None of the five turn-of-the-era authors discussed above seem particularly interested in forgiveness as an action on God's part when they interpret the story.

The Alexandrian provenance of many of these texts is interesting. Snakes were a noticeable symbol of divinity and rule, but snake symbols were also used for protection along the Nile.[362] It makes sense that their image is something Jewish and Jewish-Christian writers in Egypt would have had to grapple with.

For Christian Frevel, in the story told in Numbers 21 the threat of the justified wrath of God ceases and the murmuring of the people is replaced with repentance and trust in the mediation of their leader Moses. This story turns a corner that signals the end of the wilderness wandering and the beginning of the successful conquest of the Promised Land. Frevel suggests that "the emergence of narrative traditions is not restricted to the early phase of Israel and can be assumed to be contemporary to the redactional process."[363] This idea along with the interest in this story in Alexandrian circles may suggest an Egyptian origin to the snake story. It also highlights the uncertainty behind the text-types interpreted by our various authors. Philo is the only author who quotes enough of the Septuagint to give certainty that it is the text he is interpreting. The other authors may have been using forms of the story that come from traditions predating both the Septuagint and the Hebrew text. Similarly, while Jean Danielou points out that the *testimonia* "represent the prophetic argument for the continuity of the two Testaments,"[364] more current scholarship on these texts makes one wonder whether the *testimonia* may predate the New Testament and be part of its development.[365]

362 Charlesworth, *The Good and Evil Serpent*, 17.

363 Christian Frevel, "Understanding the Pentateuch by Structuring the Desert: Numbers 21 as a Compositional Joint," 130.

364 Jean Danielou, *The Theology of Jewish Christianity* (Philadelphia: Westminster Press, 1964), 271.

365 There are a set of variants to Numbers 21:8 and 9 that replace the word σημείου (sign, probably indicating a standard for a flag) to ὕψους (in this case probably

A this point it seems of value to discuss one other aspect of snake imagery, not in the Judeo-Christian tradition, but very widespread and popular across the Greco-Roman world. The prominence of the cult of Asclepius in the centuries around the turn of the era, makes it important to include a brief discussion of him here.

The earliest record of Asclepius appears to be a mention in Homer's *Iliad* (8th Century BCE). There Asclepius is a human; a physician and the father of two great physicians who take a contingent of ships from the region of Thessaly in Greece off to Troy.[366] As time passes Asclepius' deeds and reputation accord him the status of a demi-god. By the 5th Century BCE a complete mythology has grown up around him. Asclepius becomes known as the son of Apollo and a mortal woman Coronis. Coronis is killed by Apollo when he discovers that she has been unfaithful to him, but as she is dying she pleads for their unborn child and Apollo rescues Asclepius from her body before it is burned.[367] Apollos leaves Asclepius with Chiron the centaur, who teaches him the healing arts, as do the snakes who live on Mount Pelion and guard Asclepius as an infant.[368] Asclepius' healing powers draw favorable attention from Athena, who gives him some of the Gorgon's blood so that he can revive the dead, but this in turn evokes the ire of Hades, who feels that his realm is in danger

best translated "on high"). While this word is interesting because ὕψους is a cognate of ὑψόω, (lift up) all of these variants occur in manuscripts that are quite late. One is a miniscule from 1125 CE and the others are all associated with a translation by Symmachus. The earliest of these manuscripts with the variant is from the 7th Century CE. Given the late dates for these manuscripts it seems likely that if there is any connection with the Fourth Gospel at all, the influence flows from John to the Greek version of Numbers, but given what is known about Symmachus it seems likely that the variants reflect the same usage as Targum Neofiti described above. (John William Wevers, ed., *Septuaginta, Vestus Testamentum Graecum, Auctoritate Academiae Scientiarum Gottingensis editum, Vol. III, 1 Numeri* (Göttingen: Vanderhoeck & Ruprecht, 1982), 254-255 and Karen H. Jobes and Moisés Silva, *Invitation to the Septuagint*, 2nd Ed. (Grand Rapids: Baker, 2015), 29-30.

366 Gerald D. Hart, *Asclepius, the God of Medicine* (Lake Forest: Royal Society of Medicine Press 2000), 3.

367 Hart, *Asclepius, the God of Medicine*, 7-8.

368 Hart, *Asclepius, the God of Medicine*, 42.

of being depopulated. So, Zeus kills Asclepius with a thunderbolt. Apollo retaliates, so Zeus appeases him by making Asclepius a new constellation within Scorpio. Though there is now no story that explains it, Asclepius is apparently also allowed to return to earth to practice medicine.[369] By the 2nd Century CE, Asclepius is worshipped throughout the Greco-Roman world.[370]

Serpents became a particular symbol of Asclepius in part because of his story and because of the belief that the gods had bestowed special favors on serpents. The shedding of their skin came to symbolize the casting off of death, recovery from illness, and rebirth and regeneration. Their tunnels were thought to be entries to the underworld, making it possible for them to communicate with the gods under the earth. That their bodies could form a circle made them a symbol of eternity. That they had no visible genitalia meant that they had supreme reproductive powers. The belief that serpents had keen vision and did not sleep meant that they were vigilant. Their habitat among the bushes made it possible for them to know the medicinal powers of plants.[371] Asclepius is associated with one particular snake, thought by herpetologists to be *Elaphe longissima,* a harmless snake that can grow quite long and is known to be adept at climbing.[372] Asclepius is frequently depicted holding a staff with a snake coiled around it or with a snake rearing up in front of him. It is the snake-intwined staff that has become the symbol of many medical associations. The caduceus, two serpents entwined around a winged staff, is the symbol of Hermes, the messenger, and this became a symbol of communication, peace and commerce.[373] Its present day use as a medical symbol may be the result of a confusion between the two or it may be used on emergency vehicles as a symbol of swiftness. As Christianity became more dominant in the 4th

369 Hart, *Asclepius, the God of Medicine*, 10.

370 Hart, *Asclepius, the God of Medicine*, 165; Wendy Cotter, "Miracle Stories: The God Asclepius, the Pythagorean Philosophers, and the Roman Rulers," in *The Historical Jesus in Context*. Amy-Jill Levine, Dale C. Allison Jr. and John Dominic Crossan, eds. (Princeton: Princeton University Press, 2006), 168.

371 Hart, *Asclepius, the God of Medicine*, 41.

372 Hart, *Asclepius, the God of Medicine*, 42.

373 Hart, *Asclepius, the God of Medicine*, 41.

Century CE, worship of all the Greco-Roman gods began to decline and medicine continued to develop outside of Asclepieions, temple compounds that practiced healing. The snake coiled around a pole was recovered as a symbol of medicine during the Renaissance. Its conflation with Moses' bronze serpent very likely aided its public acceptance.[374]

There are striking parallels between Asclepius and Jesus:[375] they both have divine fathers and mortal mothers; they both died and rose again; they both were healers with miraculous powers; they were both portrayed as compassionate and willing to serve humankind. They were both accused, tried, and executed because of jealousy from others within their own community. Both were described as saviors.

So, what can be said at this point about how serpents were viewed in the 1st Century CE? As discussed in the literature review given in Chapter 1 above, James Charlesworth feels that he has successfully demonstrated that there is a typology between Jesus and the bronze serpent that Moses made and that this typology is intended as a positive comparison between Jesus and a symbol of life and rebirth. He believes that John was drawing on the positive images of serpents within the Greco-Roman culture at the time of his Gospel's composition.[376] According to Charlesworth the author of the Fourth Gospel uses the typology to say that Jesus comes from above to bring life in the present and eternal life in the future to those on earth. Charlesworth leans heavily on iconography and symbology in his argument.

While it may be correct that serpents were looked upon as positive symbols in parts of the Greco-Roman world and that over all Christ on the cross can be seen as a positive symbol – a symbol of God's healing, new life, and the conquest of evil and death – it is not at all evident that the serpent is an unambiguous symbol of goodness in John or other Jewish writings. All of the writers closest

374 Hart, *Asclepius, the God of Medicine*, 45.

375 Hart, *Asclepius, the God of Medicine*, 183-185.

376 Charlesworth points to the fact that Zeus, Apollo, Athena, Hermes, Asclepius and Hygeia were closely associated with serpents. Charlesworth, *The Good and Evil Serpent*, 30-31.

to John in theology and culture wrestle with the ambiguity of the serpent as a symbol. Philo tells us that the serpent's creation had a good purpose but that purpose went off track – the serpent ultimately led to spiritual death. The other four authors considered here make an even stronger connection with disobedience and death than Philo does. There is also a clear difference between the serpent of Asclepius, which was known to be harmless and the serpents described in Numbers 21 and elsewhere in the Old Testament, as well as interpreted by Philo, Pseudo-Solomon, Paul, Barnabas, and Justin Martyr. Charlesworth argues that the connection between snakes and evil was a later Christian development, but the evidence of the writings of Jewish and Jewish Christian authors at the turn of the era is that the connection between the serpent, evil, and death occurred even before the possibility of 'Christian thinking' existed.

Before Jesus walked the earth, the story told in Numbers 21 was a difficult one for Jewish writers to interpret. For them it became a story about God providing a way for God's people to turn back from disobedience and receive God's promised blessings. For the earliest followers of Christ it was the cross that was difficult to explain. They insisted on a connection between Jesus and the story of God's salvation told in the Jewish scriptures, but according to those scriptures crucifixion was the death of one cursed by God. To them the story of Moses and the bronze serpent was useful because it spoke of how a bad thing could become, by God's power and command, a good thing. The serpent was in Jewish thought primarily a symbol of danger, evil, disobedience, and death. Christ as the commanded and sent antitype of the serpent, became the symbol of the conquest of death and the destruction of evil. Belief in Jesus as the one sent from God became, for his followers, the way to turn to God and receive the promised blessing of eternal life in God's kingdom.

John is clearly a hellenized Jewish writer and thus very likely to be aware of Greco-Roman imagery and ideas. If these come into play at all in his Gospel it seems to be as more of an unstated one-upmanship. The gods of Rome are not mentioned in John's portrait, but Jesus is shown to be greater than Asclepius since he can heal with a touch, with a word and at a distance; greater than Bacchus, who needed grape juice to make wine; greater than Mars, paradoxically, because Jesus drives out his opponents in and through defeat. There may be a similar element of this one-upmanship in both Paul and the Wisdom of Solomon. Paul lists many parts of the body of Christ in 1 Corinthians 12. This very specific list may reflect the votive body parts displayed in the Asclepieion in Corinth, reenforcing Paul's assertion that members of the body of Christ (both individual body parts and whole persons in the Corinthian community of believers) are incorporated into the God of Israel through Christ and can no longer have anything to do with Asclepius.[377] Pseudo-Solomon states explicitly that only the God of Israel has "authority over life and death and [can] lead down to the gates of Hades and raise up (Wisdom 16:13)," a rather direct denial of existing accounts of Asclepius raising the dead[378] and the story that Hades became angry with Asclepius for de-populating the place of the dead, prompting his execution by Zeus' thunderbolt.

Conclusion

What, if anything, can be added to what has already been said about the reference in John's Gospel to the serpent lifted up by Moses based on the above review of its closest contemporary references? It might be helpful to begin by summarizing the discussion with a table:

377 Hart, *Asclepius, the God of Medicine*, 193-194.

378 Wendy Cotter, "Miracle Stories: The God Asclepius, the Pythagorean Philosophers, and the Roman Rulers," 170.

Table: Summary of References to Moses' Serpent in Near Turn of the Era Literature

Source	Number of References	Type of Reference	Possible Intent
Philo	2 (*Allegorical Interpretation* 2.71ff and *Husbandry* 98ff)	Extended allegorical interpretation including quotations	Encourage observance of the law
Wisdom of Solomon	1 (Wisdom of Solomon 16:5-14)	Extended interpretation, retelling Israel's story	Comfort and encourage continued practice of Jewish faith
Paul	1 (1 Corinthians 10:9)	Brief allusion in a retelling Israel's story	Exhortation to abstain from pagan rituals
The Epistle of Barnabas	1 (Epistle of Barnabas 12:5-7)	Extended typology between Jesus and the bronze serpent	Exhort Jewish followers of Jesus not to return to Judaism
Justin Martyr	3 (*First Apology* 60, *Dialogue* 91, and *Dialogue 112)*	Extended explanations of the bronze serpent as a type and sign	Apologetic – to convince others that Jesus is the promised Messiah
John	3 (John 3:14, 8:28, and 12:31-32)	Brief allusive typology reflecting sweeping theological concepts	Testimony – to bear witness to what God has done through Jesus Christ.

The investigation conducted in this chapter may have provided more questions than answers, but it does give a fuller picture of the immediate context in which the story of the bronze serpent was interpreted by the author of the Fourth Gospel. John's quote of the story is so brief that it is impossible to identify with any certainty whether he had the Septuagint or some other source available to him. While John has many explicit quotations from the Septuagint, he also uses many things that appear to be either his own free quotes or quotes that come from other unknown sources.[379] John's use of the story has many resonances with the writers surveyed here. John is interested in the serpent as a way to turn to God in belief (John 3:14-18), understanding this as the way to be born from above. And John is interested in the cross as the destruction of evil (John 12:31-33). There may be a common source for the connection between the cross and the glory of Jesus that is present in both John and *The Epistle of Barnabas.* But John is also innovative in his interpretation of the story. He alone employs the irony of 'lifting up' (ὑψόω) as both the physical event of the crucifixion and the exaltation of the Incarnate One. He alone speaks of the crucifixion, coupled with the resurrection and ascension, as a unique revelation of Jesus as God (John 8:28).

One thing that stands out in the discussion above is the concern, particularly in the more Jewish interpretations of the story of Moses and the serpent, with ethics. Philo, Pseudo-Solomon and Paul all see the snakes sent by God in response to the disobedience of Israel as corrective, as God's way of turning Israel back to God by changing their behavior. For these three authors, the people who disobey are part of Israel (and for Paul also part of the body of Christ) and their disobedience doesn't change that. The narrated death of the Israelites doesn't even enter Philo or Pseudo-Solomon's interpretation; the focus is on God's saving act. For Paul, as for the author of the Numbers 21 account (as discussed in Chapter 3) the disobedience of Israel does have consequences. Disobedience, or as Paul puts it, testing Christ, means that some of Israel falls short of the goal of gaining the promised land or of being in Christ. In all these cases

379 Köstenberger, "John," 415-421.

right action is a component of salvation. If salvation can be defined as "I will be your God and you shall be my people," (Exodus 6:7, Jeremiah 7:23, Jeremiah 11:4, Jeremiah 30:22, and Ezekiel 36:26) only in the case of Exodus 6 is the promise entirely decoupled from God's expectation of certain standards of behavior for God's people. God's steadfast love (חֶסֶד) reigns when Israel participates faithfully in the covenant. This sense seems less strong in Barnabas and Justin Martyr with their sharper focus on belief in Christ as the key to salvation. Is the link between looking to the uplifted Christ and right behavior to be found in John's Gospel? It will be the argument of the next and final Chapter that the typological connection between Jesus Christ and the serpent on the pole, at least for present-day readers of the Fourth Gospel, does indeed address the connection between faith in Christ and the consequences of disobedience. In the present circumstances, right relationship with God and one another comes about when one faces, in the cross of Christ, both the God who loves humanity and the consequences of humanity's refusal to trust God. This face to face acknowledgement of humanity's failing allows for restorative dialogue as will be discussed in the next and final chapter.

Chapter 5

Atonement and Justice in the Gospel of John and Public Theology

Introduction

This last chapter aims at accomplishing three things. The first will be to summarize the thinking in the previous four chapters and review what has been discovered there about the typology first expressed in John 3:14. The second will be to discuss what has been discovered here that may contribute to the current discussion of atonement theology in the North American context in which this author is located. This author believes that a theory of "restorative atonement" presents a scripturally sound alternative to the penal substitutionary atonement theory that currently undergirds most of society's thinking about God. The final objective will be to revisit the discussion of the process of translation attempted here – from narrative to theology – to evaluate the purpose and possibility of Scriptural Theology.

The Typology of John 3:14

The work conducted in Chapters 2 through 4 has uncovered a number of things. 1) The typology first expressed in John 3:14 most likely directly correlates Jesus and the serpent rather than some broader metaphor. Both the grammar of the Greek and the work of later interpreters bears this out. 2) This typology is central to the structure of John's Gospel, occurring three times in significant places and intertwined with many of the important themes throughout the Gospel. 3) It is very likely that serpents were viewed negatively by John. The portrayal of the serpents/serpent in Numbers 21 is negative as they bring death, albeit a death that leads to repentance, to the Israelites. Many interpreters, both "Jewish" and "Christian," link these serpents to the serpent in Genesis 3. The serpent, who caused Eve to doubt God and thus brought death to the first humans is also viewed negatively by these interpreters. This being the case, the comparison between Jesus and the serpent is ironic, leaving room for tension, questions, and misunderstanding. It displays the irony that God uses the rejection of the Incarnate One to save the world and glorify God's self.[380] 4) The 'lifting up' of Jesus just as the serpent was "lifted up" also tells the reader that one sees the glory and presence of God in the cross, resurrection and ascension. It is Jesus' hour to be glorified and God is glorified in him. 5) The typology contributes to the theme of Israel in the Wilderness that is at the core of John's witness to Jesus. In John, this theme speaks of the journey from slavery to freedom for all of God's people then, out of Egypt to life in the land of promise, now, out of slavery to sin and death into eternal life in Christ.

Ultimately what John says through the figure of Jesus as the serpent is that facing the rejected and crucified one and thus facing up to one's rejection of God, allows the birth from above that brings about authentic faith and thus eternal life. This is true because in Christ, God becomes an offended human victim, no longer far off, but one who can meet human offenders face to face, calling them to account. This Jesus, as the only human who was entirely faithful to God, is confirmed as the Incarnate One by his resurrection and ascension. Thus he also makes possible true forgiveness, reconciliation and restoration of broken relationships.

---

380 This irony is stunningly displayed in a brilliant piece of Scriptural theology conducted by Karl Barth in his *Church Dogmatics Volume II, Part 2,* Chapter VII, 35. 4, "The Determination of the Rejected." (Karl Barth, *Church Dogmatics*, Volume II, Part 2 (Edinburgh: T&T Clark, 1957), 456-506.

Restorative vs Retributive or Rehabilitative Atonement

In Chapter 1 of this work it was discussed that Timothy Gorringe agrees with the image of atonement as restorative justice, though he arrives at his conclusions from a constructive theology rather than a strictly scriptural approach. Using the lens of restorative justice to examine the Gospel of John, particularly the 'lifting up' of Jesus as the serpent has opened up new possibilities for seeing the Christ event as restorative rather than retributive.

The work of Adonis Vidu offers a counter example to this work. Vidu, also working from a constructive theology perspective, examines the "ongoing conversation with the history of thinking about justice and the law" but he does so in broad agreement with a penal substitutionary model.[381] For Vidu, atonement theology presents a doctrine of God. Disagreements about the nature of what happened on the cross are disagreements about the nature of God.[382] Vidu begins his exploration with the theological construction that God is simple and 'is' God's attributes. "God is present in [God's] actions in a different way than we are present in ours."[383] What is definitive in the debates about atonement, for Vidu, is the idea of divine simplicity; that God's actions spring uniquely from God's nature.[384] Vidu seeks to shore up the theology of a simple God, one who is identical with all of God's attributes. This God as the origin of all attributes, is entirely independent and free, is in complete control even when acting through human proxies, and never changes. Vidu insists that "the language of Scripture itself has to be understood in the light of the absolute uniqueness of God."[385]

For Vidu the crucifixion is both a crime and the will of God; this is possible because of the different planes of agency between humans and God. Vidu thinks that those who want to deconstruct law deprive themselves of the means of doing justice. For him the

381 Adonis Vidu, *Atonement, Law, and Justice: The Cross in Historical and Cultural Contexts* (Grand Rapids: Baker, 2104) Kindle Electronic Edition: Location 95.

382 Vidu, *Atonement, Law, and Justice*, Location 143.

383 Vidu, *Atonement, Law, and Justice*, Location 152.

384 Vidu, *Atonement, Law, and Justice*, 240.

385 Vidu, *Atonement, Law, and Justice*, 246.

forms of love and justice are inherently exclusionary on a human level, but through the doctrine of simplicity God's love and justice are at least partially visible as one and the same.[386]

Vidu's work demonstrates clearly that the lens ones uses to read scripture controls what one finds there. This is the great challenge of scriptural theology and of dialogue between readers of scripture.

The work of Gorringe and Vidu demonstrates that it is legitimate to consider atonement theory and theories of law and justice to be in dialogue with one another, as they have been demonstrably throughout human history. Their two separate writings show how scripture and context, up to this time, have resulted in basically two strands of understanding in atonement theology and criminal justice. The first, descended from Anselm is retributive. This strand yields an atonement theory that says sin cannot be forgiven and washed away without punishment, but that it can be punished by proxy, God can take the punishment so the sinner can go free. The criminal justice system that is intertwined with this theology accepts that the appropriate reaction to crime is punishment. When the punishment is complete, the offender has paid his debt to society and can go free. The second strand, following Abelard, can be termed rehabilitative. In this way of thinking, Jesus' death on the cross provides an instruction in love or reveals the human mechanisms of scapegoating in a way that allows humanity to change. In the criminal justice system this meant in the past a change from execution to prison and efforts to reeducate offenders and return them to society.

Beyond this general agreement to the witness of history, Gorringe and Vidu part company. Gorringe, Gilliss, and this author find that neither retributive or rehabilitative justice work in practice nor are either of the atonement theories that support them completely satisfying. Retributive justice drives the offender farther away from society and fails to reduce the injury to the victim. Violence appears to breed violence and repeat offending is a significant problem. Rehabilitative justice has also often proven ineffective and is prone to problems of overstepping the rights of offenders and resulting in abuse. Between the two historic strands of retribution and

386 Vidu, *Atonement, Law, and Justice*, 271.

rehabilitation stands restorative justice, which perhaps can address the weaknesses of each. With restorative justice both the victims' and offenders' needs are addressed, along with the needs of the community that created them. The consequences of the offense are not ignored, rather they are addressed by mediated dialogue that can address the harm along with what proceeded and follows it. The actions of the offender cannot be deflected, thus seeming to turning the offender into a victim. The victim can express the harm and ask for appropriate restitution. The community is called upon to address both the circumstances that led to the crime and ways to heal in the aftermath.

The reading of John's Gospel provided above can contribute to the dialogue concerning criminal justice in today's western society. It provides a opening and invitation to wonder and rethink how God deals with the problem of human disobedience and rejection of God and humanity's horrendous mistreatment of one another. John's vision is that in Jesus' incarnation and crucifixion, God enters into God's creation and becomes the victim of humanities self-interested rejection of God. But Jesus' resurrection and ascension demonstrate God's power to overcome all of humanity's failings. Death and rejection are not the end; life with and in God is. Jesus gives the Holy Spirit's reconciling powers to the disciples and sends them back out into God's beloved cosmos.

The events and lives described in Scripture have a certain brutality to modern readers, particularly in America and Western Europe. This is partly because the events of the history recounted are brutal, but also because many white people living in the western context often have the privilege of shielding themselves from the brutality that is still operating in this world, much of it institutionalized in racism, classism, and particularly, perhaps, in the criminal justice system. The aspect of brutality in the scriptural stories is understood by many to include an aspect of retributive punishment. But if resurrection and God's rule are the future, as they are for John (as demonstrated above by his continual backward looks), then everything that was lost in violence and brutality will be drawn up into God, restored to life. What then is left to return creation to health but reconciliation?

Scriptural Theology Revisited

Scriptural theology is a complicated task, and, perhaps, a hopeless one. After all, the Gospel writers chose narrative as the best way to express what they had to say about Jesus, as did the writers of the Old Testament, who often selected narrative as the genre of choice. The brief reference to the serpent that Moses made, evokes multiple layers of meaning and resists one firm interpretation, even when the context in John's Gospel and that of Numbers 21 are taken seriously. One of the take-aways of the exercise performed in this work is that a sense of certainty must be banished. The unknowns are many and difficult. What was the form of the Numbers story that the author of John knew? Was John aware of Philo, Pseudo-Solomon, Barnabas or any form of Targum? Did John see snakes as positive, in keeping with his Hellenistic context; or as negative, which seems to be the attitude in the Old Testament and Rabbinic literature? None of these questions can be answered with certainty. A scriptural theologian makes decisions based on careful scholarship, listening to the Holy Spirit. Such a theologian also will, hopefully, be open to listening to the opinions of others and value their perspectives. Paying attention to the interpretive practices of ancient interpreters also requires a certain openness and willingness to hold historical questions gently; to step into the greater story of scripture with a willingness to see, particularly, type and antitype in a wholistic way. This can make the process a joyous and creative one. One can listen to scripture, taking seriously its context then and now, taking seriously its interconnections and literary features. One can enter into its story, attempt to see the world through its eyes, and bring one's own reality into that story in ways that can shape one's engagement with the surrounding world. The theology expressed through this listening process may be very different from theologies developed in other times and places. It will be a dialectical theology, one that is in conversation with other theologies. It will be a theology that seeks to move the conversation in ways that build up the church and transform society's presuppositions and activities in life giving ways.

Thus one's atonement theology is shaped, not only by one's lenses, but also by how one encounters scripture through those lenses: if scripture is read propositionally, a propositional atonement theology will be discovered. If scripture is read as experiential story, one's atonement theology may be shaped very differently.

The conversation above has demonstrated that one's starting point very much determines one's end point. It also points out a fundamental difference in how scripture can be read. This author reads seeking to find what was most likely the intent of the author of the Fourth Gospel, an encounter with Jesus and in him the God who sent him. Vidu's image of reading scripture (though that is not the focus of his work) is one of obtaining facts about God and God's actions. For Vidu, the reading is controlled by theological ideas about God that have been previously determined, presumably from prior readings of Scripture in combination with philosophical and theological thought. In his system there appear to be things that Scripture may say about God that must be explained away, based on the superior knowledge of God obtained from theology. This way of reading works very strongly to protect the status quo. Vidu uses the example of the debate about the doctrine of hell as a place of eternal conscious torment. But he states upfront that what one decides about the existence of an eternal hell cannot change one's understanding of God; God is beyond understanding, so if one decides there is an eternal hell, it must be an expression of God's love combined with God's justice.[387] Vidu, with his starting point of the simple, transcendent, otherness of God, finds this in all his portraits of God in the different time periods. Thus he overestimates the "transcendence" of God in some parts of the scriptures and excludes any possibility of the development of the idea of transcendence there.[388] Vidu seems to attempt to move his doctrine beyond dialogue. Because one starts with the simplicity of God, neither the words of scripture nor human experience can have much to say before this monolith of the simple God.

This returns one with gratitude to the critiques, flawed as they may have been, offered so long ago by Gabler and Wrede. Each new generation needs to allow scripture to speak using all the tools at its

---

387 Vidu, *Atonement, Law, and Justice*, 257.

388 Vidu, *Atonement, Law, and Justice*, 45.

disposal, both historical and literary. Each generation, empowered by the Spirit of the living Christ can feel free enough and faith-full enough to try on new lenses, lenses that allow them to focus on the text itself and hear it anew.

Conclusion

Both Gorringe and Vidu have demonstrated that theories of atonement are in constant dialogue with politics, law, and penal systems and thus strongly influence one another. Different theologies of atonement arise from a contextual reading of scripture in dialogue with the social climate in which it is read and the problems that a society is seeking to overcome. After the patristic era, which tended to shy away from theories of atonement, such theologies have tended to fall into two streams, one retributive (requiring some sort of punishment) and the other rehabilitative (believing that Christ reveals an alternative that can be carried out by humans). Atonement as restorative justice appears to mediate between these two streams, addressing weaknesses in both. "Restorative atonement" takes the consequences of an offense seriously without the violence of punishment. It understands the incarnation and death of Jesus as God entering as victim into the human predicament so that with Christ's resurrection and ascension, God, by the Holy Spirit, can become a participant in granting forgiveness, asking for reparation, and transforming society in ways that promote justice.

One of the very important features of a restorative atonement model that arises both from a literary reading of John's Gospel in the current context, but also from critical examinations of atonement theology and the current justice system, is that everyone is important to the process of finding justice once an infraction, whether it be crime or sin, has occurred. Offender and offended, God and the community, gather face-to-face to express their hurts, to ask for and receive forgiveness, to determine what reparations are possible, and decide how their community can be transformed. These are all activities that can happen within the family of God and can be modeled by the church.

Public theologians can enter this dialogue by advocating for a place in the legal process for both victim, offender, and community;

creating a safe space for dialogue. They can articulate that the God of creation is also the God of restoration. They can express to the world that 'God so loved' that God descended into it and became the victim of all of its violence and rejection so that God could not only forgive, but also draw all of creation up into God's self through Jesus' resurrection and ascension, thus reconciling the world in God.

Bibliography

Alison, James. *Raising Abel: The Recovery of the Eschatological Imagination*. New York: Crossroad Publishing, 1996.

Alison, James. *On Being Liked*. New York: Crossroad Publishing, 2004.

Agourides, Savas. "Structure and Theology in the Gospel of John," *Greek Orthodox Theological Review* 47/1-4 (Spring-Winter 2002): 111-137.

Anderson, Paul N. *The Riddles of the Fourth Gospel: An Introduction to John*. Minneapolis: Fortress Press, 2011.

Ansell, Nicholas John. "The Call of Wisdom, The Voice of the Serpent: A Canonical Approach to the Tree of Knowlege," *Christian Scholars Review* 31 1 (2001): 31-57.

Aster, Shawn Zelig. "'Bread of the Dungheap': Light on Num. 21:5 from the Tell Fekherye Inscription," *Vestus Testamentum* 61 (2011): 341-358.

Barker, Margaret. *The Gate of Heaven: The History and Symbolism of the Temple of Jerusalem*. London: SPCK, 1991.

Barth, Karl. *Church Dogmatics, Volume II, Part 2*. Edinburgh: T&T Clark, 1957.

Barton, Stephen C. "Johannine Dualism and Contemporary Pluralism," in *The Gospel of John and Christian Theology*, ed. Richard Bauckham and Carl Mosser. Grand Rapids: Eerdmans, 2008. Kindle Electronic Edition.

Bauckham, Richard. "Messianism According to the Gospel of John" in *Challenging Perspectives on the Gospel of John*, ed. John Lierman, 34-67. Tübingen: Mohr Siebeck, 2006.

Bauckham, Richard. "The Holiness of Jesus and his disciples in the Gospel of John" in *Holiness and Ecclesiology in the New Testament*, ed. Kent E. Brower and Andy Johnson, 95-113. Cambridge: William B. Eerdmans, 2007.

Bauckham, Richard. *Jesus and the Eyewitnesses*. Cambridge: William B. Eerdmans, 2006.

ben Meir, Samuel. *Rashbam's Commentary on Leviticus and Numbers: An Annotated Translation*. Translated and Edited by Martin I. Lockshin. Providence, RI: Brown Judaic Studies, 2001.

Berner, Christoph. "Die Eherne Schlange: Zum literaischen Ursprang eines mosaischen Artfakts," ZAW 124 (2012): 341-355.

Beyerle, Stefan. "Das Eherne Schange: Num 21, 4-9: Synchron und diachron gelesen," *Zeitschrift fur die alttestamentliche Wissenschaft* 111/1 (1999): 23-44.

Bingham, D. Jeffrey. "Christianizing the Divine Aseity: Irenaeus Reads John," in *The Gospel of John and Christian Theology*, ed. Richard Bauckham and Carl Mosser. Grand Rapids: Eerdmans, 2008. Kindle Electronic Edition.

Bird, Micheal F. *Four Views on the Apostle Paul.* Grand Rapids: Zondervan, 2012.

Borgen, Peder. *Philo, John and Paul: New Perspectives on Judaism and Early Christianity.* Atlanta: Scholars Press, 1987.

Borgen, Peder. "God's Agent in the Fourth Gospel" in *Logos was the True Light and Other Essays on the Gospel of John*, 121-132. Trondheim: Tapir, 1983.

Boyarin, Daniel. *A Radical Jew: Paul and the Politics of Identity.* Berkeley: University of California Press, 1994.

Boyarin, Daniel. "Logos, A Jewish Word: John's Prologue as Midrash" in *The Jewish Annotated New Testament*, ed. Amy-Jill Levine and Marc Zvi Brettler. New York: Oxford University Press, 2011. Kindle Electronic Edition.

Boyarin, Daniel, "The Gospel of the *Memra*: Jewish Binitarianism and the Prologue to John," *Harvard Theological Review* 94/3 (2001): 243-284.

Boyarin, Daniel. *The Jewish Gospels: The Story of the Jewish Christ.* New York: The New Press, 2012.

Brant Jo-Ann. *Dialogue and Drama: Elements of Greek Tragedy in the Fourth Gospel.* Peabody: Hendrickson, 2004.

Brettler, Marc Zvi. "The New Testament Between the Hebrew Bible (Tanakh) and the Rabbinic Literature" in *The Jewish Annotated New Testament*, ed. Amy-Jill Levine and Marc Zvi Brettler. New York: Oxford University Press, 2011. Kindle Electronic Edition.

Brown, Jeannine K. "Creation's Renewal in the Gospel of John," *The Catholic Biblical Quarterly* 72 (2010): 275-290.

Brown, Raymond. *The Gospel According to John (i-xii)*. New York: Doubleday, 1966.

Brown, Raymond. *The Gospel According to John (xiii-xxi)*. New York: Doubleday, 1970.

Brunson, Andrew C. *Psalm 118 in the Gospel of John*. Tübingen: Mohr Siebeck, 2003.

Bluesman, Rudolf. *The Gospel of John: A Commentary*. Philadelphia: Westminster, 1971.

Bultmann, Rudolf. *The Gospel of John: A Commentary.* Philadelphia: Westminster, 1971.

Caird, G. B. "The Glory of God in the Fourth Gospel: An Exercise in Biblical Semantics," *New Testament Studies* 15, (1969): 265-277.

Carasik, Michael. *The Commentators' Bible: the JPS Miqra'ot Gedolot.* Philadelphia: The Jewish Publication Society, 2005.

Carson, D. A., *The Gospel According to John*. Grand Rapids: W. B. Eerdmans, 1991.

Charlesworth, James H. *The Good and Evil Serpent: How a Universal Symbol Became Christianized.* New Haven: Yale University Press, 2012.

Childs, Brevard S. *Biblical Theology of the Old and New Testaments: Theological Reflections on the Christian Bible.* Minneapolis: Fortress Press, 1992. Kindle Electronic Edition.

Childs, Brevard. *The Church's Guide for Reading Paul: The Canonical Shaping of the Pauline Corpus.* Grand Rapids: Eerdmans, 2008.

Cheon, Samuel. *The Exodus Story in the Wisdom of Solomon: A Study in Biblical Interpretation.* Sheffield: Sheffield Academic Press, 1997.

The Christian Apologists; A Digital Version of Selected Works from Jacques-Paul Migne, Patrologiae Graecae (Paris, 1866). Volume 6. Morphologically tagged by Rex A. Koivisto, Multnomah University, Portland, Oregon USA. Copyright © 2009 OakTree Software, Inc. Version 1.8

Clements, Ronald E. "The Book of Deuteronomy" in *The New Interpreter's Bible in Twelve Volumes*, ed. Leander E. Keck, Volume II. Nashville: Abingdon Press, 1998.

Cohen, Shaye J. D. *From the Maccabees to the Mishnah.* Louisville: John Knox, 2006.

Cohn, Robert L. *2 Kings.* Collegeville: The Liturgical Press, 2000.

Collins, John J. *Encounters with Biblical Theology.* Minneapolis: Augsburg Fortress, 2005.

Coloe, Mary L. "Temple Imagery in John," *Interpretation* 63/4 (October 2009): 368-381.

Cook, Edward M. "The Interpretation of the Hebrew Bible in the Targums," in *A Companion to Biblical Interpretation in Early Judaism*, ed. Matthias Henze. Grand Rapids: Eerdmans, 2012.

Cotter, Wendy. "Miracle Stories: The God Asclepius, the Pythagorean Philosophers, and the Roman Rulers," in *The Historical Jesus in Context.* Amy-Jill Levine, Dale C. Allison Jr. and John Dominic Crossan, eds. Princeton: Princeton University Press, 2006.

Countryman, L. William. *The Mystical Way in the Fourth Gospel: Crossing Over into God.* Harrisburg: Trinity, 1994.

Culpepper, R. Alan. *Anatomy of the Fourth Gospel: A Study in Literary Design.* Philadelphia: Fortress, 1983.

Culpepper, R. Alan. *The Gospel and Letters of John*. Nashville: Abingdon, 1998.

Culpepper, R. Alan. "The Quest for the Church in the Gospel of John," *Interpretation* 63/4 (October 2009): 342-354.

Danby, Herbert. *The Mishnah*. Oxford: Clarendon Press, 1933.

Danielou, Jean. *The Theology of Jewish Christianity*. Philadelphia: Westminster Press, 1964.

Davis, Ellen F. "Teaching the Bible Confessionally in the Church," in *The Art of Reading Scripture*, ed. Ellen F. Davis and Richard B. Hays, 9-26. Grand Rapids: Eerdmans, 2003.

Dodd, C. H. *The Interpretation of the Fourth Gospel*. Cambridge: University Press, 1953.

Dozeman, Thomas B. "The Book of Numbers: Introduction, Commentary and Reflections" in *The New Interpreter's Bible, A Commentary in Twelve Volumes*, Volume II. Nashville: Abingdon, 1998.

Dunn, James D. G. *The Theology of Paul the Apostle*. Grand Rapids: Eerdmans, 1998.

Enns, Peter. "Wisdom of Solomon and Biblical Interpretation in the Second Temple Period," in *The Way of Wisdom: Essays in Honor of Bruce K. Waltke*, ed. J. I. Packer and Sven K. Soderlund, 212-225. Grand Rapids: Zondervan, 2000.

Elowsky, Joel C. ed. *Ancient Christian Commentary on Scripture: New Testament IVA: John 1-10*. Downers Grove: InterVarsity, 2006.

"The Epistle of Barnabas, Chapter XII," in *The Anti-Nicene Fathers Volume I – Enhanced Version*. ed. Philip Schaff. Early Church Fathers, Jun 8, 2009, Kindle Electronic Edition.

The Epistle of Barnabas, Apostolic Fathers, 3rd ed: Greek Texts and English Translations edited and translated by Michael W. Holmes, Grand Rapids: Baker Books, 1992, 1999, 2007, Accordance 9 Bible Software Version 9.6.6, Oak Tree Software, 2012.

Eskenazi, Tamara Cohn, and Andrea L. Weiss. *The Torah: A Women's Commentary*. New York: Women of Reform Judaism, Federation of Temple Sisterhood, 2008.

Evangelical Lutheran Church in America. *A Social Statement on: The Death Penalty*, 1991. http://download.elca.org/ELCA%20Resource%20Repository/Death_PenaltySS.pdf?_ga=1.42980781.983052087.1410786767 (Accessed on February 14, 2017).

Evans, Craig A. *Ancient Texts for New Testament Studies: A Guide to the Background Literature.* Peabody: Hendrickson, 2005.

Fee, Gordon D. *The First Epistle to the Corinthians.* Grand Rapids: Eerdmans, 1987.

Fishbane, Michael, *Biblical Interpretation in Ancient Israel.* New York: Oxford, 1985.

Flesher, Paul V. M. and Bruce Chilton. *The Targums: A Critical Introduction.* Waco: Baylor University Press, 2011.

Forde, Gerhard O. *On Being a Theologian of the Cross, Reflections on Luther's Heidelberg Disputation, 1518.* Grand Rapids: Eerdmans, 1997, Kindle Edition.

Forrester, Duncan B., William Storrar, and Andrew Morton. *Public theology for the 21st Century: Essays in Honour of Duncan B. Forrester.* London: T&T Clark, 2004.

Fowl, Stephen E. *Theological Interpretation of Scripture.* Eugene, Oregon: Cascade Books, 2009, Kindle Electronic Edition.

Frei, Hans W. *The Eclipse of the Biblical Narrative: A Study in Eighteenth and Nineteenth Century Hermeneutics.* New Haven: Yale University Press, 1974.

Fretheim, Terence E. *First and Second Kings.* Louisville: Westminster John Knox, 1999.

Fretheim, Terence E. "The Book of Genesis: Introduction, Commentary, and Reflections" in *The New Interpreter's Bible in Twelve Volumes*, ed. Leander E. Keck, Volume I. Nashville: Abingdon Press, 1995.

Frevel, Christian. "Understanding the Pentateuch by Structuring the Desert: Numbers 21 as a Compositional Joint," in *The Land of Israel in Bible, History, and Theology: Studies in Honor of Ed Noort.* ed. Jacques van Ruiten and J. Cornelis de Vos, 111-135. Leiden: Brill, 2009.

Friere, Paolo. *Pedagogy of the Oppressed*, New York: Continuum, 1994.

Gabler, J. P. "On the Proper Distinction Between Biblical and Dogmatic Theology and the Specifie Objectives of Each" tr. John Sandys-Wunsch and Laurence Eldredge in Johann P. Gabler on Biblical Theology, http://jimhamilton.info/wp-content/uploads/2012/05/Gabler-ProperDistinction-BiblicalTheology.pdf, 495 (Accessed on July 2015).

Gaiser, Frederick J. *Healing in the Bible*. Grand Rapids: Baker Academic, 2010.

Gieschen, Charles A. "The Death of Jesus in the Gospel of John: Atonement for Sin?" *Concordia Theological Quarterly* 72 (2008): 243-261.

Gilliss, Martha Schull, "Resurrecting the Atonement" in *Feminist and Womanist Essays in Reformed Dogmatics*, ed. Amy Plantinga Pauw and Serene Jones. 125-138. Louisville: Westminster John Knox, 2006.

Glickman, Andrew T. *The Wisdom of Solomon 10: a Jewish Hellenistic Reinterpretation of Early Israelite History through Sapiential Lenses*. Boston: de Gruyter, 2011.

Goppelt, Leonhard. *Typos: The Typological Interpretation of the Old Testament in the New*. Grand Rapids: Eerdmans, 1982.

Gorringe, Timothy. *God's Just Vengeance*. Cambridge: Cambridge University Press, 1996.

Grabbe, Lester L. *Wisdom of Solomon*. Sheffield: Sheffield Academic Press, 1997.

Gunn, David M. "Narrative Criticism," in *To Each Its Own Meaning: Biblical Criticisms and their Applications*, ed. Steven L. McKenzie and Stephen R. Haynes, 201-229. Louisville: Westminster John Knox, 1999.

Hall, Douglas John, *The Cross in Our Context, Jesus and the Suffering World*, Minneapolis: Augsburg Fortress, 2003.

Harrisville, Roy A., *Fracture*, Grand Rapids: Eerdmans, 2006.

Harrill, J. Albert. "Cannibalistic Language in the Fourth Gospel and Greco-Roman Polemics of Factionalism (John 6:52-66)," *Journal of Biblical Literature* 127/1(2008): 133-158.

Hart, Gerald D. *Asclepius, the God of Medicine.* Lake Forest: Royal Society of Medicine Press 2000.

Hays, Richard B. "Can Narrative Criticism Recover the Theological Unity of Scripture?" *Journal of Theological Interpretation* 2.2 (2008): 193-211.

Hays, Richard B. "Can the Gospels Teach Us How to Read the Old Testament?" *Pro Ecclesia* Volume XI, Number 4 (2002): 402-418.

Hays, Richard B. *Echoes of Scripture in the Gospels.* Waco: Baylor University Press, 2016.

Hays, Richard B. *Echoes of Scripture in the Letters of Paul.* New Haven: Yale University Press), 1989.

Hays, Richard B. *The Conversion of the Imagination: Paul as Interpreter of Israel's Scripture* (Grand Rapids: Eerdmans), 2005.

Hefling, Charles. "'Why the Cross?' God's at-one-ment with humanity." *Christian Century* March 20 (2013): 24-27.

Heim, S. Mark, *Saved from Sacrifice, A Theology of the Cross.* Grand Rapids: Eerdmans, 2006.

Hengel, Martin, "The Prologue of the Gospel of John as the Gateway to Christological Truth," in *The Gospel of John and Christian Theology*, ed. Richard Bauckham and Carl Mosser. Cambridge: Eerdmans, 2008. Kindle Electronic Edition.

Hoskins, Paul M. "Deliverance from Death by the True Passover Lamb: A Significant Aspect of the Fulfillment of the Passover in the Gospel of John," *Journal of the Evangelical Theological Society* 52/2 (June 2009): 285-299.

Jobes, Karen H. and Moisés Silva. *Invitation to the Septuagint*, 2nd Ed. Grand Rapids: Baker, 2015.

Joines, Karen Randolph, "The Serpent in Gen 3" *Zeitschrift für die alttestamentliche Wissenschaft*, 87 1 (1975): 1-11.

Joines, Karen Randolph, "Winged Serpents in Isaiah's Inaugural Vision" *Journal of Biblical Literature*, 410-415.

Josephus, *Josephus, The Complete Works*, trans. William Whiston (BN Publishing, 2010), Kindle Electronic Edition.

Justin Martyr, "The First Apology," in *The Anti-Nicene Fathers Volume I – Enhanced Version,* ed. Philip Schaff. Early Church Fathers, June 8, 2009, Kindle Electronic Edition.

Justin Martyr, "Dialogue with Trypho," in *The Anti-Nicene Fathers Volume I – Enhanced Version,* ed. Philip Schaff. Early Church Fathers, Jun 8, 2009, Kindle Electronic Edition.

Käsemann, Ernst. *The Testament of Jesus: A Study of the Gospel of John in the Light of Chapter 17,* London, SCM, 1968.

Koenen, Klaus. "Eherne Schlange und goldenes Kalb: Ein Vergleich der Überlieferungen," *Zeitschrift fur die alttestamentliche Wissenschaft* 111/3 (1999): 353-372.

Koester, Craig R. "Jesus the Way, the Cross, and the World according to the Gospel of John," *Word & World* XXI/4 (Fall 2001): 360-369.

Koester, Craig R. *Symbolism in the Fourth Gospel: Meaning, Mystery, Community*, 2nd ed. Minneapolis: Fortress Press, 2003.

Koester, Craig R. *The Word of Life: A Theology of John's Gospel.* Grand Rapids: Eerdmans, 2008.

Kolarcik, Michael. "Sapiental Values and Apocalyptic Imagery in the Wisdom of Solomon," in *Studies in the Book of Wisdom*, ed. Geza G. Xeravits and Jozsef Zsengeller, 23-36. Leiden: Brill, 2010.

Köstenberger, Andreas J. *John*. Grand Rapids: Baker, 2004.

Köstenberger, Andreas, J, "John" in *Commentary on the New Testament Use of the Old Testament,* ed. G. K. Beale and D. A. Carson, 415-512. Nottingham: Apollos, 2007.

Kugel, James L. *Traditions of the Bible: A Guide to the Bible as it was at the Start of the Common Era*. Cambridge: Harvard University Press, 1997-1998.

Kysar, Robert, *Voyages with John, Charting the Fourth Gospel.* Waco: Baylor University Press, 2005.

Larsson, Tord. "Glory of Persecution: The God of the Gospel of John in the History of Interpretation," in *The Gospel of John and*

Christian Theology, ed. Richard Bauckham and Carl Mosser. Grand Rapids: Eerdmans, 2008. Kindle Electronic Edition.

Latz, Andrew Brower. "A Short Note toward a Theology of Abiding in John's Gospel," *Journal of Theological Interpretation* 4/2 (2010): 161-168.

Lee, Dorothy, *Flesh and Glory: Symbolism. Gender and Theology in the Gospel of John.* New York: Crossroad, 2002.

Lee, Won. Punishment and Forgiveness in Israel's Migratory Campaign. Grand Rapids: Eerdmans, 2003.

Lienhard S. J., Joseph T. ed. *Ancient Christian Commentary on Scripture: Old Testament III: Exodus, Leviticus, Numbers, Deuteronomy.* Downers Grove: InterVarsity Press, 2001.

Leveen, Adraine. " Reading the Seams," *JSOT* 29.3 (2005): 259-287.

Levine, Amy-Jill and Marc Zvi Brettler eds. *The Jewish Annotated New Testament*. New York: Oxford University Press, 2011.

Levine, Baruch A. *Numbers 21-36: A New Translation with Introduction and Commentary.* New York: Doubleday, 2000.

Lewis, Alan, E. *Between Cross and Resurrection, A Theology of Holy Saturday*. Grand Rapids: Eerdmans, 2001.

Lewis, Karoline M. *Fortress Preaching Commentaries: John.* Minneapolis: Fortress, 2014.

Lincoln, Andrew, T. *The Gospel According to Saint John*. London: Continuum, 2005.

Lincoln, Andrew T. "The Beloved Disciple as Eyewitness and the Fourth Gospel as Witness," *Journal for the Study of the New Testament* 24: 85, London: Sage (2002): 3-26.

Lincoln, Andrew T., *Truth on Trial: The Lawsuit Motif in John's Gospel.* Peabody MA: Hendrickson, 2000.

Lieu, Judith. "Anti-Judaism, the Jews, and the Worlds of the Fourth Gospel," in *The Gospel of John and Christian Theology*, ed. Richard Bauckham and Carl Mosser. Grand Rapids: Eerdmans, 2008. Kindle Electronic Edition.

Lose, David J. *Making Sense of the Cross*. Minneapolis: Augsburg Fortress, 2011.

Lozada, Francisco, Jr. *A Literary Reading of John 5: Text as Construction*, Studies in Biblical Literature Vol. 20. New York: Peter Lang, 2000.

Lowry, S. "The Confutation of Judaism in the Epistle of Barnabas," in *Studies in Early Christianity: A Collection of Scholarly Essays*, ed. Everett Ferguson. New York: Garland, 1993.

Lundbom, Jack R. *Deuteronomy: A Commentary*. Grand Rapids: Eerdmans, 2013.

Luther, Martin. *Luther's Works, Volume 34: Career of the Reformer IV.* ed Lewis William Spitz, Minneapolis: Augsburg, 1960.

Luther, Martin. "'Concerning the Letter and the Spirit' from Answer to the Hyperchristian, Hyperspiritual, and Hyperlearned Book by Goat Emser in Leipzig" in *Martin Luther's Basic Theological Writings*, ed. Timothy Lull, 74-103. Minneapolis: Augsburg Fortress, 1989.

Luther, Martin. *Luther's Church Postil Volume II: Gospels, Epiphany, Lent and Easter Sermons.* Translated by John Nicholas Lenker. Minneapolis: Lutherans in All Lands Co, 1906.

Luther, Martin. *Luther's Church Postil: Gospels, Pentecost or Missionary Sermons, Volume III*, Translated by John Nicholas Lenker. Minneapolis: Lutherans in All Lands, 1907.

Luther, Martin. *Luther's Works*: *Devotional Writings I, Volume 42*. St. Louis: Concordia 1969.

Luther, Martin. *Luther's Works*: *Lectures on Galatians 1535 Chapters 1-4*, Volume 26. St. Louis: Concordia 1963.

Luther, Martin. *Luther's Works*: *Sermons on the Gospel of John, Chapters 1-4, Volume 22*. Edited by Jaroslav Pelikan. St. Louis: Concordia 1957.

Luther, Martin. *Martin Luther's Complete Church Postil*, trans. ed. John Nicholas Lenker, 1905, http://www.lutherdansk.dk/1%20Web-AM%20-%20Introduction/Kirkepos.htm (Accessed on November 11, 2012).

Luther, Martin. "Prefaces to the Old Testament" in *Luther's Works, Volume 35*. Philadelphia: Muhlenberg Press. 1960.

Luther, Martin. *Sermons of Martin Luther: The House* Postils, *Volume 2*, Translated by Eugene F. A. Klug et al. Grand Rapids: Baker Books, 1996.

Malina, Bruce J. and Richard L. Rohrbaugh. *Social-Science Commentary on the Gospel of John.* Minneapolis: Fortress, 1998.

Marshall, Ronald F. "Our Serpent of Salvation: The Offense of Jesus in John's Gospel," *Word & World* XXI/4 (Fall 2001): 385-392.

Matera, Frank J. "Christ in the Theologies of Paul and John: A Study in the Diverse Unity of New Testament Theology," *Theological Studies* 67 (2006): 237-256.

McNamara, Martin. *Targum and Testament Revisited: Aramaic Paraphrases of the Hebrew Bible: A Light on the New Testament.* Grand Rapids: Eerdmans, 2010.

Meeks, Wayne A., "The Divine Agent and his Counterfeit", in *Aspects of Religious Propaganda in Judaism and Early Christianity*, ed. Elisabeth Schüssler Fiorenza, 45-49. London, University of Notre Dame Press, 1976.

Meeks, Wayne A., *The Prophet-King: Moses Traditions and the Johannine Christology*. Leiden: E. J. Brill, 1967.

Metzger, Bruce G. *A Textual Commentary on the Greek New Testament*, 2nd Ed. Stuttgart: Deutsche Bibelgesellschaft, 2001.

Milgrom, Jacob. *The JPS Torah Commentary: Numbers, The Traditional Hebrew Text with the New JPS Translation*. Philadelphia: The Jewish Publication Society, 1990.

Miller, Patrick D. "The Book of Jeremiah: Introduction, Commentary, and Reflections" in *The New Interpreter's Bible in Twelve Volumes*, ed. Leander E. Keck, Volume VI. Nashville: Abingdon Press, 1995.

Miller, Paul, "'They Saw His Glory and Spoke of Him' The Gospel of John and the Old Testament," in *Hearing the Old Testament in the New Testament*, ed. Stanley E. Porter, 127-151. Cambridge: Eerdmans, 2006.

Moberly, R. W. L. "How Can We Know the Truth: A Study of John 7:14-18," in *The Art of Reading Scripture*, ed. Ellen F. Davis and Richard B. Hays, 239-257. Grand Rapids: Eerdmans, 2003.

Moberly, R. W. L. "Did the Serpent Get it Right?" *The Journal of Theological Studies* 39 1 (1988): 1-27.

Moloney, Francis J. *Belief in the Word: Reading John 1-4*. Minneapolis: Fortress, 1993.

Moloney, Francis J. *Glory Not Dishonor: Reading John 13-21*. Minneapolis: Fortress, 1998.

Moloney, Francis J. *Signs and Shadows Reading John 5-12*. Minneapolis: Fortress, 1996.

Moloney, Francis J. *The Gospel of John*. Collegeville: The Liturgical Press, 1998.

Moloney, Francis J. "The Gospel of John: The 'End' of Scripture," *Interpretation* 63/4 (October 2009): 356-366.

Moltmann, Jürgen, *The Trinity and the Kingdom*. San Francisco: Harper and Row, 1981.

Motyer, Stephen. "Bridging the Gap: How Might the Fourth Gospel Help Us Cope with the Legacy of Christianity's Exclusive Claim over Against Judaism?" in *The Gospel of John and Christian Theology*, ed. Richard Bauckham and Carl Mosser. Grand Rapids: Eerdmans, 2008. Kindle Electronic Edition.

Motyer, Stephen. "The Fourth Gospel and the Salvation of Israel: An Appeal for a New Start," in *Anti-Judaism and the Fourth Gospel*, ed. Reimund Bieringer, Didier. Pollefeyt, and Federique Bandecasteele-Vanneuville, 83-100. Louisville: John Knox, 2001.

Moyise, Steve. *The Old Testament in the New: An Introduction*. New York: Continuum, 2001.

Mussner, Franz, *The Historical Jesus in the Gospel of John*. Freiburg: Herder, 1967.

Myers, Alicia D. and Bruce G. Schuchard. *Abiding Words: The Use of Scripture in the Gospel of John*. Atlantá: SBL Press, 2015.

Neyrey, Jerome H. *The Gospel of John*. New York: Cambridge University Press, 2007.

Neusner, Jacob. *Mekhilta According to Rabbi Ishmael: An Analytical Translation, Volume Two*. Atlanta: Scholars Press, 1988.

Nickelsburg, George W. E. "Philo among Greeks, Jews and Christians," in *Philo und das Neue Testament Wechselseitige Wahrenehmungen*. ed. Roland Deines and Karl-Wilhem Niebuhr. Tübingen: Mohr Siebeck, 2004.

Noll, Mark A. "Common Sense Traditions and American Evangelical Thought." *American Quarterly* 37:2 (1985): 216-238.

O'Day, Gail R. and Susan E. Hylen. *John*. Louisville: Westminster John Knox, 2006.

O'Day, Gail R. *Revelation in the Fourth Gospel.* Philadelphia: Fortress Press, 1986.

O'Day, Gail R. "John" in *The New Interpreter's Bible in Twelve Volumes*, ed. Leander E. Keck, Volume IV, 491-866. Nashville: Abingdon Press, 1995.

O'Keefe, John J. and R. R. Reno, *Sanctified Vision: An Introduction to Early Christian Interpretation of the Bible*. Baltimore: Johns Hopkins, 2005.

Olson, Dennis T. *The Death of the Old and the Birth of the New: The Framework of the Book of Numbers and the Pentateuch,* Brown Judaic Studies 71. Chico, California: Scholars Press, 1985.

Paget, James Carleton. *The Epistle of Barnabas: Outlook and Background.* Tubingen: Mohr Siebeck, 1994.

Painter, John. "Johannine Symbols: A Case Study in Epistemology," *Journal of Theology for Southern Africa* 27(1979): 26-41.

Pamment, Margaret, "The meaning of *doxa* in the Gospel of John", in *Zeitschrift für die Neutestamentliche Wissenschaft und die Kunde der Älteren Kirchen* 74, Berlin: Walter de Gruyter & Co, (1983): 12-16.

Pancaro, Severino, "People of God" in St. John's Gospel", in *New Testament Studies* 16, London: Cambridge University Press, (1970): 114-129.

Pancaro, Severino, *The Law in the Fourth Gospel.* Leiden: E. J. Brill, 1975.

Parsenios, George. *Departure and Consolation: The Johannine Farewell Discourses in Light of Greco-Roman Literature (Supplements to Novum Testamentum).* Leiden: E. J. Brill, 2005.

Parsenios, George. *Rhetoric and Drama in the Johannine Lawsuit Motif.* Tubingen: Mohr Siebeck, 2010.

Phillips, Elaine A. "Serpent Intertexts: Tantalizing Twists in the Tales," *Bulletin for Biblical Research* 10.2 (2000): 233-245.

Philo, "Book 3 Allegorical Interpretation, 2" in *The Works of Philo Judaeus of Alexandria: A contemporary of Jesus, Paul and Josephus.* ed. E. C. Marsh, trans. C. D. Yonge. Common Man's Prospective, Oct. 7, 2010, Kindle Electronic Edition.

Philo, Allegorical Interpretataion II, English Text, *The Works of Philo,* Completed and Unabridged. New Updated Edition. Translated by C. D. Yonge. Copyright © 1993 by Hendrickson Publishers, Inc. Electronic text prepared by Oaktree Software, Inc. Version 1.1.

Philo, Greek Text, *Works of Philo,* The Norwegian Philo Concordance Project, Copyright © 2005 Peder Borgen, Kåre Fuglseth, Roald Skarsten, Updated portions copyright © 2009 OakTree Software, Inc. Version 2.9

Porter, Stanley E. *John, His Gospel, and Jesus: In Pursuit of the Johannine Voice.* Grand Rapids: Eerdmans, 2015.

Rahlfs, Alfred ed. *Septuaginta,* Editio altera by Robert Hanhart, Deutsche Bibelgesellschaft, Stuttgart, 2006, Bernard A. Taylor and Dale M. Wheeler, Kraft/Taylor/Wheeler Septuagint Morphology Database v. 4.7, 2012, Accordance 9 Bible Software Version 9.6.6, Oak Tree Software, 2012.

Reinhartz, Adele. "Judaism in the Gospel of John," *Interpretation* 63/4 (October 2009): 382-393.

Reynolds, Benjamin, E. *The Apocalyptic Son of Man in the Gospel of John.* Tübingen: Mohr Siebeck, 2007.

Romanowsky, John W. "'When the Son of Man is Lifted up': The Redemptive Power of the Crucifixion in the Gospel of John," *Horizons* 32/1 (2005): 100-116.

Sandy-Wunsch, John. *What Have They Done to the Bible? An History of Modern Biblical Interpretation.* Collegeville: Liturgical Press, 2005.

Sampley, J. Paul. "The First Letter to the Corinthians" in *The New Interpreter's Bible in Twelve Volumes*, ed. Leander E. Keck, Volume X, 773-1003. Nashville: Abingdon Press, 2002.

Schipper, Bernd U. "Die Eherne Schlange: Zur Religiongeshichte und Theologie von Num 21, 4-9" ZAW 121 (2009): 369-397.

Schneiders, Sandra M. "The Lamb of God and the Forgiveness of Sin(s) in the Fourth Gospel," *The Catholic Biblical Quarterly* 73 (2011): 1-29.

Schnelle, Udo. *Apostle Paul: His Life and Theology.* trans. M. Eugene Boring, Grand Rapids: Baker Academic, 2005.

Seitz, Christopher R. "The Book of Isaiah 40 - 66: Introduction, Commentary, and Reflections" in *The New Interpreters Bible: A Commentary in Twelve Volumes, Volume VI* (Nashville: Abingdon Press, 1994.

Seow, Choon-Leong. "The First and Second Book of Kings" in *The New Interpreter's Bible in Twelve Volumes*, ed. Leander E. Keck, Volume III. Nashville: Abingdon Press, 1999.

Septuaginta, Alfred Rahlfs, ed. Editio altera by Robert Hanhart, Deutsche Bibelgesellschaft, Stuttgart, 2006, Bernard A. Taylor and Dale M. Wheeler, Kraft/Taylor/Wheeler Septuagint Morphology Database v. 4.7, 2012, Accordance 9 Bible Software Version 9.6.6, Oak Tree Software, 2012.

Septuaginta, Vestus Testamentum Graecum, Auctoritate Academiae Scientiarum Gottingensis editum, Vol. III, 1 Numeri, ed. John William Wevers. Göttingen:Vanderhoeck &Ruprecht, 1982.

Skarsaune, Oskar. *The Proof From Prophecy: A Study in Justin Martyr's Proof-Text Tradition: Text-Type, Provenance, Theological Profile.* Leiden: Brill, 1987.

Smith, D Moody. *John*. Nashville: Abingdon, 1999.

Spiritual Levity. "Baseline Assessment for Visioning Process," Prepared for St. John's Evangelical Church of Mahoning, Mahoning Valley, PA, 2014.

Stackhouse, Max L., Deirdre King Hainsworth, and Scott R. Paeth, eds. *Public Theology for a Global Society: Essays in Honor of Max Stackhouse*. Grand Rapids: Eerdmans, 2010.

Staub, Jacob J. "The Healing Serpent: Recovering Long Lost Jewish Fragments: Parashat Hukkat (Numbers 19.1-22.1)," in *Torah Queeries: Weekly Commentaries on the Hebrew Bible,* ed. Gregg Drinkwater, Joshua Lesser, and David Shneer. New York: New York University Press, 2009, Kindle Electronic Edition.

Sterling, Gregory E. "The Place of Philo of Alexandria in the Study of Christian Origins," in *Philo und das Neue Testament: Wechselseitige Wahrnehmungen.* ed. Roland Deines and Karl-Wilhelm Niebuhr. Tübingen: Mohr Siebeck, 2004.

Steinmetz, David C. "The Superiority of Pre-Critical Exegesis" in The Theological Interpretation of Scripture, ed. Stephen E. Fowl, 26-38. Cambridge MA: Blackwell, 1997.

Storrar, William F., Peter J. Casarella, and Paul Louis Metzger, eds. *A World for All? Global Civil Society in Political Theory and Trinitarian Theology.* Grand Rapids: Eerdmans, 2011.

Sturdy, John. *Numbers.* New York: Cambridge, 1976.

Talbert, Charles H. "The Fourth Gospel's Soteriology between New Birth and Resurrection," *Perspectives in Religious Studies* 37/2 (Summer 2010): 133-145.

Taylor, Mark Lewis. *The Theological and the Political: On the Weight of the World.* Minneapolis: Fortress Press, 2011.

Thiselton, Anthony C. *The First Epistle to the Corinthians: A Commentary on the Greek Text.* Grand Rapids: Eerdmans, 2000.

Thompson, Marianne Meye. "'His Own Received Him Not': Jesus Washes the Feet of His Disciples," in *The Art of Reading Scripture,* ed. Ellen F. Davis and Richard B. Hays, 258-273. Grand Rapids: Eerdmans, 2003.

Treier, Daniel, J. *Introducing Theological Interpretation of Scripture: Recovering a Christian Practice.* Grand Rapids: Baker Academic, 2008, Kindle Electronic Edition.

Trelstad, Marit, ed., *Cross Examinations, Readings on the Meaning of the Cross Today.* Minneapolis: Augsburg Fortress, 2006, Kindle Electronic Edition.

Turnage, Marc. "Is it the Serpent that Heals?" in *Israel in the Wilderness: Interpretations of the Biblical Narratives in Jewish and*

Christian Traditions, ed. Kenneth E. Pomykala, 71-88. Leiden: Brill, 2008.

Van Ness, Daniel W. and Karen Heetderks Strong, *Restoring Justice: An Introduction to Restorative Justice.* New York: Routledge, 2015.

Vidu, Adonis, *Atonement, Law and Justice: The Cross in Historical and Cultural Contexts*, Grand Rapids: Baker Academic, 2014, Kindle Electronic Edition.

Volf, Miroslav. "Johannine Dualism and Contemporary Pluralism," in *The Gospel of John and Christian Theology*, ed. Richard Bauckham and Carl Mosser. Grand Rapids: Eerdmans, 2008. Kindle Electronic Edition.

von Loewenich, Walther. *Luther's Theology of the Cross.* Translated by Herbert J. A. Boumen. Minneapolis: Augsburg, 1976.

Wallace, Daniel B. *Greek Grammer Beyond the Basics: An Exegetical Syntax of the New Testament.* Grand Rapids: Zondervan, 1996.

Waweru, Humphrey Mwangi. "Jesus and Ordinary Women in the Gospel of John: An African Perspective," *Swedish Missiological Themes*, 96/2 (2008): 139-159.

Webster, Jane S. *Ingesting Jesus: Eating and Drinking in the Gospel of John.* Atlanta: Society of Biblical Literature, 2003.

Wenin, Andre, "Le serpent de Nb 21,4-9 et de Gn 3,1. Intertextualité et élaboration du sens" in *The Books of Leviticus and Numbers,* ed. Thomas Römer, (Leuven: Peeters, 2008): 545-554.

Wevers, John William, ed., *Septuaginta, Vestus Testamentum Graecum, Auctoritate Academiae Scientiarum Gottingensis editum, Vol. III, 1 Numeri* (Göttingen:Vanderhoeck &Ruprecht, 1982).

Williams, Rowan. "Anglican Approaches to St. John's Gospel," in *The Gospel of John and Christian Theology*, ed. Richard Bauckham and Carl Mosser. Grand Rapids: Eerdmans, 2008. Kindle Electronic Edition.

Witherington III, Ben, *Jesus the Sage.* Minneapolis: Augsburg Fortress, 1994.

Witherington III, Ben, *Jesus the Seer.* Minneapolis: Augsburg Fortress, 1999.

Wrede, William. "The Task and Methods of "New Testament Theology" in *The Nature of New Testament Theology: The Contribution of William Wrede and Adolf Schatter*. tr. Robert Morgan. London: SCM Press, 1973.

Yarchin, William, *History of Biblical Interpretation: A Reader*. Peabody: Hendrickson, 2004.

Zetterholm, Magnus. *Approaches to Paul: A Students Guide to Recent Scholarship*. Minneapolis: Fortress Press, 2009.

Appendix I

Love So
AMAZING
Join Us This
EASTER
SERVICE TIMES
Sunday, March 31st
11:00 am | 6:00 pm
LIGHTHOUSE BAPTIST CHURCH

YOU CAN KNOW YOU WILL GO TO HEAVEN

1) RECOGNIZE YOUR CONDITION

Romans 3:23 "For all have sinned, and come short of the glory of God."
No one is good enough to go to Heaven on his own merit. No matter how much good we do, we still fall short.

2) REALIZE THE PENALTY FOR SIN

Romans 6:23 "For the wages of sin is death..."
Just as there are wages for good, there is punishment for wrong. The penalty for our sin is eternal death in a place called Hell.

3) BELIEVE CHRIST DIED FOR YOU

Romans 5:8 "But God commendeth His love toward us, in that, while we were yet sinners, Christ died for us."
Christ's great love for us was shown when He died on the cross to pay our debt.

4) TRUST CHRIST ALONE AS YOUR SAVIOUR

Romans 6:23 "...but the gift of God is eternal life through Jesus Christ our Lord."
Romans 10:13 "For whosoever shall call upon the name of the Lord shall be saved."
Everlasting life is a gift purchased by the blood of Jesus and offered freely to those who call upon Him by faith.

Let us help you word a prayer. (Realize that it's not mere words that save you, but your faith in Jesus Christ.)

"Dear Lord Jesus, I know I am a sinner. Please forgive me for my sin. Jesus, come into my heart and save my soul from Hell. I am trusting you, and you alone to take me to Heaven when I die. Thank you for saving me, Jesus. Amen."

Lighthouse Baptist Church
1349 Green Street (near Beltzville Lake)
Lehighton, PA 18235
(610) 377-0641
www.lbclehighton.org

Appendix II

Outline of John's Gospel

I. Prologue (John 1:1-18).
II. The Book of Signs (John 1:19-12).
   A. The Testimony of John the Baptist (John 1:19-34).
   B. The Calling of the Disciples (John 1:35-51).
   C. The Cana to Cana *inclusio* (John 2-4).
      1. Jesus changes water to wine at a wedding (John 2:1-12).
      2. Jesus performs a sign in the temple (John 13-25).
      3. Jesus encounters Nicodemus at night (John 3:1-21).
         a. Dialogue with Nicodemus (John 3:1-13?).
         b. Discourse: the sending of the Son (John 3:13?-3:21).
         c. First "Passion prediction" (John 3:14-15).
      4. Jesus and John the Baptist (John 3:22-35).
         a. Dialogue between John and his disciples (John 3:25-30).
         b. Discourse: the one from above (John 3:31-35).
      5. Jesus and the Samaritan woman (John 4:1-42).
      6. Jesus returns to Galilee (John 4:43-54).
         a. Jesus heals the son of the βασιλικός (ruler/official, a Gentile?) at Cana.
   D. Jesus as the new Temple.
      1. Jesus heals on the Sabbath (John 5:1-47)

a. Healing of the man by the Pool of Bethzatha (John 5:1-18)
b. Discourse: the Son does what he sees the Father doing (John 5:19-47)

2. The 2nd Passover: the feeding of the five thousand (John 6:1-71).
   a. Jesus feeds the five thousand (John 6:1-15)
   b. Jesus walks on water (John 6:16-21)
   c. Discourse: "I am the bread of life" (John 6:22-40)
   d. Conflict with "the Jews" and the falling away of many disciples (John 6:41-71)
3. Jesus at the Festival of Booths (celebrating water and light in the wilderness) (John 7:1-10:21?).
   a. Jesus' teaching and dialogue at the Festival: "rivers of living water" (John 7)
   [[The later inserted story of the woman caught in adultery. (John 8:1-11)]]
   b. Jesus continues to teach and dialogue at the Festival: "I am the light of the world" (John 8:12-59)
   c. Second "Passion prediction" (John 8:28)
   d. The healing of the man born blind (John 9:1-41)
   e. Discourse: "I am the Good Shepherd" (John 10:1-21)
4. Jesus at the Festival of Dedication (probably what is now called Hanukkah); a dispute over his identity (John 10:22-41).

E. The death and raising of Lazarus (John 11:1-54).

F. The 3rd Passover: Transition into the Book of Glory (John 11:55-12:50).
   1. Mary anoints Jesus (John 12:1-8)
   2. Jesus' entry into Jerusalem (John 12:12-50)
      a. Some Greeks ask to see Jesus (John 12:20-26)
      b. Third "Passion prediction" (John 12:31-32)

III. The Book of Glory (John 13 - 20).

A. Jesus last night with his disciples (John 13:1-17:26).
   1. Jesus washes his disciples feet (John 13:1-20)
   2. Jesus predicts his betrayal (John 13:6-30)

   3. Jesus' Farewell Discourse (a new commandment, "I am the Vine," the promise of the Holy Spirit (John 13:31-16:33)
   4. Jesus' final prayer (John 17)
B. The Passion narrative (John 18-19).
   1. Jesus' betrayal and arrest (John 18:1-12)
   2. Jesus' trial before "the Jews" and Peter's denials (John 18:13-27)
   3. Jesus and Pilate (John 18:28-19:16)
   4. Jesus' crucifixion and burial (John 19:16a-42)
C. The Resurrection (John 20).
   1. Mary comes to the tomb, then brings Peter and "the beloved disciple (John 20:1-10)
   2. Mary encounters Jesus (John 20:11-18)
   3. Jesus appears to the disciples and gives them the Holy Spirit (John 20:19-23)
   4. Jesus and Thomas (John 20:24-29)
D. The closing of the Book of Glory and statement of purpose for the book. (John 20:30-31).

IV. Epilogue (John 21).